GRACE REVEALED

a memoir

Greg Archer

NorLightsPress
762 State Road 458
Bedford IN 47421

Printed in the United States of America

ISBN: 978-0-9906862-4-8

Cover Photo by Duncan Walker
Book Design by Nadene Carter
Edited by Sammie L. Justesen

First printing, 2015

Dedication

To my resilient grandparents, Jadwiga and Jacenty Migut, all of their children—Ted, Mary, Janina, Joe, Stanley, John and Bernice—and to all generations of Wilks and Miguts near and far, past, present, and future.

And to the nearly 2 million deported Polish people whose lives were affected by Joseph Stalin's political decisions in the 1940s.

Acknowledgements

A very deep, heartfelt thank you to the following souls and entities that helped bring this story to life by lifting up this mood-swinging blond:

John Migut (It began with you.); my mother, Bernice Gorder (For the homemade pierogi, the binges they spawned and so much more.); NorLights Press; the Kresy-Siberia Foundation; The Hoover Library at Stanford University; Raine Luciano (Here's to lighthouses.); Duffie Bart (Here's to self-inquiry.); Kathleen Walker (Everything is material.); Renee and Karl (Two miracles & Belle. We'll always have North Oaks!); The Toms of Minneapolis (For Menomonie, with unending thanks.); Suna Lock (With love and Thursday nights.); Joshua Fischer (Napa? Yosemite? Really?); Eric Sassaman (Few words can aptly convey your significance in this. Thank you.); Jane Sullivan (To "feelings."); Jeff Dinnell (Friend. Truly! TYATM.); Rebecca Lampi-Fisk, John Odlum, John Amaral and Patrick Gillis (Angels all of you.); Christine and Bethany (To 4's and 6's and edits! With deep thanks.); my "office" at the Menlo Park, California, Starbucks by the Guild Theater; my "office" at Marion's Legacy Chocolate Coffeehouse in Menomonie, Wisconsin; 11:11 (a.m. & p.m.), the following personalized license plates—IMGIDED and LYTNUP; streetlamps with personality and a gaggle of other "signs."

And Jadwiga Migut (you have been here the entire time.)

Author's Note

To understand and fully comprehend my Polish family's story over the decades required listening to countless tales of survival and eventually conducting numerous interviews about the events that unraveled in their lives between 1940 and 1950, as well as researching Stalin's mass deportation of the Poles. The result is *Grace Revealed: a memoir.* Memory, translation and creativity all meet here, particularly in Part Two of the book, which illuminates my family's odyssey as I envisioned it unfolding based upon their first-hand accounts and significant research.

Contents

PROLOGUE

A small village in eastern Poland, September 2012

THE CHURCH DOORS WERE LOCKED. *Locked!* A procession of flamboyant Polish sayings made a mad dash through the forefront of my mind—and none of them were holy. Well, this was certainly awkward. I couldn't very well swear out loud in front of God and the angels when what I needed was the Supreme Being's help with parting the church doors wide open.

Temptation crippled me momentarily and I hissed "dog's blood" in Polish—rather playfully. Technically, I was not cursing. Not really—more like expressing extreme aggravation over something. And why a dog was involved in this curious Polish maxim remained a mystery. A mental posse of other, more colorful Polish phrases sprang forward—spunky ones with Swear Word Pizazz—particularly "lightening light." However, nothing more passed my lips. Just as well. Considering all of the brouhaha with thunderclouds in the Old Testament, the last thing I needed at this juncture of my journey was to be struck down by the Heavenly Father.

Locked doors—I mean, *really!* There just had to be a way to get inside the Church of Saint Onufry. After all, I was on a Mission From God and everything, and the mission had specifically led me to *this* church in bucolic Poland—not St. Mary's Basilica back in Kraków, and not St. Peter and Paul and Joseph and Henry and Henrietta and Whoever over in Warsaw. I was led to *this* church. This one!

What the hell was I supposed to do? Just stand in the entryway of the 300-year-old haven and contemplate my navel? *Again?* Good God, I was not sure I had it in me.

I grabbed the silver door handle one more time and gave it a good tug, thinking I may have been way too blond the first time I tried to get in—when Pulling should have been Pushing. Nothing.

Well, there just had to be a chivalrous priest on stand-by.

Holy water on IV-drip?

Confessional?

Anything?

My gaze ever so slowly crept upward. Surely I was being watched. Either that or I was on the receiving end of a super-sized cosmic joke. Why else would The Universe so blatantly toss me the under-reported story about Joseph Stalin's diabolical mass deportations of nearly two million Poles during the 1940s and haul my Polish ass 12,000 miles across several oceans to further investigate the war crime's impact on my family, and then deposit me within the confines of a ten-square-foot chamber of a church I could not enter?

I was never good at doing the math and, apparently, it was not about to begin now. But I did know this: The spiritual numbers were not adding up here and I had to consider my next move.

Break down the doors?

Well, that would be *trés* Superman and all those pierogi I consumed back in Kraków had added layers of flab to my weakened thighs.

"Accidentally" smash my hand through the glass?

So dramatic. And, really, just too pushy, especially for a guy who was raised in a Polish-Catholic home.

Sighing, I pressed my forehead against the windowpane, peered through the glass, and was instantly distracted by an embarrassment of eye candy. A red carpet with gilded gold accents stretched dramatically toward the main altar, which rested serenely underneath an umbrella of cathedral-like sensation that was the church's rounded ceiling. Finely detailed, painted scenes of angels and the heavens played out there with ethereal Biblical revelry. The altar's backdrop—a dark green, marble-like shrine—protruded outward diagonally, its columns and framework a powerful mix of soft, lily-white and bold golden hues. I assumed the image within the centerpiece—a crestfallen man sporting long, unkempt hair and an overgrown beard—was Jesus Christ, but upon deeper scrutiny, I wondered if it could very well be the saint after which the church was named: Onufry—known in these parts as Onufrego.

Fighting my rising impatience, I fetched my iPhone from my coat pocket and snapped several pictures of the church's interior. When I turned around, I realized I was not alone in the entryway. Jesus was there—deeply carved right into the back wall, in fact, arms stretched, head turned downward, his beaten body attached to a wooden crucifix.

"Shouldn't you be up front?" I remarked, indicating the locked church behind me.

I held up a hand and apologized. Clearly not the time to be glib. I sat down on the bench underneath The Lord and leaned forward.

"Look," I continued to express my innermost thoughts—out loud, because, of course, talking to oneself and/or some invisible Higher Power with good hearing and strong psychic senses, seemed to be the most perfectly natural thing to do for a confused, middle-aged blond, Polish person with a history of mood swings. "I *have* to get inside the church. You know that. I know that. I came all this way—for my family, for myself, for some mysterious, somewhat esoteric, and can I just say, downright crazy, journey you strongly suggested I pursue!"

I considered the locked doors for a moment and then my head dropped in defeat. Perhaps it was best to take the hands-off approach on this one. There is nothing worse than Hanging On when you know full well you're supposed to be Letting Go. It wastes precious time and besides, your fingernails become unbelievably soiled from all the time spent clawing at the dirt of the cliff of which you are strongly being urged to let go.

Let go.

Let God.

Let it be?

Worth a try.

I sat there in silence for several minutes, inhaling and exhaling—deeply, smoothly, metaphysically, like any good Chicago transplant living in Northern California would. But then … it occurred to me that maybe I had not been clear enough.

With God, that is.

"Listen, it's fine if you don't want me to go inside of the church. Really, it is. Finding this place was enough. I will turn it over to you. Completely."

A beat.

"But *c'mom!* You know you want me inside of the church. So, what do you say? How about pulling out a little miracle from your robe?"

Nothing. Aside from the psychobabble inside of my head, it was so quiet I could have heard the smallest droplet of holy water fall upon the carpet just on the other side of the locked doors.

The back of my head found Jesus's feet on the cross behind me.

Just give me a sign!

"Ha!"

A sign!

That was precisely what got me into this predicament.

~ ~ ~ ~

Part One

The Signs

CHAPTER ONE

THIS STORY BEGAN WITH A BROKEN picture frame and actor Ewan McGregor. But not at the same time. And a photograph of Ewan McGregor was not even in the picture frame. Nor did the Hollywood hotshot have anything to do with breaking it.

Allow me to explain…

It was the autumn of 2011…

One morning, I walked into my third-floor office of the weekly magazine for which I was the editor in Santa Cruz, California. To my surprise, the double picture frame housing two different black-and-white photos of my Polish family lie face up on my desk with the glass from the frames broken, the remnants arranged in a clumsy collection of jagged shards right there atop it.

My Polish grandmother's indomitable eyes stared up at me with haunting concern from one of the photos; her tightly drawn lips refused her powdered, solemn face to soften. Next to her lie a group portrait of my grandmother, my aunt, my three uncles, and my mother, all at various ages in their youth, sitting on a bench outdoors in Tanzania, Africa, during the 1940s.

I sat down behind my desk and quickly assessed the situation, glancing at the top-hanging shelf on the wall nearly five feet away. The picture frame typically resided there and during the course of any given week, I would peer up at those photos more times than I could accurately assess, and ruminate—on my family's strength, their will, how World War II affected them. At times, these deep thoughts temporarily helped me avoid a life-long habit: Mood Swinging.

I would not necessarily call myself bipolar.

Emotional? Of course. But bipolar. No. (Not yet.)

Actually, I was truly intrigued with the term my therapist and friend, Dan, had once used during one of my emotional downturns.

"Greg, you have labile mood disorder. That's all."

I fell back in the loveseat as Dread stumbled over Annoyance in the pit of my tummy.

"That's all? How could that be all? And how could I have a labia mood disorder? I'm a guy!"

My friend laughed so hard a tear ran down his face.

"Labile—it's *labile* mood disorder. Not labia."

I gazed down at my privates. "Oh."

Regardless, the news did not sit well. Later that evening I found emotional refuge in a delectable pint of Ben & Jerry's frozen yogurt. Cherry Garcia, if you must know. I looked up this disorder that I apparently had, also dubbed ED—Emotional Dysregulation, something about "an emotional response that is poorly modulated, and does not fall within the conventionally accepted range of emotive response; also referred to as labile mood (marked fluctuation of mood)."

Labile mood disorder—the nerve!

Now, as I inspected the broken picture frame in my office, my suspicion rising like Lindsay Lohan's blood alcohol level, I wondered how that frame could have traveled from its restful perch across the room to the very center of my desk. And how did it break, freeing the pictures from their protective glass?

The cleaning crew? It must have been their doing. They *could* have accidentally bumped into the frame when they were dusting the high shelves, thereby forcing it to tip over. But then again, the office cleaning crew never dusted the high shelves—good help apparently is still hard to find—and besides, if they had, how did the broken frames find their way onto the very center of my desk?

I sat there and stewed about it for a few more minutes until the only reasonable conclusion found its way into the forefront of my mind: The broken picture frames were a "sign."

Yes. A sign.

I get them.

Sometimes.

And usually when my labile mood is not in disorder.

And not because I am special. The signs just … happen.

Occasionally.

Think Haley Joel Osment à la *The Sixth Sense*. You know, that kid in the popular movie from the 1990s; the one who always saw dead people? It is something like that. Except I do not see dead people. I get "signs."

But let's not get off track here. The point is this: I ask for help, I ask for signs—perhaps far too often—and sometimes I get them. Look, I boast just enough smarts to realize that somebody up there/out there/in here is probably exhausted from hearing from me and would love for me to get off the spiritual phone line what with all the other requests for assistance and guidance around the globe and everything. But there is a very good reason for what I do.

I'm curious.

Either that, or I'm an addict.

"Hello, my name is Greg and I am a 'sign' addict."

It is just that I have a deep craving to be led by something divine—my Higher Self, God, The Universe, whatever you want to call it. Let's face it: The route from A to Z is never void of spiritual goodies. I believe they are there for the taking if you are open to see and receive them. There has to be something greater than myself willing to toss me an occasional breadcrumb or miracle along the path.

Whenever I find myself on the receiving end of a "sign," it's usually delivered by one of two couriers: synchronicity or serendipity. (There is also Divine Intervention, which, at times, can be messy, and I fear opening that Pandora's Box—really, it's too early in our relationship to dirty our hands with that now.)

C.G. Jung typically receives credit for coining the term synchronicity back in the 1950s, having explained it as the simultaneous occurrence of events that appear significantly related but have no discernable connection. But as far back as the mid-1700s, Horace Walpole in his work, "The Three Princes of Serendip," illuminated that serendipity was the occurrence and development of events by chance in a happy or beneficial way.

So, whenever I find myself experiencing a moment of serendipity that simply cannot be explained away as mere coincidence (there is no such thing!), I see it as an opportunity to pause and take notice.

The broken picture frames. My Polish family. It had to be a sign. Why?

Because just a few hours before that discovery on my desk, while sweating out my emotional angst in a Bikram Yoga class, I silently albeit insistently asked for guidance on *what* I should be focusing. Now, my gut was now telling I'd been given a clear lead— that I must focus on my family. But there was a catch.

How do I put this?

Quite simply: I did not like the sign I'd just been given.

This is never a good—for lack of a better word—*sign*. Because it's not as if you can take your Sign From God back to Wal-Mart and exchange it for, well, a better sign. Although, I have not checked in with Deepak, Oprah, Caroline Myss, Marianne Williamson, Tony Robbins or Wayne Dyer about the real return policy, so who knows, anything is possible.

Regardless, Divine Law seems to suggest that A Sign From God is not exchangeable.

Period. The end.

Why did this bother me? Several reasons.

But the Mother Of All Reasons was this: I knew within every fiber of my being that by receiving the "sign," I would have to do the one thing I had been avoiding for several years: Explore, embrace, and fully deal with my Polish family's past.

In other words: I was totally screwed.

~ ~ ~ ~

CHAPTER TWO

ACTOR EWAN MCGREGOR PLUCKED several plump grapes off of the healthy fruit cluster and tossed the juicy deep blue-violet morsels into his mouth. As he noshed away, his cerulean blue eyes lit up dreamily and the sides of his mouth rose in pure delight.

"Mmmm. So good."

I studied him for a moment, realizing there was not one flaw on the creature. Not one. Clad in black jeans, a cream-colored T-shirt, and a snug coal-colored jacket, his dark blond hair sprouted upward in various directions with intentionally messy bravura.

He sat back, wonderfully confident in his chair. His eyes fell down to the fruit platter and then up at me. "Take some," he was telling me with his gaze, but I resisted. Pineapple and apple slices were in fine company with robust strawberries and it was all tempting, but I felt out of sorts, completely off. And I was annoyed for having the awareness to realize it as Mr. McGregor and I sat across from each other at a marble table in a posh suite of the St. Regis Hotel in Downtown San Francisco.

I wasn't nervous. I had interviewed countless celebrities before, and this interview, I had convinced myself, would be one of the highlights of the season. I was there to interview Mr. McGregor for his role in the film *Salmon Fishing in the Yemen*, a love story about an unlikely couple who fall in love while on a far-away mission to do good, but whose chances of success are questionable.

I quickly chalked up my mood to fatigue and proceeed with the interview, which would run on *The Huffington Post*.

"I never played this kind of role before," Mr. McGregor casually remarked. "I never worked with director Lasse Hallström."

I nodded, feigning interest.

"My costar Emily Blunt is so divine. She's very similar to the way I do things—able to really throw herself into a scene."

A "hmmm" out of me, another cheery grin from Mr. McGregor.

"You can make a poor film out of a great script but it's difficult to make a great film out of a poor script. I really do believe it's the foundation of everything. The script has to be something you really…"

My elbow found the table as my chin plopped into the palm of my hand. "I see," I politely offered.

But inside, a storm rumbled. *Good God. I am soooooooooooooo bored!*

Well, what cruel inner gale force wind was this? It nearly shoved me out of my chair. Did I really just have that thought?

I glanced Mr. McGregor, fearing he could read my mind. He had played Obi Wan Kenobi in a *Star Wars* trilogy, after all. One never knows how much an actor picks up by creative osmosis. I cleared my throat, composed myself, and did my best to appear as calm as could be.

On and on the man went—about the film, about the love story, about surviving against all odds.

And on and on I brooded—about having such a harsh thought, about being a horrible person (*Bad interviewer! Bad interviewer!*), about being … *bored?*

I checked in with myself again, just to be certain. Clearly I was mistaken.

Greg—you're bored with a capital B!

Well, I would not have it. It simply was not so. Tired? Yes. Bored? No.

PUHLEASE … when are we getting the hell out of here?

Jesus, Mary, and Farrah Fawcett—may she rest in feathered-hair peace!—I *was* bored. Or was I simply disinterested?

Or worse: positively depressed?

All at once, interior missiles were launched.

What the hell is wrong with you? How could you be bored? Big movie star! A-list actor. Trainspotting! Star Wars! Beginners! This man is the Gregory Peck of modern cinema—classy, arty, the real deal. You love press junkets! You love doing celebrity interviews! This is what you do, Greg. This IS you!

Mr. McGregor chuckled at something I had asked, but for the life of me, I had no recollection of my question.

"Lasse Hallström," McGregor went on, "he's sort of bonkers."

Bonkers. Yes.

That's exactly what I must be, for how else could I explain my curious indifference. I was sitting across from one of Hollywood's most striking, interesting and eloquent actors—and against a backdrop of studly skyscrapers and a layer of lingering San Francisco fog. I could not be BORED!

Just then, Shame and Confusion crawled into bed with each other and gave birth to Mega Worry—a quick pregnancy if ever there was one. And then, from the deep pit of my belly, came the realization that my Boredom Newsflash was hardly Breaking News.

Months had passed since the Broken Picture Frames Incident—getting "the sign" and not doing a damn thing about it—and since that time, I became increasingly less enthusiastic about the work I was doing. At first, I thought it was burnout. But I quickly tossed aside that idea upon the arrival of dismal realizations I had trouble fully accepting: That I was trapped within the Slow Lingering Death Of Journalism As I Knew It; that all of the "advances" in Social Media and flurry of online portals, many of which do *not* pay their contributors, had somehow watered down a significant chunk of my creative life, stripped it of value, and insisted it be condensed into nothing more than 140-character Tweets or a throng of Selfies to post on Facebook.

Somehow, a period had been placed at the end of the flowery sentence that was my writing career. Now, it felt as if I was lost in the ellipses.

And this Mr. McGregor—he of fame and fortune and resilient hair gel— only seemed to remind me that something had been *way* off inside of me for years. I had experienced similar feelings sitting across from John Travolta, Bruce Willis and a number of other great actors and actresses—but never in front of Diane Lane, never, I swear to God and Wonder Woman's lasso of truth.

Perhaps it was time for me to face the obvious—that my growing indifference had nothing to do with the stars I was interviewing; that it had everything to do with me. How had I gone from being the person who had worked so hard to establish himself as an entertainment journalist, somebody who had chatted up Joan Rivers, Betty White, Anderson Cooper and a slew of other notables, only to arrive in a posh hotel suite across from one of the world's finest actors and just be plain ol' *bored?*

A male film publicist opened the door slightly and popped his head inside. "Five minutes left."

I offered my broadest fake yet soothing smile.

"One last question: What's some of the best advice you've been given about life?"

I always concluded my interviews with that question because after interviewing so many people over the years, I realized two things:

1. The answer to that question could expose a rare glimpse into their depth.

2. Inevitably, most of the responses eerily related to something I had to hear, based on what I'm going through in my own life at the time.

Mr. McGregor sat there for a moment and pondered the question. His gaze lifted. To which I immediately thought: *Why is it that, whenever we search for an answer, more often than not, we can always be found looking up?*

"I don't know what it would be," McGregor mused. "A lot of people give you advice by how they are—by how they act. Don't they? The people you love and respect are supposedly advising you by example."

I left the St. Regis thinking about that.

The people you love and respect are supposedly advising you by example.

How had my family served me by example?

As I slipped into the front seat of my low-resting Mazda Miata, cursing the fact that despite nearly a decade of Bikram Yoga, middle age was beginning to have its way with my Polish hips, I thanked the Universe for the interview. And, seeing that I had arrived at such a dramatic turning point—*bored; how could you be bored?*—I naturally asked for a sign on what I needed to do.

The broken picture frames flashed before my eyes.

I had been given a sign months ago. How many more signs did I need to receive? The message was clear: "Look at your family; look at their past."

What? Did I want a flashier sign? Something like, "Hey, you're going to be on the receiving end of buckets of cash if you turn right instead of left at the next traffic light?"

Yes. Yes I did want *that* sign.

Still, when The Powers That Be instruct you to do something, you must do it. I had avoided doing what I was told and now I was weary, tired, listless, and unhappy.

I turned the key in the ignition and sighed in frustration.
How the hell did I get here?

♦ ♦ ♦

Growing up on the Westside of Chicago in the late 1960s, I often stuffed into my mouth dozens of Polish kiełbasa and potato pierogi doused with melted butter. I quickly morphed into the polite but klutzy, chubby Polish kid I was destined to become. Food was not my only vice. I also wandered into the fantastic alternate reality of sixties television. *Here Come The Brides, I Dream of Jeannie, Bewitched, Laugh-in, The Brady Bunch*—these were a few of the television shows I watched religiously, pining to live in their dreamy, magical worlds. I never wanted to attend kindergarten or Sunday mass. I wanted to play with Greg, Marcia, Peter, Jan, Bobby and Cindy Brady—and then fall asleep inside Jeannie's super groovy, magic bottle.

There were just four of us—my father, my mother, my older brother, Rich, and I. We lived in a modest two-bedroom home on Altgeld Street, near the thoroughfares of Fullerton and Laramie, in a neighborhood filled with a diverse mix of ethnic families, parks in which to frolic and friendly neighbors to appreciate. My father was a Polish immigrant who worked as an engineer for General Telephone & Electronics. My mother, also a Polish immigrant, took a part-time job at a nearby bakery and, eventually, the popular corner dime store known as Louie's 5 & 10.

Summers were filled with playful neighborhood parties and chasing fireflies with other kids or my many Polish cousins. Winters afforded us the opportunity to build substantial snowmen and lose ourselves in monstrous snowdrifts brought on by the occasional blizzard. Several times a week, I could be found playing "school" in the basement of the home of my very first friend on the planet, Nancy Marek—who was always the teacher. Afterward, I marveled at how savvy Nancy was in convincing her tall, brunette mother, Barb, to make Kraft Macaroni & Cheese, which would be piled, piping hot, in mounds on our paper plates. I never understood why Nancy poured nearly half a bottle of ketchup over her mac & cheese and I was too fearful to attempt to do so myself. I couldn't even bring myself to dip an Oreo cookie into a glass of milk. I must have been an Add No-moisture Binge Eater. Expect for the melted butter on the pierogi, of course.

Once a month, on Saturday nights, my parents arranged a jolly get-together for their Polish friends and my mother's siblings. En masse they arrived at our house, stylishly dressed, impeccably proud, and sat on the edges of our foam-cushioned sofas and chairs. Lit cigarettes made repeated trips to and from their lips. Full ashtrays collected around the house. Empty highball glasses begged to be refilled. And attention almost always fell upon my gregarious father, Bill, who, after just one Scotch and soda, could recite a rhyming Polish joke and have the guests howling with laughter.

These Poles were loud.

They were expressive.

They were joyous … on the outside.

But beneath the surface lurked tales—both dark and menacing—I was too young to fully grasp.

However, one of those tales surfaced during Christmas of 1969.

I was five when I first heard about "the family story"—how my mother, three of her brothers, her two sisters, and their parents, endured some kind of "adventure" when they were children. My interest piqued upon hearing extravagant words such as "Poland" and "Siberia" and "Uzbekistan" and "Tanganyika."

I was curious—but positively clueless—about what happened to them. Later, when I was eight years old and my family relocated to the nearby suburb of Elmhurst so my father could be closer to work, the combination of my parents' marital challenges and my ever-expanding waistline diverted my interests elsewhere.

My parents divorced when I was 15 and I acquired a strong desire to escape, partially because of the demise of my parents' marriage, but more so because I always felt like such an outsider in the few conventional midwestern jobs I held as a teenager. Being an Ace Hardware clerk was fine—for a while. But my mind always wandered from nuts and bolts to who really murdered Peter Campbell on the primetime sitcom *Soap*. As a telemarketer for Montgomery Ward Life Insurance Company, I fantasized about living in Thousand Oaks, California, rather than just calling someone there. And I never really met the quotas my other telemarketing coworkers achieved. Instead, I preferred to talk about how everybody was *feeling*.

A traditional Midwestern job? It felt like a prison sentence.

I will not be imprisoned, I thought proudly, not really certain why. For I was young and how could I possibly know anything about prison? I wanted to be a writer, which was considered unconventional to most adults around me.

Rather than fight against the grain, which I did not feel strong enough to do at the time, I allowed my emotions to rule the day. I decided it would be better to explore life elsewhere. I just had no idea that within three years, it would take me more than 2,000 miles away from home.

At eighteen, I moved to Arizona to attend Arizona State University as a journalism student. I never thought of myself as a sign tramp at the time. Sensitive and desperately hungry to be understood—yes—but always seeking guidance from the Universe? Not so much.

Fate was kind, however. My cousin and Godmother, Chris—a soulful, giving blond with model-like flair—lived in Phoenix, near the university. Living in close proximity to her seemed like a good idea. During my college years, my visits with Chris, my Aunt Janina's only child, often included observations about our Polish family—from their boisterous spirits and wonderfully endearing methods of communicating with each other (read: loudly) to their compelling tale of survival during in the 1940s, which we often discussed.

When I left the familial comfort of that college nest and moved to San Francisco in my early twenties, I noticed I was doing something more repetitively than I ever did before: Ask for guidance. I did this silently as I walked to and from my job as a publicist in a public relations firm that handled regional film publicity.

Lead me, guide me, show me...

I was not certain why I began the mantra. I was just aware I had begun reciting it to and from home.

Home.

After several years living in San Francisco, it no longer felt like "home," which may have been why I kept asking for guidance. But, as they say: Be careful what you ask for. Eventually my spiritual barking took me away from the PR job I had so eagerly grabbed and tossed me into a curious trifecta:

1. A temp job at Charles Schwaab. (Chuck: please forgive me for using that time to pen a TV script.)

2. 12-step meetings. ("Hi. My name is Greg and I would be more than honored to be your Al-Anon pal!")

3. A small, rent-controlled one-bedroom apartment I shared with a recovering female alcoholic who had two dogs and a cat with a million fleas.

The deeper message? When the Universe gives you fleas, you scratch.

During this time, I considered returning to writing, but lacked the confidence and courage. I convinced myself I was fine—just fine, thank you very much—amid my otherwise lack of real direction and purpose. But deep down, I was confused and searching for answers.

Asking for guidance became my go-to; my default mechanism.

One day my beloved college friend Raine, phoned. She had just moved to Pacific Grove, near Carmel, California, with her then-husband and she was desperate to share some news with me.

"Hey, I think you should move down here. I have the perfect job for you."

I took the bait. "What is it?"

"You would be working in a coffeebar—in a bookstore. It's really charming. For some reason, I think I got the job part-time so you could eventually take it over."

I laughed so loudly she must have moved the phone away from her ear.

"Are you serious? I went to the Walter Cronkite School of Journalism. I'm deep. I'm soulful. I'm creative! And you want me to the schlep coffee for a bunch of lonely souls living in Mayberry RFD?"

I chased back my vehement disapproval with a loud, resounding: "No way!"

One week later, I was schlepping coffee for a bunch of lonely souls living in "Mayberry RFD."

Ah, but as it turned out, they weren't *that* lonely. They were kind, interesting and—this surprised me—interested in me and what I had to say. Bookworks was one of the first bookstores in America that served coffee and pastries around an old-fashioned coffeebar in the back of the store. This was long before Borders and Barnes & Noble stormed onto the scene. It smacked of a West Coast *Cheers*—without the booze—and for the first time in a long while, I was truly happy.

In between shifts, I moonlighted as a fitness instructor and attempted to write the great American novel—by hand. I changed my name. *Archer had a good ring to it*, I thought. After all, I was a Sagittarius and I no longer felt like a Gregory Robert Krzos or that the name captured the person I thought I was. Not that I knew—not really. But Archer did sound fetching.

Life was good.

And everything would have remained good, until, one day, four years later, I asked for a specific sign.

A big one.

I wondered if it was time to move on. But where to this time? I couldn't move back to Elmhurst, Illinois.

"My family doesn't understand me!" I always told myself, thinking the distance between us offered me a better opportunity to fully express myself as a writer and fitness instructor.

On a whim, I quit the job at the bookstore. Looking back, it wasn't the most brilliant thing to do without much of a game plan, but, on the plus side, it did boost my need for guidance on what to actually do with my life at that point. As a Sign From God freak, this was the most ideal situation in which I could put myself.

Fortuitously, before I left my post at the bookstore in the summer of 1994, I had already purchased a ticket to Hawaii for a September vacation.

A thought emerged: *Why not just move to Hawaii?*

A counter-offer was born.

Move to Hawaii? You're nuts! You don't have any money! If we're supposed to pack up everything and move to Hawaii, then why don't you just ask the Universe for a sign to make sure it's the right thing to do!

At last! The voice of reason.

I was standing on Lighthouse Avenue in Downtown Pacific Grove on a cool, slightly foggy summer night, gazing up the heavens when I did it: "God, Universe … if I'm supposed to move to Hawaii, just give me a sign by midnight that…"

(Please allow me to explain: I knew perfectly well that giving a time limit to something as vastly intelligent as The Universe sounds like an absolutely ridiculous thing to do. But it wasn't as if I was demanding it—well, not that much. I was merely *suggesting.* And, if I did not receive the sign by midnight, then I would simply, well, continue venturing forth with the same befuddled, childlike vehemence I had always exuded.)

"So, if I do not receive a sign to *move* to Hawaii by midnight. I will just go there on vacation as planned."

Five minutes later, parched and slightly exhausted—people think asking for signs is such an easy thing to do!—I sauntered into a local liquor store with the sole purpose of purchasing a bottle of water. I opened the glass door of the cooler and reached for the first bottled water available.

My heart skipped a beat.

The label on the bottle read: Hawaii Bottled Water.

The next day, I began packing what few belongings I owned.

Weeks later, by the time I settled into the Waikiki Beach YMCA and strolled through the park nearby, I was experiencing a full-blown panic attack. I was twenty-nine and practically homeless. What had I done?

I searched for a pay phone and immediately called my friend Raine, who had since moved back to the Midwest.

"I still can't believe you moved to Hawaii!"

"How many times do I have to tell you—I got a sign!"

She chuckled.

"Very funny. I'm freaking out about this," I went on.

"Well, you could always buy another bottle of water."

How rude!

I had given away most of my belongings and the only real possession I had left was an oversized, heavy suitcase, which I dragged— looking utterly foolish in the process—all the way across Waikiki Beach to the YMCA.

I needed support. I needed encouragement.

"Is there anybody you know in Hawaii?" Raine asked.

I thought about it. There were, in fact, a few people I knew. Immediately after the call, I connected with a young married couple, Rob and Kelly, whom I met at the coffeebar back in Pacific Grove. They happened to be living in Hawaii at the time and invited me to stay with them until I found permanent residence. I soon found a job teaching fitness classes. Things began to click.

But none of it sat well with my Polish mother back in Chicago, still concerned about my "rash" behavior.

"Move back home—right now. You're roaming the world like a Gypsy!"

"There's nothing wrong with being a Gypsy, mother."

"You belong here, and not thousands of miles away from home."

I don't know where I belong, I wanted to say, but that would have only triggered more concern. Besides, Oahu was lovely and my friends were wonderful hosts.

What's the saying: The Universe works in mysterious ways?

So mysterious, it seems, that two months later, after my blond locks had grown out to shoulder-length and my money supply dwindled, I returned to California with $29.02 in my bank account. But I never regretted the experience. I realized that "the sign" I received presented me with a wonderful game of multiple-choice. I could a) Trust it and follow it and acquire evidence that everything would work out just fine; b) Ignore it completely; or c) Realize a power bigger than myself was operating in my quirky life and that this power and I could actually be relating to each other.

A and C won out.

Back on the Mainland, as another few years sped by, my writing became more prolific, my life more "California." I developed a deeper interest in spiritual things. I acquired a female roommate with a penchant for recalling past lives. (And, really, why wouldn't that happen? I was in Northern California, after all.) My roommate insisted I had been in many past lives with her. I never received a real sign as to whether any of that was true but good Lord: China circa 500 A.D. sounded über dramatic. Still, there are no words to describe how immensely grateful I was for our time together—in this lifetime, that is.

As if picking lint out of my spiritual navel had not already become a full-time job, I noticed that, at times, street lamps went out whenever I passed underneath them. I occasionally caught the time at precisely 11:11, too. I did not think any of it happened because I was "special;" my fluctuating self-esteem never allowed me to feel that valued or hold much ego. But I felt as if I had somehow intersected with a little bit of synchronicity during theses occurrences. Maybe it was an indication I was on the right track.

Or something…

It felt natural for me to hang my life on a cool cosmic coat rack. I may not have been financially prosperous, but at least I thought The Universe had my back. To others, I must have appeared to be an extremely naïve, sensitive creature.

Five years later, I felt called upon to accept the position of Editor-in-Chief of a prominent weekly magazine in Santa Cruz, California and a new set of circumstances began to unfold. I resisted the change at first, fearing it would take me away from my true calling as a writer. But eventually, I embraced the new tasks and the opportunity to help improve a publication that had been in the community for, at that time, twenty-five years.

Outside of the paper, I freelanced for magazines, interviewing top stars— Ellen DeGeneres, Robert Pattinson, Cyndi Lauper, and many others. I managed to connect with the right publicists and attend Red Carpet events or conduct backstage interviews with celebrities. Over time, I packaged myself as an entertainment journalist.

The thing about celebrity features is there can never be too many of them. More publicity is well, just more publicity. And more publicity tends to equate with more star wattage. Or value. In the 21st century, celebrities are now akin to modern works of art. And the job of the Hollywood publicity business (and it's just that—a business if not a wonderfully well-oiled machine)—is to make sure the spotlights are shining down ever so brightly on their works of art.

But by late winter of 2012, a vast majority of publications and online arenas succumbed to being content-driven rather than quality-driven. Journalism on all fronts was in the midst of a massive identity crisis, and ad dollars were the only thing that seemed to matter for those in charge. Times had changed. Anyone and everyone could write about *anything*. Modern media's slow crawl toward mediocrity had officially transformed into a major sprint. As a writer who once felt valued for his contributions, suddenly, I felt pushed aside, unwanted—and also unpaid.

Not a good thing for my labile mood. I could not muster enough energy to keep shining a bright light on anything—or anyone.

Mood swinging with reckless abandon, I turned to what I knew how to do best: Asking for signs.

The broken picture frame!

Yes, but not *that* sign!

◆ ◆ ◆

In spring of 2012, in an immaculate Ritz Carlton suite in San Francisco, actor Chris Pine—his piercing eyes a rugged steel blue—sat beside director Alex Kurtzman, who was at the helm of the film *People Like Us*. Pine was the main headliner of the movie, which revolved around his character serendipitously discovering he has a half-sister.

After introductions, I sat across from the duo and pressed record on my digital recorder, but my inner self felt weighted down by the heavy anvil I had just caught in my most recent game of Catch the Sign with The Universe.

"What made you say yes to the role?"

"What did you find most alluring about it?"

"What do think of the picture now that you've seen it?"

I was robotic in my delivery of the questions.

When Mr. Pine uttered the word "serendipity," my head tilted to the side like a curious puppy. He had my attention. I softened.

"Do you believe in serendipity, in twists of fate?"

Mr. Pine leaned forward, resting his arms on his thighs.

"I definitely believe that if you put something out there into The Universe, in whatever way you think that means—praying, writing it down, or visualizing or whatever—that it will come to fruition in some form or another. And if it doesn't, there is a reason why it doesn't … but you will be led toward that thing you need to realize."

The broken picture frame!

Here's the thing about taking detours from your Signs From God: Eventually, they lead right back onto the road you are supposed to be traveling in the first place.

～ ～ ～ ～

CHAPTER THREE

FORGIVE ME, FATHER FOR I SPOKE TOO SOON. It may not have "all began" with the broken picture frame and Ewan McGregor. It may have *all* began when I received a large envelope from my Polish uncle in 2002.

I had encouraged my mother's older brother, John Migut, to write down what he and the family encountered in the 1940s. But when, on that fateful fall day at the Santa Cruz post office, I found myself staring at the floppy disk he had mailed and read the Post-It note attached to it—"Here it is Greg. Some things that happened!"—I swallowed hard and thought: "Dear Lord, he actually did it!"

Well, I did the most sensible thing I could. I hid the envelope in a filing cabinet and refused to insert and open the disk on my computer, fearing what I would discover. But I must have been interested because I asked my uncle to share some family history. Still, something about him actually documenting that history frightened the hell out of me.

Why?

I did not have answer.

But I had memories, many of which all came rushing back to me.

That Christmas of 1969—my Polish clan: The Miguts, loud, happy, hungry and cavorting in our living room on Altgeld Street in Chicago. I began holding my focus there—on that scene.

A celebratory bunch, the entire crew consisted of my mother, Bernice, the youngest of seven children—Ted, Mary, Janina, Joe, Stanley and John. Eldest brother, Ted, was the distant sibling—misplaced during the war, later found. Mary spent much of her young adult life struggling to stay alive. Janina (Jenny in English) was social and expressive—a bona fide 1960s Zsa Zsa Gabor with a bright smile and infectious hug. Joe was direct, Stanley sensitive and John, a loveable prankster.

And my mother, outgoing yet practical.

My uncles Joe, Stanley, and John were present that Christmas. Aunt Jenny was "fashionably late."

"I can 'splain everything," she chuckled in broken English as she stormed through the front door with a striking, six-foot-something middle-age man with gray hair.

"I have surprise for you all!" she beamed.

Much later in life, I realized that if one has as much *joie de vivre* as my playful aunt, somebody who had endured a hellish childhood and managed to walk out of it still able to smile, why not arrive late? Few people knew how to master a grand entrance and my Aunt Jenny was certainly one of them. Her surprise that evening? She had just gotten engaged to her new suitor.

Mother quickly escaped back into the kitchen—the pierogi needed her attention more than my aunt did. Meanwhile Aunt Jenny gushed over her newfound love and eventually found an empty spot on our lime green sofa from Sears Roebuck & Co. She spotted me on the floor and immediately flung her arms out in front of me.

"My darling Gregory! Come to Auntie. I love you with all my heart!"

Smothered there in her bosom, rocked back and forth like an infant, she moistened my cheeks with more than a dozen kisses. Giggling, gasping for air, I fell back onto the shag carpet, relishing the warm, loving glow consuming every fiber of my being.

Aunt Jenny reached down and wiped some lipstick off the side of my cheek.

"See what Auntie has done. You look like a clown."

"Like Bozo?" I quipped.

"Exactly sweetheart. Like Bozo the Clown!"

Somewhere between the disbursements of green olives—fitting appetizers at the time—and Scotch on the rocks for the adults, one of my relatives mentioned something about living in a place called Africa.

Africa?

What was that? A nearby town?

It sure sounded mysterious. If it was anything like my aunt, with her infectious smile and stylish demeanor—white pearl necklace and ash-blond, Aqua Netted hair—then I wanted to know more about it.

My brother immediately fetched the small globe from our bedroom and placed it down in front of me. It spun around and around and around until my Uncle John intervened. He tapped a large multi-colored shape on the globe several times.

"Tanzania. We were there. But it was called Tanganyika back then."

"What did you do there?" I asked.

"Oh, many things. We lived in huts."

"Huts? Like on *Gilligan's Island*?"

I wanted to know more.

Yes. It all began right there—at that precise moment.

Over the years, during other holidays, my occasional inquiries revealed more details about my family's past.

Elmhurst, 1978. Thanksgiving dinner.

My Uncle Stanley—the middle Migut brother. He waved at me from across the dining room table.

"Let me show you the Masai handshake we learned in Africa," he said.

Masai? I had never heard of such a word.

"It's the African name of the tribe that lived near our huts in the orphanage," he went on.

"You lived in an orphanage—in Africa?"

"Yes, Tanzania. Remember? Now come here!"

My Uncle John chimed in: "There were thousands of misplaced Polish children living in Eastern Africa during the 1940s, Greg."

Had I already been told this fact? Why did it seem new to me? And how on earth did my family get to Africa?

I approached Uncle Stanley, his cheeks flushed from devouring rich Polish food. He set down his fork and found my eyes. I stood there completely captivated if not amused by the texture of the moist, half-eaten piece of stuffed cabbage that was trying to disappear inside of his mouth. He quickly licked his fingers, wiped his face with a napkin and extended his slightly greasy hand toward me. I took it. He squeezed hard and swiftly pulled down my hand and arm. Next, he gripped my hand in his fist and pulled my arm down again. He returned to the standard handshake—all the while reciting a Masai saying. He wrapped it all up by placing one hand at the base of my neck and gently pulling my forehead toward his forehead.

"Now … that's the way the Masai greeted each other!"

Fascinating. What other things had my family been taught in Africa? More importantly, what were the actual events that led them to that place on the planet? By the time I was in high school, after a series of inquiries, the missing pieces fell into place.

In early 1940, under Joseph Stalin's orders, my family was taken by force from their farm in eastern Poland by Russian soldiers. They were treated like criminals, locked in one of hundreds of boxcars crowded with other Polish citizens, and carted off to a Siberian labor camp thousands of kilometers away. Nearly 2 million Poles suffered these mass deportations. For eighteen long, dismal months, the family endured brutal conditions in the labor camp, conditions so harsh that, eventually, it robbed them of their health and vitality—and for some, their lives. In the summer of 1941, a surprising turn of events found these imprisoned Poles—those who survived their confinement—released from the camps. They were left to wander southern Russia in search of aid. Some of them found it in Uzbekistan. A vast number of them perished. Those who, either by twists of fate or unshakeable faith, managed to escape Russia, found refuge in the Middle East, India and, later, the eastern stretches of Africa or in more distant locales such as Mexico or New Zealand.

The mass deportations of the Poles during the 1940s was, and to some extent still is, one of the most under-reported stories of Stalin's wrath.

"Most of the world knows what Hitler did to the Jewish people," my Uncle John often told me. "But hardly anybody knows what Stalin did to our people."

There was something portentous in that statement.

I must have paid attention to it the first time I heard it back in high school. Perhaps this knowledge embedded itself so uniquely within my psyche and lay dormant there until an ideal moment in time presented itself. Sparked either by naiveté or divine guidance, that inner knowledge must have nudged me to ask my uncle to document his memories.

The floppy disk. I remained baffled by my resistance to look at it. Up until the precise moment in time I received that disk, my family's story was just that—a story. It smacked of an ethereal fairy tale filled with a mythic villain in dark corners of The Universe. It had been comfortably out of reach, a safe distance away from me.

The floppy disk became a haunting invitation into a house of horrors.

Eight months from its arrival, I forced myself to read what was on that disk—all of it. A few months after that, I wrote about my family's experiences in a published essay. In May of 2004 the article won a major journalism award.

And that was that. I thought I had done what I needed to do: Tell my family's story.

I could not have been more wrong.

Four years later, vowing to explore and write about the ordeal in more detail, I allowed my ignorance to lead me into something I wasn't truly equipped to follow through on. During a holiday visit back in Chicago, I videotaped interviews with several family members who recalled their journey in even more vivid detail.

"Wonderful," I thought at the time. "This will be good."

But was it?

Upon returning to California, several more months passed before I could will myself to take action and have the video file transferred onto a DVD. Like the floppy disk before it, I refused to give it even a quick glance. More than a year later, the DVDs were still buried underneath a sloppy arrangement of paperwork in the bottom drawer of my desk.

Time passed.

A lot of it.

I kept myself busy—career, status, bright lights, and Hollywood red carpet events; interviews with the likes of Piers Morgan, Martha Stewart, Joseph Fiennes, and hosting community TV shows. All good. But a broken picture frame ignored ... cannot stay ignored.

I may have buried the DVDs, but for some reason, my family's bona fide We Survived Stalin procession continued to make an insistent stroll down the streets of my mind.

Poland.

Stalin.

Siberia.

Uzbekistan.

Africa.

There is a saying made popular by C.G. Jung: "What you resist persists."

And now, The Universe was suddenly taking delight in speaking to me through a celebrity—Chris Pine? "You will be led towards that thing you need to realize."

What did I need to realize?

I kept asking myself that question. The answer? In passing along the information to me, my Uncle John had inadvertently made *me* an integral character in their tale. I was now part of *their* story.

I recalled the famous 12-step saying: This too shall pass ... but first, it will PISS.

YOU.

OFF!

Like some kind of perverse chain letter that must remain circulated, had my uncle simply been the messenger? Were all cosmic fingers now pointing at me, asking me to investigate something more deeply?

But what? And why? I turned to another celebrity for inspiration.

John Wayne said: "Courage is being scared to death ... and saddling up anyway."

I had no other choice. Not really.

On a chilly, foggy afternoon in Santa Cruz in late spring of 2012, I located Uncle John's original notes yet again. I placed them near other transcriptions of interviews I had conducted with my Uncle Stanley, Aunt Jenny, and my mother, Bernice. I retrieved the DVDs that contained some of those interviews and opened their cases, fully prepared to watch them—again and again.

As long as it took. It was as if I had been handed an elaborate, historic jigsaw puzzle whose intricately shaped pieces with jagged edges had just been tossed up into the air and the fragments had fallen down on top of me ... and I had to assemble them all back together again.

I locked the doors of my cottage house. I pulled the drapes over the windows. I lit several white votive candles and burned small strands of white sage. If I was really going to travel back in time—*really* look at this stuff—best to do so using as many spiritual accouterments as possible. Besides, if God, The Universe, and the millions of Poles who suffered during the 1940s as a result of Stalin's madness truly wanted to show me something more than I thought I already knew—that red and white were Poland's color scheme and that their Polish Eagle always flies high—well, this was the only way I knew how to officially report for duty.

First stop: Ground Zero—eastern Poland, early February in 1940, the moment when my family's "once upon a time" swerved horribly off course and their "happily ever after" turned into a fractured fairy tale—once all theirs, but now, suddenly mine to experience. I pressed play on a DVD filled with recorded family interviews. Moments later, words turned into animated images and the images pieced themselves together, boldly projecting onto the big movie screen of my mind. My eyelids fell shut.

Funny. Sometimes that's the only way to see everything more clearly.

~ ~ ~ ~

Part Two

The Story

CHAPTER FOUR

JOHN: *February 10, 1940*

I was six years old when it happened. It was very early in the morning, before dawn, and my five brothers and sisters and I were still asleep in our farmhouse in eastern Poland when our Mother came into our room and woke us up. Outside, we heard noises—people, vehicles, something. "Be quiet," Mother told us. Her voice was filled with concern. From the window we saw soldiers on the road and sleds being pulled by horses. One by one, the sleds branched off to individual houses in the area. When one of those sleds stopped right in front of our farmhouse, we all turned to our mother. We didn't know what to think of it. And then came the pounding on the door. Boom! Boom! Boom! "Quickly now, hide!" our mother urged and we obeyed, finding a spot beside the built-in stove by the wall in the front room.

There was more pounding at the door, and when my father opened it, two Russian soldiers barged into our house, bringing in the freezing cold with them. Immediately, one of the soldiers grabbed my father by the neck and shoved him right up against the wall. The soldier held him there. I think he may have even lifted my father off the floor a little bit. Somebody gasped—my mother, my sister, I cannot recall. We all stood there shaking, not so much from the cold air, but from the shock of it all. We feared for our lives.

The soldier had an armband with the letters NKVD on it. Later, I learned he was part of the secret Russian police. The soldier leaned in, his face right up to my father's, and said: "I will give you half hour to pack up some of your belongings. You are giving us this house and we are taking you to another place!"

My father just stared back at him. He was unable to speak. What could he do? This soldier meant business. He could kill him.

The soldier squeezed my father's neck harder. "Do you understand?"

And then ... he released his grip and my father dropped to the floor. Right away, my mother rushed up to him but we children stood back not knowing what to do; not knowing what was happening; not knowing what these soldiers would do next.

We felt completely helpless.

The soldier headed for the door. "Thirty minutes!" he reminded us.

Mother told us to go and pack; that we had to leave; we should hurry. She was a strong-willed woman: a God-fearing Catholic. Both my parents were. You knew better than to disobey my mother. She loved us. But she was also in charge. So, we obeyed her—rushing around like mad. Frantic, we stuffed some of our clothes and other belongings into empty pillowcases. My mother grabbed some bread and other food—potatoes and other vegetables—from the kitchen. And then my father took my older sister, Mary, out back to the chicken coop, where my other sister, Janina, also kept her pet goose. They came back with a sack filled with eggs and dead chickens. I could not believe it. My father had twisted the necks of the chickens, killing them. I guess he thought we would need food wherever we were going.

We heard the soldiers outside. Mother took me by the arm while carrying my younger sister Bernice, who was just three years old, and then all of us—my father, my older brothers Joe and Stanley and sisters Mary and Janina—walked out of our house we loved so much and right into the bitter cold. The sled was there on the road and I noticed a machine gun attached to the front of it.

"Get in!" one of the soldiers shouted. I could not take my eyes off his hands; they were clutching a bayonet.

My mother stood there for a few seconds, gripping the small wooden cross she had taken from her bedroom wall. The soldier noticed it.

He walked right up to her, looked my mother directly in the eyes and then grabbed the cross out of her hand and threw it into the snow.

"You will not need that where we are taking you!"

♦ ♦ ♦

ONCE UPON A MIDSUMMER'S HOLY DAY, a day filled with gracious thoughts and one of exceptional heat and humidity, a little boy and a little girl noticed each other for the very first time in the stuffy confines of an old church in a village in eastern Poland. How could it be, thought young Jadwiga, herself no more than seven years of age, that she had never seen the boy before? The village of Łąka was small, after all, and surely she would have noticed him with his family at one of the festivals held in the courtyard. But there he was, sitting right there in the pew directly in front of her, stealing glances at her while he knelt on the dreadful angled kneeler that she herself never truly enjoyed kneeling on at all.

As her mother fanned herself with a handkerchief, Jadwiga studied her new acquaintance with enquiring eyes, he with his dark brown hair combed back and eyelashes so much more thick and full than other boys. The next time the boy observed her, Jadwiga smiled. The innocent gesture startled the bashful creature and his chin immediately sunk into his chest. He kept his hands locked in prayer and prayed.

Silly thing, Jadwiga giggled, perhaps a bit too loudly for her stern mother scolded her for it on their walk back home with her father and sisters.

"Child, if I catch you laughing in church again, or at that boy…"

"But Mamma, he looked at me first!"

Head shaking in disapproval, her mother issued a stern warning: "Look to God. Forget the boy."

But it was not in the stars.

Months folded into years and the years created memories and the memories gave birth to a friendship and love that destiny deepened. And so, when Jacenty and Jadwiga were in their early twenties, after the Great War and just before the year of 1920, they exchanged marriage vows in the beloved church in which they met. They resided with Jacenty's family in the neighboring village of Łukawiec. Ted was their firstborn. And then came Mary, Janina, Joe, Stanley, John and Bronia, two to three years apart.

When Jacenty was informed that for his service in the Austrian Army during World War I, he could receive a plot of land in eastern Poland for a relatively modest price, Jadwiga encouraged him to take it. However, there was great risk. The land, some three hundred kilometers east of their villages, was close to the newly established borders of Poland and Russia, and with all of the political instability surrounding them, Jacenty feared taking it, even though Russia and Poland had agreed on a peace treaty in the early 1920s.

"My Beloved," Jadwiga pointed out. "Certainly more land will help our growing family. With seven children, how much longer would you have us stay with your mother and father? This land in the East … it will be a new beginning for us."

And so it came to pass that in the spring of 1939, Jacenty reluctantly surrendered. He took the land that was offered and the modest farmhouse that came with it in pastoral Liczkowce, near the village of Tarnopol. Soon, the entire family was enjoying life on the quaint acreage. The older boys tended to a cow and chickens. Janina coveted her white goose, distinctly marked with splashes of gray on its tail. They planted potatoes and cabbage and beets.

My God in heaven, Jadwiga often prayed, *thank you for our good fortune. Everything about our home is perfect and nothing will disturb us here.*

She had no idea how horribly wrong she was.

As Jadwiga slid across the snow-speckled seat in the sled and the frigid February morning air stung her cheeks, instinct took over. Quickly, she pulled the blankets over young John and little Bronia. They were still babies, she fretted, no more than six and three years of age. And what of her other children? Janina, not quite a teenager; Joe, so determined at ten; Stanley still in need of guidance from his elder siblings. At least her dear Mary had grown into a young woman, but even at eighteen, she still lacked the confidence to stand up for herself.

What could the soldiers possibly want with their family?

Jacenty, Joe and Stanley filled the sled in front of Jadwiga and suddenly Ted, her eldest son, flashed before her eyes. He had left the farmhouse several days ago to visit her mother back in Łąka in the west. Had Russian soldiers stormed into that area as well?

Was Ted safe?

Was her mother?

The fierce crack of a whip startled everyone. Suddenly, the horses began pulling the sled, blazing a trail through the countryside. Jadwiga dare not turn back, for she could not bring herself to watch the home she had come to love disappear in the darkness.

And where would they stop? The village of Tarnopol? Lwów was a much larger town but so far away. One of the soldiers had informed them they were being given another house; new land somewhere else. But how could they believe the Russians? Ever since fall, when reports came that Stalin's military had invaded parts of eastern Poland, the nerves of their countrymen had been tested. And rumors that Polish intelligencia had been arrested in Lwów did little to alleviate their growing fears.

Jadwiga pressed her palm against her coat, holding her heart, where she could feel the rosary necklace resting. *Mother of God, be with us now.*

An hour passed, perhaps two. When daylight arrived, it offered little solace, for now everything around them was more visible and the shock of winter white in the middle of the forest was foreboding. The sled stopped abruptly. Young John attempted to stand up, but Jadwiga's hand immediately fell upon his shoulder, forcing him back down. When Jacenty glanced back at her, Jadwiga followed her husband's distressed gaze onto the horizon where, less than a kilometer away, she saw the crowded train depot. Her eyes widened suspiciously at the sight of so many people at the station at such an early hour, but there was no time to reflect upon it because the sled was moving, rushing against a torrent of chilling wind. They stopped again, this time just several meters from the depot and the noisy fuss there demanded everybody's attention.

Jadwiga's heart skipped a beat upon sight of the long line of shaken, shambolic individuals. Poles! Their neighbors. Comrades. Hundreds of them, perhaps more.

Seemingly all at once, the soldiers, their breaths labored and their bayonets raised, were beside the sled, demanding they vacate the vehicle. Jadwiga instructed the children to move cautiously and remain close to her. One of the soldiers—tall, disarming, his face long, his brow furrowed—stretched his arm outward, insisting they all walk toward the back of the line. Everybody obeyed. Now positioned at the rear of a massive enclave, the family moved with methodical melancholy alongside approaching boxcars on the tracks. The entire herd lumbered awkwardly through the thick snow, distracted only by the intermittent pleas for mercy from some of the frightened souls in the line with them.

"Spare us!"

"Where are you taking us?"

"My children! Please—do *not* separate us!"

Futile appeals. They plodded into the desolate winter morning, unattended, and quickly disappeared into the void.

The cattle line moved on, but animals on a farm were better consideration, Jadwiga thought bitterly.

Several more soldiers approached.

"Get in line!"

"Stay in line!"

"We see everything!"

And so, the procession ambled across the snow on the walkway.

The family was beside the last boxcar on the track, but one gaze at the length of the row ahead was enough to induce panic. And just meters away, in several open boxcars, any question about what would happen to them next immediately became clear by a band of soldiers that found twisted delight in asserting their directives.

"Idiots!" some of them scoffed. "Get in the car! Now! Do not make us pull you aside!"

Into the cars their comrades went—men, women, children, old, young. If one of the boxcars was already been packed full, the guards saw nothing ill about grabbing other human beings and quickly shoving them up into the crammed compartment. A few unfortunate people hung clumsily from the inner sanctum and begged to be sent into another car, but their cries were ignored. Better to surrender to fate and allow oneself to be sucked through the gates of hell than endure an unpredictable soldier's wrath.

However, a few Poles resisted. As promised, they immediately encountered blunt force. Either the soldiers forced them back into the crowded cars or they were dragged out into the center of the walkway and beaten enough until their blood soiled the white snow on the platform underneath them.

"Get in the car!"

Jacenty locked eyes with the Russian soldier in front of him now, and then he tilted his head back so he could see his family behind him. But it only seemed to incense the soldier, who lurched forward. Immediately, Jacenty cleared a path for Jadwiga with little Bronia in tow.

Jadwiga took one look at the hysteria in the boxcar and was instantly filled with dread. It was full. How on earth did the soldiers expect any more bodies to fit inside of it? She glanced at her Beloved and then … all at once she was being lifted up into the congested cell. Carefully cradling Bronia's head with her free hand, she struggled to find her footing in the boxcar. She knelt on the floor for a moment, her back to the others below, and then hurriedly collected herself. By the time she was on her feet, young John was already being hoisted into the car, an expression of sheer terror on his face.

Stanley, Joe, and Mary followed in swift succession. Jacenty flung his arms up in the air and several men in the car raised him up straightaway. Jadwiga touched his shoulder, but the small comfort immediately vanished.

Janina! Where was their daughter?

Down below, the girl stood there, overcome with fear yet oddly fascinated … for in the distance, between a scurry of frenzied legs and boots, her eyes fixed on the delicate creature moving toward her along the platform amidst the chaos. Dodging the dance of madness before it, an anxious ruffle of its feathers and several audible *rronks* revealed its true identity.

Her goose!

Had it followed the family all the way from the farm?

The shock pierced Janina's heart so deeply that she momentarily lost her breath. Oh, how she adored her goose. She had held the goose egg before the creature hatched; warmed the egg with her own hands. She had cupped the gosling in her palms not long after it was born; cherishing it with all of heart. She had fed it; watched it grow.

In that split second arose a possibility: could she bring the goose with her?

"Janina!"

"JANINA!"

She turned. Someone grabbed hold of her and into a flurry of chaos Janina went. But the strong will of the child would not be broken. She was back on her feet in an instant, her head peering out of the boxcar.

Where was it? Her goose! Where?

Arms outstretched, she willed the creature to fly right up to her.

Pointless. The doors of the car were closing. One rapid tug on her coat collar and she was pulled back into the bedlam.

A moment later, everything turned a horrible shade of black.

~ ~ ~ ~

CHAPTER FIVE

JANINA:

They just shoved all of us into the boxcar. We were packed like sardines in a can. Horrible.

There were four wooden shelves, two on each side of the car, and one wood-fired stove in the middle, which some people fought to be near to keep themselves warm. Our family—not so fortunate. We were pushed to the side of the boxcar, and some of us shared the top shelf, the coldest place in the boxcar, it seemed to me.

The train was going full speed for some time, passing many towns and villages, but we could not know for sure. There were no windows in the car and we did not know day from night because there was never much light inside of the car; sometimes only a few rays of daylight coming through cracks in the walls. We could only judge what was happening from the noises we heard outside.

So many days passed. We were all very cold, and very very hungry ... and so very thirsty. I did not understand why this was happening to us. I just cried and prayed to God. We did not know what else to do. We prayed to be taken back home. We prayed for food. We prayed for water.

♦ ♦ ♦

AND SO IT CAME TO BE that on a train heading east toward a place far, far away from anywhere that remotely resembled anything safe and familiar, the ominous row of boxcars traveled into the unknown. The Poles had been traveling for several days, but despite the ongoing torrent of cries and prayers, not one among them knew where they were being taken. On a few occasions when the train did stop at a station, the doors of the boxcars roared open and an intense burst of bright white light forced everyone to cover their eyes. The blast of fresh air, although frigid and unkind, was welcome.

At several of these stops a Russian soldier made a brief appearance, either tossing into the car several buckets filled with snow or, if luck and supply collided, perhaps some bread. These were short-lived states of grace, but nobody argued for more. Instead, their curiosity persisted.

"Where are you taking us?"

"Why are you holding us against our will?"

"Do not let us die in here!"

Pointless.

The doors always slammed shut with hardly a word from the soldiers on the platform.

But the bucket of snow—what a bountiful gift from God it was. Immediately, it was passed around. Mothers broke off smaller pieces of the collected snow and like Holy Communion, placed it on the tongues of their young, thirsty children. Others grabbed a hearty handful of snow and swallowed it whole, oblivious to the souls in the rear of the car, or at the sides of the car, who remained less fortunate. Like the bread supply, which almost always ran out too quickly, the snow rarely found its way back to them. More enterprising creatures resorted to other measures to quench their thirst.

From a dank wooden shelf Young John shared with some of his family members, the boy had everything he needed. He would never be thirsty for long for all he had to do was stick out his tongue, place it on a nail on the side of the wooden post of his shelf and lick the ice that had formed there. Oh, how he began to relish those tiny cold droplets of moisture on his tongue.

"Brother, what are you doing? You have lost your mind!"

John contemplated his older sister Janina. "I am thirsty! You should try it."

"Well, I will never do it!"

John shrugged. More icy nails for himself.

However in the days that followed, the frozen nails were briefly forgotten, temporarily replaced by the foul stench permeating the car. Not one among them in the compartment had properly bathed in more than a week's time and the air reeked like an unkempt latrine in back of an old farmhouse. Any lingering remnants of dignity faded altogether as there was no proper place to relieve oneself in the boxcar, save, perhaps for a hole in the floor in one corner or the rise of hay in another corner, which had become an area for urination.

Parents resorted to escorting their small children to the hole or the hay. More often than not, the adults strongly suggested that children "hold it in" for as long as they could, quite possibly hanging on the thinnest strand of hope that when the doors of the boxcar opened again the soldiers would demonstrate a modicum of mercy and allow some of the occupants to relieve themselves outside in the bushes or by the trees near the station. But it was unwise to entertain such thoughts. The train had not stopped in days, and the children were always escorted to the hole by one of their parents or an older sibling, often having to force their way through the horde.

On one occasion, as Joe finished his business at the hole, he ambled by his father and brother, chin to chest. He did not utter a word.

Jacenty nudged John forward. "Now you go!"

"But Tata," he begged, his face flushed with embarrassment.

"Quickly now."

One gape at the hole in the floor and John dare not move another step. The sight of the icy tracks rushing below made his stomach turn. What if the hole in the floor broke open? What if he fell under the train? He would be crushed in an instant! John turned away and buried his head into his father's thigh, but Jacenty had grown weary of their ordeal and there was no time to properly console the child.

"Enough. Come now. I will hold onto the back of your coat. Just like last time."

Hastily, John turned his back to the crowd, loosened his pants and attempted to urinate through the hole. But the train was moving too fast and he nearly lost his balance.

"I got you," Jacenty assured him from behind.

Somehow John managed. When he finished, his father handed him the wool blanket that had been draped around his neck and shoulders.

John was confused.

Jacenty stared back at him. "Hold it up in front of me so that nobody will see me."

"But Tata!" John pleaded, not wanting to do it. If he had to hold up the blanket that meant that his father had to do more than just urinate. And everybody in the car was watching. He could feel it—all of the eyes just … staring at them.

"Hold it up!" Jacenty told him again, and proceeded to squat down.

Reluctantly, John lifted the blanket as high as his arms would allow and shut his eyes, blocking out the image of all the others around him. He could feel the tears trying to break through, but he would not cry. Not now. Not in front of all of the strangers.

When his father's hand found his shoulder again, John knew that his father was finished, and he immediately began plodding through the crowd, back to the family; back to his shelf. With any luck, he would not have to return to the hole for several more days and would not have to listen to the worried adults.

"We were at a station yesterday, but they did not open the doors."

"They are just trying to frighten us!"

"Why don't they kill us now! Why drag it out?"

One day, John noticed something occurring at the other side of the boxcar. A stout, plucky gentleman in a long black winter coat fussed over an empty bucket, his gaze fixated on the ceiling. John's attention lifted upward ever so slightly until it landed on a hole in the roof above the man. Transfixed, he watched as the man flung the bucket up to the ceiling. A second later, the object tumbled right back onto the floor. Three, four, five times the man tried to get it through the hole but with no success. The bucket dropped to the floor and rolled toward somebody's foot.

"Dammit!" cursed the man. "God help me!"

On and on the exasperated character went for some time, each attempt seemingly more frustrating than the last until, finally, the bucket passed through the hole in the roof.

The crowd erupted into cheers. Quite unexpectedly, John chuckled, the very act of which startled him. Nobody had smiled or laughed since that day the soldiers came.

"Pull it back. Pull it back!" the crowd urged the man with the bucket.

A few tugs on the rope that had been attached to the object and the pail returned to the man. Grinning ear to ear, he proudly showed off the bucket, now filled with snow that had collected on the roof of the boxcar. The group could barely contain their joy for it was as if they were being offered a very special Christmas present.

John rolled his tongue over his parched lips. *Water!*

No more frozen nails today.

~ ~ ~ ~

CHAPTER SIX

STANLEY:

We were traveling for nearly two weeks and people were getting sick. There was no food, so we were all hungry. What could we do? You go to sleep hungry. You wake up hungry. Many people died and the bodies were piled up on the side of the car. I could not stand the smell of the dead bodies.

One day, my mother asked my sister Janina to reach for Bronia from the top shelf of the car, where we were situated, and hand her down to her. Bronia was young—just turned three years old. Janina grabbed Bronia, but all of a sudden, the boxcar rocked and she lost her grip. Boom—Bronia fell to the floor face first. She hit her head on one of the shelves on the way down.

My mother screamed so loudly we had to cover our ears. And then, Bronia was crying. There was blood everywhere. I could not look at it.

My mother screamed for help; screamed to the guards. But the train was moving and there were no guards. Somebody handed my mother a wet rag and told her to hold it against Bronia's forehead— she had a gash right there in the middle, just above her nose and between her eyes. She cried and cried and cried into the night. The rag quickly became soaked in blood, so my mother ripped off part of her blouse and made another small cloth. And then another one when that one was filled with blood. She tried to comfort Bronia but she was in too much pain.

Finally, my sister settled down, but I could still see tears in my mother's eyes. She cried out for help but the Russians were not going to help us.

◆ ◆ ◆

AND SO IT CAME TO PASS that many tears were shed and so many hearts began to shatter. But within the railcar prison, not everyone lost hope. After all, there were religious people among them and by God's grace, a few prayers had been answered—a small fire in the stove emitted some heat and The Man With The Magic Bucket supplied them with snow.

One day, after the train stopped at a station and the boxcar's doors slid wide open again, two soldiers leapt into the car, startling the people near the doorway. Bayonets visible, they attended to the dead bodies in the pile and quickly dragged several of them toward the opening. One by one, the dead flew through the air and fell onto the platform below.

Nothing but unwanted scraps now.

During such demoralizing episodes, mothers clutched the rosaries around their necks, the wooden crosses firmly embedded into the flesh of their palms. A sign of the cross, a kiss, and onto another fierce round of prayer.

Jadwiga had been religious all her life. She may have lacked a warm, demonstrative representation of her true fondness for others—she had to be strong, after all, to keep her large family in order—but ever since she was a young girl, she prayed throughout each day. She had grown into a productive woman, short in stature but a force to be reckoned with. But now that her treasured home had been taken away and the family was forced into a desolate chamber without any explanation—and her youngest child nursing a head wound—she fought a rising helplessness.

Prayer was all she had.

As the doors slammed shut, Jadwiga turned away and rubbed a rosary bead in her hand. First, she mentally recited The Apostles Creed, and then The Lord's Prayer, and then three Hail Mary's, just as her mother taught her when she was a child.

Hail Mary, full of grace, the Lord is with thee. Blessed are thou among women, and blessed is the fruit of thy womb Jesus. Holy Mary, mother of God. Pray for us sinners, now, and at the hour of our death.

How long had she been at it?

Minutes?

An hour?

Mother of Mercy, our life, our sweetness and our hope! To thee do we cry, poor banished children of Eve; to thee do we send up our sighs, mourning and weeping in this valley of tears. Turn then, most gracious advocate, thine eyes of mercy toward us, and after this our exile, show unto us the blessed fruit of thy womb, Jesus. O clement, O loving, O sweet Virgin Mary!

Several days later, the doors slid open again. This time, they remained open longer than at some of the other stops. Not a soldier could be found monitoring the platform. Could it be a trick? For if anyone tried to flee, surely the Russians would shoot the culprit without hesitation.

The Man With The Magic Bucket attracted attention yet again, but he wasn't searching for snow. He peered out of the boxcar, down each side of the platform. Suddenly, he waved his hand, beckoning a man and a woman near him in the car. They approached, each holding one side of a large, faded-brown potato sack that appeared to be full.

How had the couple acquired a sack full of potatoes? For if they had food, surely they would have either shared it or been robbed?

The Man With The Magic Bucket kept vigil at the door.

"Now!" he huffed, motioning for the couple. "This is your only chance!"

Flustered, the couple anxiously handed over the potato sack and with fierce diligence, the troika carefully lowered it out onto the platform. Several of the car's occupants inched closer, studying the situation with cautious eyes. They stood there, mesmerized by the scene. And they would have remained in a trance were it not for the feverish shrill from a whistle coming from somewhere on the platform.

The soldiers—everybody could hear their approach.

All at once, the mob in the car drifted back for fear of being blamed for something in which they had not partaken. The woman at the door, her face positively panic-stricken, fell onto her knees and desperately flung her arms toward the potato sack on the platform.

"Grab it. Somebody help me!"

Three soldiers arrived, one of them firing off a round of curse words. He kicked the sack. Something inside of it moved. Audible gasps came from the crowd.

It only seemed to fuel the soldier's fury.

"Stupid peasant!" he spat and swiftly retrieved a knife from the side of his belt and proceeded to plunge it deeply into the sack.

"No!" shrieked the woman and she leapt to her feet, burrowing her head deep into her husband's chest, pounding his shoulders.

The soldier ripped open the sack.

Another scream.

"Mother!"

All eyes fell upon the delicate girl, not much older than young John, as she clumsily emerged from the potato sack unscathed. She had been inside of it the entire time.

The murmurs intensified and the grim reality sunk in—the parents were attempting to free their child. But now the girl was at the mercy of the Russian with the knife.

"Dear God, take her away from this!" the mother howled. "Let her go! Spare her!"

Desperate to settle the matter, the woman's husband handed his wife off to The Man With The Magic Bucket and stepped forward to face the guards. Perfect timing. The blow to his chest from the back end of the bayonet sent him falling back into the throng.

"Idiots! You think you can get away with such nonsense?" cursed the guard. "We see everything. We *know* everything!"

He grabbed the young girl by her coat collar and proceeded to toss her back into the car, the ripped potato sack following close behind.

"Next time, we kill her—and both of you!"

The firestorm of anger intensified as other soldiers stormed onto the scene. In the car, the woman was back on the floor, heaving through a flood of tears and hysteria as she held onto her daughter for dear life.

Moments after the doors slammed shut and the darkness returned, somebody pounded on the side of the boxcar—from the outside.

The Man With The Magic Bucket fixed his gaze through a small crack in the wall.

"They are marking our car with a big X."

The menacing silence filled every crevice of the boxcar now.

The Man With The Magic Bucket took several steps back and glared at the door in disbelief.

"A marked car means they will not open the doors—at all! They will give us nothing."

"No water!" somebody else chimed in.

Or wood, a few others may have thought, feeling the rising dread.

Grief-filled sighs circulated throughout the car. Several women began to cry. That did nothing to alleviate the situation, for each audible release only made their exhausted breaths more visible. All they could do was watch in desperate resignation as the life force left their weathered bodies only to disappear into the nether regions of their dank, frigid crypt.

~ ~ ~ ~

CHAPTER SEVEN

JOHN:

Whenever the train stopped, people in the boxcar pounded on the walls. They wanted to get food, water, or help, but nobody came to help us. Our door was marked. We were left in there to die. The Russians did not care. After a while, I could not stand looking at the dead bodies lying on the floor. I turned my head toward the wall so I would not see the bodies, but in my mind I could still see them. People were freezing, so much so that they started removing the clothes off of the dead people and put them on their own bodies. They were doing anything they could to keep warm.

I remember my mother peering at my father, tears spilling out of her eyes as if she wanted to say: "The children are shivering from cold and hunger. What are we going to do?" She was crying because she couldn't do anything for us. We were so terrified, hungry and cold, and we didn't know what to say. We were in shock. All we knew was that the Russian soldiers told us we were going to a nice place, but we didn't know where exactly and after all these weeks in a freezing car, nobody believed it any more. All that we did know was that when we asked for food, our mother and father couldn't give us anything, so we kept licking the icicles on the tops of the nails to get moisture.

Sometimes, our parents thought of ways to cheer us up, but they were in terrible shock, too, and about everybody in the boxcar was moaning and crying, and feeling the aches and pains of being sick or from being cold or frostbitten.

After about three weeks, the train arrived to the designated area and we learned we were in Siberia. And much later, that is was in the region of Novosibirsk. All the people were unloaded from the boxcars at this time and the dead were tossed off to the side, into the deep snow. The rest of us who could walk were pushed or kicked by the soldiers and ordered to march to the barracks that awaited us in the Siberian forest.

The nice place the Russians had told us about was a slave labor camp.

In our camp, we had about twelve barracks and each barrack held a number of wooden bunks, three levels high. It could house about fifty to seventy people. No mattresses or proper bedding there—just sawdust, about six inches deep in each bunk. We had no pillows to sleep on, no sheets or blankets to cover ourselves with. We slept in our clothes at night, but we kept scratching ourselves, trying to fend off all of the lice and other blood-sucking creatures that were in the sawdust. But what could we do? We just kept covering ourselves with the sawdust to keep from freezing to death. There was a large wood-fired stove in each barrack, but that did not generate much heat.

It seemed within the first day or two of being in the camp, the healthy adults were rounded up and assigned to duties. Most of the men, and people over the age of fifteen or sixteen were sent to cut down trees in the forest. In my family, only my father and my older sister Mary worked. The rest of us were too young. My mother did not work, because she had to take care of us.

What about the people who could not work because they were too sick or too weak? They didn't get anything to eat and drink. Nothing! The Russians had this saying: "Those that do not work, do not eat!"

The workers cut down the trees using long saws, all of it done by hand with old-fashion saws operated by two people, better known as push-pull action. The workers also had a daily quota to satisfy—it was called "norma." There were many men cutting down the trees. My sister Mary was eighteen years old but she wasn't as strong as the men.

THERE CAME A TIME when one among the family was to be tested.

One day, Jacenty rose before dawn and joined his eldest daughter, Mary, by the stove in the center of the barrack. They warmed their hands over the heat in silence, and Jacenty nursed a small cup of hot water. A brief respite before father and daughter went to work in the forest.

But soon, even this quiet ritual became too painful to endure, for whenever Jacenty retrieved the small portion of bread he had wrapped and kept in his coat pocket from the previous day's work, through the flickering shadows cast by the stove's flame he noticed young John across the room. The boy's head slowly rose up from the bunk he shared with his brothers, and father and son locked eyes. Jacenty cracked a faint smile through his fatigue and John lifted his head up higher in anticipation. His father peered down and considered the bread—a handful and no more than several hundred grams in all; his pay for an entire day's work. And then Jacenty began to divide the bread into several smaller pieces. He walked over to John, handed him a piece of bread, ruffled his hair, and gave more than half of the bread that remained to Jadwiga to pass out to the other children when they awakened.

Mary followed similar suit. Every morning the same: rise, warm hands, divide the bread among the family. Rote. But this was another day and they were all still alive.

Outside, other rituals unfolded.

Under the scrutiny of a commandant and his henchmen, adult males and select females of varying ages, teenage boys, and older teenage girls reported for duty. They lined up en masse—weak, solemn ghost-like—and began the nearly half-kilometer trek into the snow-covered forest beyond the camp's perimeter to a wide clearing, whereupon they were divided up.

Surrounded by trees, two men were sent to one tree, two others to another tree, and many others paired off elsewhere. They had all been given the same task: to saw down the trees. One man at one end of a saw, and another at the other end.

Push.

Pull.

One, two, three…

And again.

Push.

Pull.

One, two, three…

What misery. For often, the wood was impenetrable—seemingly frozen solid. And yet, the workers stood armed with a bitter sense of purpose, braving their soured hope so they would receive scraps of food if they met their daily norma.

How many of the trees they had to saw down always remained a mystery. As days and months passed, their greatest achievement became surviving the bitter cold. The more fortunate among them tended to the fallen trees in the clearing. There, they removed the branches and sawed the trunks into manageable batches. And all under the watchful eyes of soldiers and under a thick blanket of clouds so dismal gray and foreboding it would chill or ward off the most tenacious of evil spirits.

Few workers dared step out of place or utter a word in defiance lest they be kicked or beaten. Or worse, locked up for days and left to starve, only to be tossed right back into the assembly line of the working dead.

There was no rest during the day, save perhaps a fleeting segment of time mid-day, when the workers were offered a can of watered down porridge—just enough to provide a modest boost of energy to work for six more hours.

And what of Mary? Under normal circumstances, the teenager would have been married off back in Poland. However her fate was sealed almost immediately during her first week in the camp. She would work with the men.

As she trudged through the nearly thigh-high snow along with the others in the line on that very first day, her attention fixated on her father who was in front of her. Two by two the men began pairing off and were ordered to the base of a tree. As Mary watched her father leave with another man, her heart flooded with fear.

I am a woman. I cannot cut down a tree!

But she never allowed the words to pass her lips.

"Foolish girl," one of the other workers would have told her. "You certainly are old enough. No work. No food. That is the way it is now."

Bracing the reality of the situation, Mary clutched the collar around her coat, desperate to keep herself warm, and considered the menacing, long saw on the ground. Perhaps God would intervene. Perhaps her prayers to return back to her mother and the children in the barracks would be answered. Perhaps they could all go home again and she could marry and live a life on her own farm with her own husband.

However, the glare from a Russian soldier informed her otherwise. She would not be going back to the barracks that day—or home. Choking back tears, she watched as the man at the other end of the saw bent over and picked it up. He shot her a look of resignation and huffed. Quickly, Mary pulled her gloves beyond her wrists so they fit more snugly and lifted her end of the saw. As she and the man arrived at one of the trees along the perimeter, immediately her head fell back. She looked up and studied the gruesome height of the beast. There seemed no end to it.

When the man set the teeth of the saw against the trunk, Mary panicked. He was moving too fast. She had no idea what she should do. She searched for her father, but he was across the clearing, already working with another man.

"Do you want to get us killed?"

Killed? So shocked was she by her partner's comment, she felt the warmth completely drained from her body.

"Pull on it," the man insisted.

Nerves shattered, Mary dared not disobey him. She tightened her grip on the saw and slowly began pulling it toward her with all her strength, willing the teeth to find their way into the bark.

Push.

Pull.

One, two, three...

And again.

Push.

Pull.

One, two, three...

Immediately overcome with exhaustion, she could barely go on. Her arm and shoulder muscles burned from the sharp pain. She lifted her gaze yet again. Gray clouds everywhere. If there was a heaven above, surely the Russians had taken that away from them, too.

"Keep moving," the man prodded her.

Push.

Pull.

One, two, three...

And again.

Push.

Pull.

One, two, three...

Through labored breath, Mary struggled to keep up with him. And then, suddenly, she felt the saw blade rip deeper into the bark.

But it may as well have been her heart.

~ ~ ~ ~

CHAPTER EIGHT

STANLEY:

It was bitter cold in the camp. I never felt such an awful cold. All of the men were sent to work and the women without families went with them. The snow was above the knees, sometimes at the waist, so the workers needed that snow cleared by the trees and a few of the female workers helped with that. When the tree was finally cut and it fell down, some of the workers took off the branches and peeled off the bark. Other people sawed the tree and the logs were stacked up. Later, at or around nighttime, a flatbed truck came and the workers put the logs on the truck and they were taken away somewhere.

One time, my father was assigned to do something else. He was very weak at this time, but he took me to work with him one day when he was assigned to monitor a booth. Sometimes, a guard was inside, and in the booth there was a stove where one could heat water for tea. My father was told to stand watch and whenever the soldiers got cold, they came to that booth and warmed their hands and drank tea.

There was a stable for the commandant in our camp with horses inside. I remember how the commandant sat on the horse and told people to go to work. I shivered at the sight of that man because my father and sister were his slaves. I believe he was the same guard who, when we first came to the camp, ordered the other soldiers to tell the adults that the kids had go to school.

I will never forget that first day of school. On one wall, there was a picture of Stalin and Lenin. And on another wall, Marx. After school, my brother Joe and I, and some of the other children, came back to the barracks in tears. We told our mother there was no way to pray in the school; that the soldiers would not allow us to pray, and what would we do if we couldn't pray? My mother hugged us and told us it was going to be okay; we could still pray.

"Pray to the only God you know," our mother insisted. "Remember what I am telling you. Please, children, pray!"

But we were terrified. We wanted to pray, but we were afraid we would be punished if the guards caught us.

◆ ◆ ◆

ALL EYES WERE UPON THEM, but none of the soldiers could see into their dreams … for it was there, in their imaginations, where festive kitchen tables materialized—each filled with precious meals from the homeland. Oh, how the deported treasured such images, clinging to them as they arose each morning only to return back to the nightmare in which they were living. Food, once so plentiful back home in Poland, quickly became a precious commodity in the camp and the struggle to attain enough of it a continuous measure of strength or weakness.

Wives, woeful and tearful, watched as their husbands and older children—the majority of them already malnourished, weak, or fighting illness from their ordeals in the boxcar—left the barracks each morning and returned some ten, eleven, or twelve hours later. Exhausted, they sported not much more than a small loaf of bread to be shared among the entire family.

The chance that a Russian guard would disperse additional clothing to fend off the cold was rare. Winter coats or gloves were handed out sparingly and the unfortunate Poles who feverishly vacated their homes back in Poland without proper boots or footwear—overtaken by their fear of being killed on the spot—in just a short span of time, could not bear another long day in the snow, their feet completely exposed to Siberia's haunting cruelty. They would have to become enterprising—for their families, for themselves, for the hope of living one more day. Either that—or perish. Some of them found rags, soiled clothes, or strands of ripped garments, and wrapped the flimsy, filthy bits around their feet or weathered shoes.

What more could they do?

And yet, rare moments of levity occurred. Some were born of the women—the wives and mothers who were forced to bond together in solidarity in a battle that took place closer to the barracks.

Several dozen children of various ages were sent to school in the camp. Janina, Joe and Stanley attended. During the first few sessions, the children sat in the classroom for several hours and were told to listen attentively to the men standing at the front of the room, who addressed them in Russian.

The commandant took a long stick and pointed to a picture on the wall of a man with a thick dark mustache.

"Backo Stalin!" he told the class, his dark eyes scrutinizing the children's faces. Nobody said a word. The commandant whacked the stick against the wall, directly underneath the large picture.

"BACKO STALIN!" he screamed, prompting the room.

Petrified, the children turned to each other for clues on what to do, but that only seemed to anger the man even more.

"BACKO STALIN!" he ordered.

A young boy sitting in the front row began to sob. A moment later, the commandant's stick landed on a table, its smack igniting terror.

"BACKO STALIN!" the commandant urged, this time more pressing.

"Backo Stalin!" the class immediately repeated.

"BACKO STALIN!" the commandant barked yet again.

"Backo Stalin…" the children reluctantly recited.

Later, back at barracks, Jadwiga listened as the children relayed the story.

"Do not listen to the man," she urged. "Pray. Keep praying—just as I taught you. But do it in silence. The commandant will never know what you are doing."

Other mothers fretted, a few wept.

"They are brainwashing our children!" one of the mothers pleaded. "What hope do we have now?"

Another day. Another story to relay.

Joe said: "The Commandant says all prayer is forbidden—that if we pray, we can only pray to Backo Stalin!"

Jadwiga stood there for a moment and allowed what she had heard to penetrate her mind. She did not blink. "We shall see about that."

The following morning, after the workers had been ushered off, a Russian soldier made his rounds around the barracks. He was to escort several of the children to the classroom again, wait inside, and stand watch until they had completed their lessons for the day—a fortunate assignment for it was much warmer indoors than to being sent into the wretched forest to oversee the workers cutting down trees.

But something was not right. The soldier stopped and glanced back at one of the barracks. Earlier, he had pounded on the door but nobody had come out. He turned around, walked back and smacked his palm several times against the outside wall.

"Out! Now!"

Still nothing.

He did not have time for such nonsense. Hand gripping his military belt, he walked back to the door, forced it wide open and proceeded to walk inside.

"Outside. Come!"

However, a quick search for the children only triggered concern. The majority of the women stood in front of the bunks. Head tilting slightly, he stole a glimpse of a boy in a bunk behind one of the mothers. Scrutinizing the entire portal now, he realized all of the children were hiding behind a barricade of females.

"*Out!* The children go now!"

The women did not move.

"Quickly!" he added, heading back toward the door. "The children attend school!"

"Not today. If the children cannot pray, they will not go to school."

The soldier stopped dead his tracks. He turned around and faced the women. What nonsense was this? Who would be so foolish to defy him?

The man retraced his steps with deliberate intent, his slate eyes narrowing as he inspected each and every woman. "If the children do not go to school then we will arrest all of the adults. And how would you like that?"

Silence.

The corners of his mouth rose in satisfaction. He was back to the door in no time.

"Then arrest us!"

He spun around. "Who said that?"

Nobody breathed a word.

Jadwiga stood with the others—frozen, yet positively solid in their collective resolve. Suddenly, the armor of fear and cautiousness she'd been carrying for weeks fell off of her body and crumbled into a million little pieces onto the filthy floor beneath her. How dare the man insist on taking their children away from their only solace—their mothers? And for what? To turn them against the only faith they had ever known and proclaim their undying affection to whom—*Backo Stalin*? No. Mary had already been taken from them, dragged into the frozen abyss and forced to perform feats beyond her capacity. She would not stand for this.

Jadwiga held her focus on the wall in front of her.

"If you arrest us, where will you take us?" She mused, indicating their squalid surroundings. "Somewhere worse than this?"

The soldier remained at the door.

More time to do her bidding.

"You do not need our children. After all, you have our husbands and some of our women. Surely, that should satisfy the requirements of your people."

She paused—long enough to secure the argument.

"Of course, we will all stay out of your way, obey all of your standard camp rules, and never be a bother to you and the other important soldiers as I am sure your men have very serious things to do. Fretting about the children in our barracks would simply be a nuisance to you. They are so young, after all. They should remain here. With their mothers."

A menacing glare and yet, the soldier said nothing at all.

Nobody moved. Nobody breathed. Clearly, there would be hell to pay.

Seconds later, the man stormed out of the barrack and slammed the door. The impact forced the entire structure to rattle. Heartbeats racing, the women stood in a state of shock. One panic-stricken mother immediately rushed to the window.

"What have we done? He will have us arrested. He is going to come back!"

Jadwiga exhaled. "The man will not be coming back."

~ ~ ~ ~

CHAPTER NINE

BRONIA:

> I was too young to remember. I don't remember the soldiers coming to the farmhouse in Poland. I don't remember being taken away on the sled. I don't remember being in the boxcar with my family. I don't remember falling down from the shelf in the boxcar and nearly dying. I was too young at the time. I remember things later on, but nothing about all of that. I must be one of the few lucky ones. Now that I know what happened there in Siberia, and what some of the kids went through—what my brothers and sisters, and my parents went through in that miserable place—I thank God I do not remember one thing.

◆ ◆ ◆

AND THEY ALL CAME TO KNOW THAT Siberian winters were not for weak or timid souls. Frequent and heavy snowfalls, and temperatures that often plummeted to forty below Celsius, had assured them that Mother Nature, like the Russians, had also become a prominent foe. Confronting her was not easy. Surviving her was even worse.

As the death toll in the camp rose, the strong-willed among them survived the first winter in the camp. Those who perished were discarded, tossed out into the snow and piled against a barrack wall or on the side of the commandant's barn, until a proper transport arrived to deposit their remains in ditches in the forest or other unmarked graves. Rarely did the transports arrive in a timely fashion, and on more than one occasion, the camp workers reporting for work in the morning might spot in the pile a dead comrade who had worked alongside them the day before.

With the dead visible to the human eye, some mothers forbade their children to gape out of the barrack window, or venture too far from the barrack for fear that they would witness the horrible sight. But over time, weakened by lack of food and the monotony of daily suffering inflicted upon their husbands, brothers, older children, and single females, the women resorted to prayer, begging God that the dead bodies be removed.

By late summer of 1940, after nearly five months of confinement, Mother Nature released her vicious spell over the camp. The gray skies parted somewhat. The sun returned. Pale, frail, and crestfallen, the prisoners covered their eyes as they looked at that sun with morbid fascination. Perhaps they had believed they would never see such a glorious sight again.

The warm weather offered levity. The working conditions—still a brutal kind of hard labor—became slightly better without the deep snow. In an effort to keep their families nourished and alive, mothers were allowed to take their children into the forest just outside the camp's perimeter. It seemed to defy logic … for if the prisoners were allowed to roam freely, surely a few of them might attempt to escape for good. But where would they go, fugitives in a strange land, only to be hunted down by the soldiers who kept watch?

And so it was in the forest during spring and summer that these mothers and their children occasionally found comfort. They ripped off bark from the birch trees as anxiously as their hands would allow. The more enterprising among them punctured holes into the tree using sharpened sticks and retrieved the sap. The bark would later be used to make soup and the sap, the perfect syrup for their bread. They collected berries and gathered mushrooms. Anything remotely resembling something edible became fair game, even flowers. After all, the Russians were not about to increase the bread supply. The sojourns into the forest were a blessing.

When the cold weather and snow returned in late summer and early fall, the forest treks came less often, but on the rare occasion they did occur, Jadwiga instructed her children to dig deep into the snow and find as many frozen roots from plants and bushes as they were able—perfect ingredients for soup or porridge.

In the evenings, when Jacenty and Mary returned from work, the family and some of the others in the barrack were eager to consume whatever Jadwiga and the other women made from the scraps. Before they bowed their heads down in prayer, one among them first looked at the man or woman standing watch by the window. Several soldiers had caught other prisoners praying and they were immediately punished—beaten or sent to confinement.

"Pray to Father Stalin," the soldiers often remarked upon capturing the offenders. "He is the only one who can help you here."

A mindful soul standing watch at the window was necessary.

"All clear," he would inform them, and quickly, the Catholics in the collective made the sign of the cross and gave thanks for their daily blessings— their health, their family remaining intact, the souls of the dead who had passed and the hope that they would be set free and return to their homeland.

Before dawn, Jacenty and Mary rose for work yet again. Another day. Another quota to meet. Another few grams of bread to share.

And when snow fell steadily again during the new year of 1941; when the temperatures plummeted below zero once more, signaling the return of another long winter, the soldiers issued warm clothing to prevent people from freezing to death. Many of the Poles questioned why the soldiers bothered as it appeared the NKVD were simply waiting for the captives to quicken the pace of the slow exhausting death to which they were being subjected.

And still, no amount of prayer could have halted the twisted fate that fell among them. It seemed as if the men—those who had endured more than a year of atrocious working and living conditions; those who had ached and suffered their way through a long, hungry day of hard labor to remain alive for their family—were quickly dying off.

Widows mourned, crying relentlessly through the night.

"Where is God? Why is this happening to us? Show us mercy."

There were crueler twists: Dead children. In the family's barrack, aside from the Migut children, only three other children remained. And the other barracks had even fewer children.

Like the previous winter, soldiers collected the dead and deposited them into the snow on the side of a barrack. Often, days passed without a transport to claim the bodies. The frozen corpses remained there, piling up two, three high, forming a long doomful row. No mother could have foreseen what followed, and few were actually aware of it. How many days had young John—and the few young children who were still alive—played "Hop and Stop" among the dead?

It was a relatively easy game to comprehend, but not simple to maneuver. One among them yelled out the word "Hop." And then, one by one, the children took turns jumping over one corpse to the next—without falling onto the dead body or the snow. The frozen corpses were as stiff as tree trunks and yet very slippery. One had to concentrate. And when the prompter gleefully called out, "Stop!," all at once, the children ceased moving and did their best to remain as still as possible. A few of the little ones didn't make it. They slipped on the snow and tumbled awkwardly atop a frozen corpse.

Laughter. "Come on, let's try it again!"

When John returned to the barrack after such excursions, he never shared anything about his Hop and Stop game. Surely his mother would punish him. But as the days passed that winter and the children in the barrack seemed to disappear, never to return again, John found the courage to ask his mother something to which he feared the answer.

"Mother, where have all of the children gone?"

Jadwiga placed her hand on her son's shoulder.

"Do not worry about that now. Just know that God is listening to our prayers. God is helping us."

~ ~ ~ ~

CHAPTER TEN

JOHN:

In August of 1941, we heard the news— that Russia became an ally with Great Britain to defeat Hitler. We were told we'd been granted amnesty. Amnesty? That sounded as if we had all done something wrong. But it didn't matter. We were to be set free from that horrible camp. After eighteen months there, we were all sick and practically skin and bones.

News spread through the camp that the Polish Army in Exile was being led by General Anders and the army would fight alongside Russia to help defeat the Nazis. The young men in our camp, sick and weak as they were, wanted to fight for our country, so they enlisted and were told where to go. My father was in his forties, but he was very weak, mostly from malnutrition. Mary too. So, my father could not enlist.

We did not know where to go, but when the gates of the camp were raised and we were free to leave that place, we couldn't get out of there fast enough. We all rushed to gather as much as we could. We placed berries and bread into a cloth and tied it onto a stick. Like penniless, hungry hoboes we walked toward the gates, and I will never forget that day. Three families walked together toward the gate—our family walked in between two other families, not as large as ours. As we approached the gate, somebody took my hand.

And when I turned to see who it was, I noticed we all were holding hands—all three families locked together.

We walked through those gates in solidarity. My mother and some of the others decided to set the course south along the railroad tracks, hoping to reach some kind of civilization before nightfall. She figured if we headed south, we could eventually escape the cold. It was August and winter would be coming soon. That first evening, we all slept in a remote train station that was being used for log storage. The following afternoon, a train full of logs, probably from a Siberian camp, stopped at the station. When the train started moving again, we all jumped into the last empty boxcar and snuck a ride, pressing close together that evening so we could all stay warm. Fearing the conductor would catch us, we got off the train the following morning as it was slowing down to stop at another station. The adults thought the Russians would report us to the authorities if we were caught. Nobody trusted the Russians—amnesty or no amnesty.

My mother was not a highly educated person, but she knew that we had to move south to stay warm and survive. From the position of the sun she always pointed out the right direction. For several days we were fine, hopping on trains or walking through fields and forests near the tracks. But then the dogs came.

We were walking through a village near one station when a pack of dogs quickly sniffed us out, which was not hard for them to do because we smelled pretty bad. So there we were, with all these dogs suddenly coming at us. We ran and ran as fast as we could, but it didn't take that long for those dogs to catch up with us. They had a field day with the smelly Polish hoboes. Thank God for my older brother Joe. He found a big stick and whacked the dogs, until finally they let us be. We had to hide in the woods for the rest of the day and travel by night to avoid similar situations with dogs.

♦ ♦ ♦

THERE CAME A TIME when the storm clouds parted and from the heavens came unexpected rays of grace. For how could it possibly be true that the Poles were free to leave the camp? And yet, with no protocol in place to properly guide them on what to do or where to go next, the pocket of good fortune delivered a powerful irony—the Polish deportees had arrived at the Siberian camp in a boxcar and in a boxcar they rode to their freedom.

They stole rides in open transports they found along the railway or at train stations. They tramped from one village to the next. They searched through garbage pales for scraps of food. Young males, eager to assist their families, took measures into their own hands. Some of them created slingshots. There was no better way to kill rabbits or other small animals. After all, they needed to find food and now, everything was fair game—chickens, squirrels, gophers.

The three families that left the camp together remained together during long stretches of their new journey. Occasionally, the entourage met other wandering Poles who had been released from other labor camps. At these serendipitous intersections, information was exchanged and they discovered there were hundreds, perhaps thousands, more just like them—everyone apparently heading south, just as they were, desperate to escape the cruel clutches of their Russian captors.

Weeks passed. And then, another month or two vanished behind them.

In an effort to avoid being sighted or mocked by villagers for their wretched appearance or miserable stench, the group slept during the day and in the evening hours, walked or traveled by train whenever they could find transport. When, almost by chance they learned from other traveling comrades that the Polish Army in Exile might be gathering for military maneuvers in Uzbekistan, in southern Russia, it fueled their original intentions to head south.

One day, Joe inquired, "How much farther must we go?" His father was weak, and now he had a duty to help guide the entire family.

Jadwiga shook her head. There was no way of knowing.

"We stay the course, then," Joe said. "We will find a decent refuge."

More than two months into the odyssey and more than a thousand kilometers away from the labor camp, the physical toll was affecting everyone. So exhausted were some of the young Migut children that brother Joe took turns carrying them on his back. The endeavor was even more excruciating for Jacenty and Mary, each braving their own emotional and physical suffering from the hard labor they endured back in the camp.

The sight of her Beloved and Mary alarmed Jadwiga. She prayed God would strengthen them until they arrived safely in a larger city in Uzbekistan, perhaps near the Polish military, where they could receive proper care. A hopeful thought, but now Janina was battling her own afflictions as well. Some of their fellow travelers had also become ill, many of them erupting into severe coughing fits or lacking the strength to walk for long stretches.

But they simply kept moving.

Some days delivered small joys—the splendid appearance of a fruit tree in a meadow or a stranger on the road with a cart. Filled with optimism that the passing visitor in the arba might spare them food, Joe, Stanley and young John, rushed to the traveler's compartment. Often, these courageous whims found them returning empty-handed and, clutching her rosary, Jadwiga's heart sank. She had to feed her children.

"If there's one carriage, there will be another," she remained optimistic. "One day, there will be food in one of them."

A week later, the temperatures warmer, the sun shining brightly, young John ran up to yet another stranger in a passing arba. From a distance, Jadwiga watched as her youngest son engaged the farmer in conversation—how and in what language she did not know. Surely the farmer was Russian, but by now most of the children understood some of the language and they were able to interpret what the locals were saying.

Suddenly, John waved his arms, motioning for the family.

"This farmer is heading toward the big city and he can give us a ride part of the way," he reported enthusiastically.

Relieved, Jadwiga quickly gathered the others and they all climbed into the horse-drawn arba. Such demonstrations of grace did not go unappreciated. The clan cheerfully gave thanks to God and showered the farmer with praise. And when young John sat up to study the road ahead, the man inspected the boy more closely. Moved by the family's plight, the farmer reached into his travel bag and retrieved a small round loaf of bread, the sight of which brought keen interest. He handed it to John, who turned back to his mother.

"Thank him," Jadwiga said, "and pass it around."

Surely, good fortune shone down on them.

John ripped off a piece of bread and nearly swallowed it whole before Jadwiga swiped the remaining loaf from him and began sharing it with the others. She placed a small piece in front of Jacenty's lips and waited for him to respond. Nothing. Unshaven, his hair unkempt, his body rail thin; she willed him to take a bite.

"See how fortunate we are, my Beloved," she whispered. "Come now. Eat!"

Jacenty responded, but the victory was short-lived when another tortuous image invoked despair—Janina. Eyes sunken, her face flushed, her illness was progressing at alarming rate.

Jadwiga placed a hand on her daughter's forehead. The girl was burning with fever and the rash on her neck and shoulders seemed to be spreading. She debated if she should inform Jacenty, but it would just make him suffer all the more. They had to get to Uzbekistan. If the rumors were true, it would be their only chance to locate the Polish Army and finally receive aid. Surely their own military would not turn their backs on them. But would Janina make it? Or Jacenty and Mary for that matter?

Jadwiga moved up to the front of the arba, behind the farmer, and asked him if there was a hospital nearby. He nodded.

"How much father then?"

The farmer made references to various points down the road and, later that evening, before the man left the family at a train station, he gave Jadwiga instructions on how to locate the hospital. He was walking back to his arba when Jadwiga called out for him.

"Thank you, sir. May God be with you."

The man stood there in silence for a moment. He shrugged, turned around and offered only a loose wave of the hand. He climbed aboard the arba and soon disappeared down the road as mysteriously as he materialized.

The following morning, in the single-story hospital building with two arms stretching out from a main unit on either side, Jadwiga quickly inspected the interior. The building appeared to be decades old, but in better condition than the wretched camp from which they came. Besides, she had no other choice. Janina was so weak now that she could barely stand up on her own. Hours later, after her daughter had been admitted into a room occupied by two other patients—Poles perhaps—several nurses breezed through the hallway outside Janina's room. Their facial expressions were filled with disdain and Jadwiga wondered whether her daughter would be safe in the hands of the Russians.

She took Jacenty's hand.

"We will come back for her," she guaranteed him. "But first, we must reach Uzbekistan in time to find the Polish Army. They can help us."

The proclamation momentarily awakened Jacenty from a dismal lethargy.

"It is not right," he said, his voice hoarse. "How can we leave her like this?"

He insisted on staying there through the night, but a few of the nurses refused such an imposing idea. Through disconcerting looks, the women insisted that the family vacate the premises and return another day. The following afternoon, Jacenty attempted to exert his will yet again. He wanted to stay the night—beside his daughter. The nurses refused. Another day, another failed attempt.

"Your daughter will not be getting well any time soon," one of the nurses warned Jadwiga. "She has typhoid fever. Leave her here unless you all wish to be further exposed."

Jadwiga glanced at Janina—helpless, feverish, lips chapped, her blond hair thinning out. She turned away, not able to bear the sight of her daughter's suffering. It was Jacenty who gently took his daughter's hand, brought it up to his cheek and held it there.

"My dear daughter, I love you so much."

Jadwiga proceeded to inform one of the nurses that they were headed toward Tashkent in Uzbekistan. Oh, how she prayed the women would inform Janina of their whereabouts once she was better. But the grim decision to leave their daughter behind was killing Jacenty.

"My beautiful daughter," he wept, his hot tears dripping off his face and onto Janina's arm as she lie there in the bed. "I love you with all my heart, and I am afraid I will never see you again."

Dumbfounded, Jadwiga stepped away from the bed. Why on earth had Jacenty said that? Their daughter was not going to die. She would not. He would see her again—*they* would see her again. She stood there in silence, attempting to take it in.

And then her heart sank. Perhaps her Beloved thought that is was *he* who would be meeting their Heavenly Father. The very idea nearly took her breath away. However, such emotional blows were becoming all too common.

First their home…

And then the boxcars…

And then the camp…

And then the treacherous wanderings with seemingly no end in sight.

And now—Janina!

What more could be taken from them? Fighting back the tears, Jadwiga struggled to hold onto the smallest shred of hope, but she could feel something beginning to harden around the walls of her soul.

She turned around and walked out of the hospital room.

Janina was in God's hands.

~ ~ ~ ~

CHAPTER ELEVEN

JANINA:

My father and mother were sitting with me on the bed in the hospital. Oh, he was crying so hard that his tears kept falling onto my hand and arms. One drop. Then another. Hot tears. He thought he would never see me ever again. My heart was breaking open. What was happening? I did not understand why I was being left there in the hospital; why I could not stay with everybody. I was so sick and confused that sometimes, I could not think straight.

And then ... I was all alone.

Why had I been abandoned?

Why had my family left me?

What had I done?

One day, a nurse came up to me and ripped the religious medallions off of my neck because she and the other workers didn't believe in God. They smirked. They laughed at me, saying: "If you are so religious ... if you are such a good Catholic, why are you lying in that bed? Where is your God now?"

It went on like this for a while. Weeks went by. Maybe a month. I was still weak.

Finally, one day, I asked for a mirror, but when I held it up in front of my face, I was frightened by what I saw. I did not recognize the person staring back at me. I had lost most of my hair. I let go of the mirror and it fell onto bed. I wept, crying out to God, "Please, God in Heaven, help me. Please!"

One of the nurses heard me and began to laugh. I closed my eyes. I did not want to see her or hear her. I was raised Catholic. I was religious. My heart ached. I wanted to be with my family.

As the weeks passed, I temporarily forgot how to speak Polish. All I could hear around me was Russian. And when I thought the nurses were beginning to show some mercy, they came into the room one day and closed the door behind them. There were other patients in the room, but they were sick and sleeping. I thought the nurses were going to give me some medicine, but all of a sudden, one of them grabbed my wrist, opened my hand and thrust a small needle right underneath my fingernail. The pain was so excruciating that I screamed but another nurse just stood there and laughed.

"Nobody can hear you. Your God cannot hear you!"

The nurse with the needle found another finger and immediately forced it underneath my fingernail. I never felt such horrible pain. I started to cry.

Finally, I cried out: "What do you want from me? Why are you doing this?"

"Tell us everything that you know. Tell us what the Poles are planning."

I had no idea what she was talking about! Why was she asking me such a thing? I told her I did not know anything, but this was not what she wanted to hear. She took the needle and forced it underneath another one of my fingernails. One by one, that woman kept poking me and prodding me. It was unbearable. My face was wet from the tears.

And then she leaned in closer to me and said: "So far, your God has done nothing for you. Why don't you pray to Stalin and see how he will help you."

"No!" I screamed back. "I am Catholic. I believe in God. I do not have any secrets for you!"

The nurses just stood there leering at me, their eyes filled with contempt. They hated me.

After they left, I could not stop sobbing. I buried my head into the pillow and just cried and cried into the night. The nurses must have heard me and began plotting something because when I finally fell asleep, I was jolted awake suddenly by a black cat that had leapt onto my bed. I sat up, frightened to death. At the doorway the nurses were there—just laughing. They had thrown the black cat onto the bed to scare me.

I kept praying throughout the night, asking for help: "Under your protection, we are asking you Blessed Mother to help us with our daily needs and shield us from harm. You are our inspiration in our lives, please ask your Son Jesus Christ for the blessings and healings for your children, in your Son's precious name I pray … Amen!"

Over and over I kept saying it.

"Blessed Mother … you are our inspiration in our lives…"

"You are our inspiration in our lives."

"You are our inspiration in our lives…"

When I finally drifted off and fell asleep, I noticed it had begun to snow outside. I fell into a deep, peaceful sleep, which was strange considering what had just happened to me. Later that night, I opened my eyes and gazed out the window. The sky appeared very unusual to me now—a light glow of colors. And then, suddenly, the sky just opened up completely. I could not believe my eyes. It was the Virgin Mary! At first, I thought I was dreaming but it felt so real. How could it be a dream? I could not take my eyes off of her. She was so beautiful, there in the sky with Baby Jesus in her arm.

And then, the Blessed Mother smiled at me and reached one arm out toward me and put her hand over my bed.

"Do not cry," she told me in the most soothing voice. "You will be fine. Everything will be fine. I have heard all of your prayers. You do not need to be frightened. Remember that you are loved. You will be leaving this place soon."

And then she just disappeared.

About a week later, something happened. The doctors said I was well enough to leave. I was in that hospital for many, many months and every day was gloomy and gray—so miserable. But on the day I walked out of that hospital, the clouds were all gone and the sun was shining.

Now, I had to find my family!

◆ ◆ ◆

IN A ROOFLESS CLAY HUT on an Uzbeki farm, in the middle of an unfamiliar land, the family found an unlikely yet reliable shelter. They stumbled upon it late one evening, only to be found the next morning by an Uzbeki woman who was shocked by the sight of the filthy creatures lying in the mound of hay inside of her hut. No doubt she was also overtaken by their stench. But the woman's heart melted upon realizing the strangers might be Polish refugees. She promptly fetched a pail, filled it with water, and brought it back to the family, along with several pieces of bread.

"Thank you. Bless you," was all Jadwiga could say, for she, too, struggled to find energy through an all-consuming exhaustion.

More than a week had passed since they deposited Janina in the hospital and they had traveled for far too long. Just days before finding the hut, all of them could have been worse off had the boys not stumbled upon a cemetery along the road. The family would have quickly bypassed such a dreadful sight of open graves and kept moving, but there were objects in those graves that could not be dismissed. Lying atop the wrapped corpses was an assortment of food—fruit, bread, and meat. Jadwiga did not know what to make of it at first.

"It must be an offering for the dead," Joe mused.

And the offerings became a blessing that kept them alive for another day. Rosary in hand, Jadwiga thanked God for the discovery and told the boys to leave a few small scraps behind for the deceased.

And now, in the hut, somewhere in a foreign land, another miracle—the Uzbeki woman offered water and bread to the children.

"You are all very sick," the woman told Jadwiga.

"Typhoid," Jadwiga offered through the fatigue. She studied the women. Her gray apron was soiled and her dark hair was pulled back and tied into a bun. In some ways, the woman reminded Jadwiga of herself—back on the farm in Poland. She shook off the memory before it tore yet another hole in her heart.

"Our other daughter," Jadwiga went on. "We left her. A hospital somewhere."

The woman nodded as if she understood, but who knew for sure? Polish and Russian dialects were similar, but Jadwiga had been battling a constant stream of grief and was now finding it difficult to concentrate. She prayed the woman would allow them to use her hut, at least until the family found proper care.

The woman handed Jadwiga a tin cup filled with water and considered Jacenty and Mary who appeared worse off than the others.

"I know of a man who can take them to a hospital in the city. In Tashkent. It is not far and they can receive proper treatment there."

Tashkent? So they were in close proximity, after all.

Later that afternoon, arrangements were made for Jacenty and Mary to be taken away on an arba. From a ramshackle wooden fence near the road on the woman's property, Jadwiga watched as her Beloveds were carted away.

"I promise I will come to you," she whispered to herself. When they were out of her sight, she willed herself to return to the hut where the remaining children were still resting. Inside, she fell upon the hay and grabbed her children's hands. She contemplated the clear sky above them through their roofless new domicile. The sight of the bright blue sky above was enough to invoke praise to God— and certainly, the cool temperature was much warmer and more bearable than Siberia—but the dull ache around Jadwiga's heart simply would not cease. She feared everything was being taken away from her.

Even her health. As the week progressed, her fever lingered.

Braving the sluggishness brought on by her illness, Jadwiga did her best to tend to the children. Like her, Stanley and Joe were battling fevers. One day, in an effort to thwart the beast, she ripped off portions of her ratted dress into long strands, soaked them in a bucket of cold water, and placed the soaked strips atop her children's foreheads, begging God to halt any advancement of the illness. Disoriented, her own face flushed, she clutched her rosary.

God, please make me strong. Please heal us. Help me find Mary and my Beloved. Help Janina.

Several days later, feeling better and having enough strength to walk again, Jadwiga approached the Uzbeki woman in the open field. It occurred to her that she knew absolutely nothing about the woman. Did she live alone on the land? There were no farm hands, no husband in sight. If the woman had a spouse, perhaps he had joined the Russian military and was just as fierce and heartless as the soldiers who took the Poles from their homeland.

"My dear lady," the Uzbeki woman told Jadwiga, "you need another day or two of rest."

Jadwiga held up a hand. "There can be no more rest. I have to find my husband and my daughter. Where is the hospital?"

The woman hesitated.

"My boys will tend to the young ones. You will not be bothered, I assure you."

A nod. She gave Jadwiga the instructions to Tashkent and then told her to wait a moment, returning several minutes later carrying a bucket.

"Take it—for your children."

Jadwiga stared in shock. The bucket was filled with milk. How long had it been since she gave her children milk? She stood there holding the bucket, not knowing what to do with it. The woman placed a hand on Jadwiga's shoulder.

"Go on. I am sure they need it."

The trek to the big city began early the following morning. As Jadwiga walked along the dirt road, passing numerous fields and farms, she kept a firm grip on the rosary in her right hand and remained in continuous prayer. She prayed for a man with an arba to appear, but no such man appeared. Onward she went—meter after meter, kilometer after kilometer, occasionally stopping briefly to rest on the side of the road before moving on again. Always, she turned to the rosary beads to find the will to continue walking.

Hail Mary, full of Grace … The Lord is with thee … Blessed are thou among women and blessed is the fruit of thy womb Jesus. Holy Mary, Mother of God, pray for us sinners, now, and at the hour of our death.

Many hours and nearly twenty kilometers later, in the short distance ahead she saw the buildings of the city loomed much larger than Rzeszów back in Poland, but Jadwiga would not be disarmed. She would locate the hospital and she most certainly would locate her Beloved and Mary.

When she entered the outskirts of the city, she quickened her pace, maneuvering through bustling streets filled with a variety of shops and offices. When at last she located the hospital, she rushed through the front metal gate, ran up the steps of the main entrance, and right through the doors. As she quickly assessed the scene, searching for a nurse or an attendant, she noticed a dark-haired man behind the main counter.

She was there in a flash.

"My husband!" Jadwiga blurted out through labored breath. "His last name is Migut. He was brought here with my daughter about a week ago."

The man flipped through several sheets of paper and Jadwiga leaned forward, her palms pressing firmly into the counter.

"Do you understand what I am saying?"

An indifferent glance. The man held up a chart. "There is no man by that name here, madam."

Jadwiga took a step back, her gaze momentarily hitting the floor. "But he must be here! Look again. *Migut.* Jacenty. Please!"

"Lady, there is no man by that name. And if there was, we do not know what happened to him."

The words: daggers right into her heart.

"I beg of you. Look once again," she insisted, clutching her rosary. "What about my daughter, Mary? Can I see her? She was also brought here."

A nurse arrived behind the counter. She and the male attendant exchanged looks and inspected Jadwiga's soiled wardrobe.

"I am not your enemy!" Jadwiga wanted to scream but she held it in, fearing an outburst would prevent her from finding her Beloved. The nurse swiped the clipboard from the man and told Jadwiga to meet her down the hall.

Praise be to God!

She was led through the main infirmary where a pungent stink of urine—of sickness, of death—permeated the air. Nerves shaken, one hand covering her abdomen, the other still clutching her rosary beads, Jadwiga inspected each and every room she passed.

Strangers. All of them. Jacenty was nowhere to be found.

The nurse stopped in front of one of the rooms. The door was closed.

"Lady, the man you are looking for is not here, however, if he was bearded, he may have been mistaken for a Jew and tossed out with the dead a few days ago."

Jadwiga's heart dropped deep into the pit of her stomach. Before she could inquire further, the nurse tapped on the hospital room window and slowly, Jadwiga turned her attention to the patient lying on the bed inside. Dear God, the sickly thin pathetic looking creature was practically bald and the sunken eyes and pale skin foreshadowed a miserable and imminent death ahead. How much time left did the poor being have? A day? A few hours?

As Jadwiga studied the person much more closely, there was something hauntingly familiar about the man.

Jacenty? God in heaven!

But the nurse had just told her…

How, in such a short amount of time, had her Beloved deteriorated so greatly? And then, as if to stick the knife deeper into her bleeding wounds, the sickly being spotted her and looked right into her soul.

Jadwiga nearly fell back from the shock. For it was not Jacenty at all!

Mary?

Jadwiga leaned into the window, her hand pressing against the glass as she took in the dreadful sight of her eldest daughter—dying right in front of her eyes. But it was not her daughter. Not any more—just a faint replica of the girl she had held in her arms as a child; the girl she cherished into womanhood.

Mary extended her arm toward the glass between them. "Mother," she gasped. "Help me!"

Jadwiga felt her knees begin to tremble. She covered her mouth as the stream of tears cascaded down her cheeks.

"Mother … Give me some bread because I am dying of hunger. The only reason I am alive is because Ted brings me a piece of bread every day."

The poor girl must be hallucinating, Jadwiga thought. Ted was not with them, but now the mere mention of his name—another one of her own children possibly suffering somewhere else in the world, so far away from them, and without her, his mother—pierced her soul, splitting it in two.

Without warning, Jadwiga lost her balance, fell to the floor and was swallowed into the darkness. When she finally came to, several nurses were lifting her up to her feet. The first thing she heard was laughter. Surely, she was imagining it. For how could the hospital officials be amused by the fact that her heart had been shattered into a million little pieces upon the sight of her daughter lying there in misery?

Seconds later it hit her: She was being thrown out of the infirmary. She was back at the main entrance of the hospital. Jadwiga struggled to turn back—to go back; to tell Mary she loved her.

"Stop! Please. I'm begging you. Let me take my daughter with me!"

One of the nurses firmly held Jadwiga by the shoulders just as the male attendant arrived on the scene. And then he proceeded to physically remove her from the hospital, accompanied by a chorus from the hospital workers.

"Bum."

"Foreigner!"

"Fool!"

She stumbled outside and ran as fast as her feet would take her beyond the front gate.

Blessed Mother … why? Tell me why is this happening?

Sobbing uncontrollably, the flood of tears too much to endure, a miserable thought emerged—one so painful she feared it would completely destroy what was left of her.

Dear God in Heaven—this is all my fault! I am to blame! If I had listened to my mother; if I had not insisted that Jacenty take the land in the east; if I had not begged him to leave our colony and take the land closer to Russia … None of this would be happening!

"Oh, Father in Heaven," she heaved. "Absolve me! Take my heart. Take my soul. Why must I go on?"

Later that evening, she returned to the children in the clay hut but she had little recollection of getting there—all of it, nothing but a soul-crushing blur because each step she took led her further away from Mary and her Beloved.

Wherever he was now.

"If he was bearded, he may have been mistaken for a Jew and tossed out with the dead days ago!"

Tossed out?

Nothing more than unwanted garbage?

Back in the hut, as Jadwiga lie there on the hay, the thought of Jacenty being alone—without his family—at the moment of his death simply became too much to bear. And images of Mary and Janina lying in their hospital beds tugged on the fabric of her soul. Somehow, she found the will to inform the children what had transpired. They stood around her, shocked, mouths hanging askew.

Jadwiga shrugged, not in surrender, but in her final obliteration … For nothing remained—no home, no future, no courage, no hope, no grace. All of it had been taken away.

"Heavenly Father," she cried out, "please take me because I don't want to live on this earth!"

The sobering proclamation completely stunned the children. They gathered around their mother and held nothing back. Now, each and every one of them was sobbing.

One among them boldly proclaimed: "Mother, who will take care of us if you leave us? We want to die with you!"

~ ~ ~ ~

CHAPTER TWELVE

JANINA:

When I left the hospital, I was pale and had lost most of my hair. Somebody at the hospital gave me twenty-five rubles and took me to the Polish Embassy where I was told to go to the nearest train station; to try and get to Tashkent, where my family might have gone. I wrote down on my arm which way to go, but by the time I got to the station, the money was gone. Either somebody had taken it out of my pocket or I had lost it. My God, how I cried about that. I didn't know what to do, so I slept there on a bench at the train station that night. It was cold and didn't have a blanket.

In the middle of the night, I was awakened by several stray dogs. Their wet noses poked my thighs, my feet, my arms and when they started growling at me, I sat there shivering and afraid, my arms wrapped around my knees. I prayed they would leave me alone. In the morning, a woman at the station was kind enough to give me something to eat and then, I started walking—for a long time— fifteen, maybe twenty kilometers. It seemed as if the entire day went by. That night, I slept on a bench at another train station. Early the next morning, I began walking again. It seemed endless. I was so exhausted that I sat on the ground and cried, this time so hard I thought I would never stop. My God, how my heart ached for my mother and my family. I just wanted to find them.

A man in an arba pulled by a donkey stopped in front of me. He was wearing a turban and he asked me why I was crying.

"I want to find my mother!" I told him. And then I explained that my family might be in Tashkent. He said a nearby road went toward Tashkent; that he was going part of the way. He offered me a ride. We were traveling on the arba for some time. We didn't speak. I kept thinking about my family and prayed I would see them again. And then, in the distance, I saw a figure walking toward us down the road. My heart was racing. As we got closer to the person, I saw something and I could not contain myself—boots! I knew those boots! And the jacket. And the pants. We were about to pass the woman when I saw it—the rosary in her hands!

I sprang to my feet. "Mamma!" I wanted to scream but could not get the words out. I was so overcome with emotion that all I could spit out through my surprise was:"MA!"

My mother stopped dead in her tracks, her face filled with shock as she stared at me. She started to cry. I jumped off the arba and she took me to the side of the road and hugged me, saying, "My dear sweet daughter, I thought you were dead. I thought we had lost you."

And then she pulled something from her jacket—a piece of meat she said she found off a dead horse. It had been boiled and laced with garlic. I took it, but I wanted to know about the others. Months had passed since I had been left at the hospital. When I asked about my father, my mother looked away and said nothing. I knew something was horribly wrong.

Was he still sick? I wondered. I wanted to know where he was. I wanted to know what happened.

◆ ◆ ◆

SEVERAL DAYS AFTER JADWIGA informed the children that their father had perished, the punishing torrent of emotion became so treacherous, so unbearable that it felt as if her heart had been poisoned. When, by God's will, the agony lifted ever so slightly, Jadwiga gathered her strength and returned to Tashkent, this time with Joe, Stanley, John, and Bronia. She was determined to find where her Beloved had been buried. She would locate the grave there; she and the children would pay their respects. They would visit Mary. They would find a church; pray for Janina.

They walked for nearly the entire day and when they arrived at the hospital gates, Jadwiga instructed Joe to watch the children. She would go in the hospital and learn the whereabouts of the nearest cemetery. Once inside, she didn't recognize any of the people behind the counter but one of the nurses there allowed her to walk back into the infirmary; back to Mary's room so Jadwiga could see for herself what she already suspected in her heart to be true. Mary was gone.

Forever.

God, hover over my dear child.

At the front desk, Jadwiga begged the attendants for a clue about what happened to Jacenty and Mary, but nobody there admitted to knowing a thing about them or where they could have been buried. Exasperated, she returned to the children and began inspecting the area surrounding the hospital.

An elderly man was walking across the road. Jadwiga called out to him. "Can you help us, sir? Please? Where is the nearest cemetery?"

The man understood her pleas and pointed down the road. That was all Jadwiga needed. In an instant, she dashed off, the others suddenly burdened to keep up with her. Down the road, she came upon a wooden fence and beyond it, several tombstones rose ominously in the prairie.

Jadwiga quickened her pace alongside the fence. She ran and ran until at last, she came upon the entrance.

"Mother, Mother!" one of the children called out behind her.

But she couldn't stop now. She rushed through the cemetery entrance and stopped abruptly, her eyes falling upon several fresh mounds of dirt a few meters away from her.

Graves!

But there were no markers; no indication of those buried there. The other graves in the distance were marked, but some of them appeared to be weathered and surely, they must have been there for some time.

The children finally caught up with her, but nothing could temper the brewing storm within.

The graves.

The fresh mounds.

Mary! Her Beloved!

Jadwiga ran up to the nearest grave, dropped to her knees and immediately began scavenging through the dirt with her bare hands.

"Quickly!" she shouted back at the children. "Get down. Help me! Start digging!"

Not one of them moved. It was Joe who gathered up the courage to guardedly approach his mother. Ever so cautiously, he placed his hand on her shoulder.

"Mother," he whispered.

"Do as I say!" Jadwiga spat. "I *will* find him. I will dig every grave in here until I uncover his face. Do you hear me? As long as it takes! Now, get down and help me!"

Like a hound determined to uncover precious sticks, she feverishly clawed away at the dirt. There was no stopping the woman. Not now.

"Faster!" she heaved, specks of loosened soil landing on her face, her neck, in her hair. "Help me. Help!"

The others just stood there, the fear of God rushing through their veins.

So fierce became the burrowing that suddenly Jadwiga began sinking slightly into the soil she had been clawing. But she would not relent. No. And when, from the foul portal beneath her, the stench of death escaped the earth, brutally attacking her senses, she turned her head away, fought back an urge to gag over the horrid stink and shook off the diversion. She was close to finding her Beloved. She could feel it.

Flooded with a sudden burst of adrenaline, Jadwiga's hands plunged even deeper into the ground. She continued the fierce attack until, at last, the brief glimmer of a corpse's head startled her so much that she nearly lost her balance and fell back from the wretched sight of it.

"Jacenty?"

But it was not her Beloved.

Nor Mary.

Defeated, her fists landed atop of the mound and she pounded it with all of her might.

No! I will find him!

Struggling to her feet, she stumbled, took several steps, landed atop another fresh mound and immediately began digging up the grave.

"Mother…"

Joe—*again*.

She ignored him and remained focused.

On she went, grave after grave, tossing back into the air twigs, pebbles, small insects—anything blocking her path.

And in return, Jadwiga found nothing.

Not her Beloved.

Nor her daughter.

Some time later, her face, hands, arms and clothes soiled with damp earth that had blanketed the dead around her, she fell back from exhaustion. Sitting there on the ground, knees turned to the side, her head hanging in surrender, nothing could halt the explosion of tears.

"God, why are you sending me this pain?" she heaved uncontrollably. "Where are you? Please let me die so I don't have to suffer any more!"

The adamant demand shook the children to their core. But there was nothing they could do but stand helplessly and watch in silence as their mother completely unraveled right before their eyes.

~ ~ ~ ~

CHAPTER THIRTEEN

JOHN:

Over time, we got to know the Uzbeki woman better. My brothers, Joe and Stanley, had the job of watching her cows out in the field. A few other Polish families were still traveling with us, and as the months passed, we were happy we were in a warm climate and had more food. Even though we had no real roof over our heads, we prayed to God, thanking him for all the good things.

My sister, Bernice, and I were enrolled in the Uzbeki kindergarten, which we attended five days a week. My mother and women from two other families were always busy gathering food for everybody, often going out to the fields or to ponds far away to catch turtles. Whenever they collected enough of those turtles, they tied them together with some rope and dragged them along the road for miles, bringing them home for dinner.

The Uzbeki people were prohibited by their religion to eat the turtles, so whenever they saw the women dragging them, they just spat on the ground and turned and looked away. They could not stomach the sight of them.

We set up a large container on the rocks in our mud hut so we could cook the turtles. I was tasked with splitting their shells after they were cooked and I never knew turtle meat tasted so good. Fortunately, it was more than what we ever had back in the Siberian camp. One time, we even managed to get some steak from a dead horse lying in the ditch. The meat was baked in the sun for three days or so, but when the flies and maggots were washed away, we cooked it, and there was plenty of food for everybody.

In kindergarten class, Bernice and I learned the Uzbeki language, some songs and played games with the other kids. We received free lunches there, too. One day, our teacher hung a large picture of Jesus on the cross on the wall and she asked us to pray to Jesus for food. Well, we prayed—very sincerely for over ten minutes, saying over and over, "Oh, Jesus, please give us a lot of food so we can enjoy our party." But we did not get any food. And then the teacher took the picture of Jesus off of the wall and hung a picture of Stalin in its place and asked us to pray again—this time to Backo Stalin. We did. Suddenly, the doors sprang wide open and a big cart of food was being rolled in for us—cookies, fruits. I could not believe my eyes. It looked so delicious.

The teacher asked, "Children, which God is better, Jesus or Backo Stalin?"

Well, immediately, the children replied: "Backo Stalin! Backo Stalin!"

When I got home, I told my mother about it and she took one look at me and said, sternly, that Stalin was not God. The look in her eyes—I knew she meant business. I told her I understood, but inside, I knew that it was also good that we got some food.

A few months later, I befriended our teacher's son. He told me that he liked mud hamburgers dried in the sun. This sounded very unrealistic to me, but at once, I put my mind to work. I began producing clay hamburgers for my new friend and I traded those clay hamburgers for his sandwiches. Everything was fine for a couple of days. He ate the clay hamburgers I made for him and I ate his sandwiches—until his mother suspected something wrong with his bowels. The teacher watched her son more closely after that and she finally caught me. She punished me by not allowing me to eat anything for an entire day.

This kind of fun and games kept me amused.

Other times, on the way home from the kindergarten, my sister and I stopped by a hut along the road. Outside, there was a man who had tied a horse to a post in the middle of a large round tin tub. He walked around in a circle with that horse and eventually, he squeezed oil from peanuts from a device. Bronia and I always stood quietly and waited for the exact moment when the horse was on the other side of the post so we could steal some of the pulp—the waste product from the oil that was extracted from the peanuts and used to feed the cows and pigs. But to us it was delicious food.

Sure enough, the operator of that peanut mill spotted us stealing some of that waste product. One time, he got so mad that he cracked his whip and let us have it. Yes, it hurt, but being hungry hurt even more.

◆ ◆ ◆

"QUICK. THE AUTHORITIES ARE looking for all of you!"

The announcement startled Jadwiga. She left Joe and Stanley to attend to the cows in the field and walked back toward the road with the Uzbeki woman.

"The officials have been coming into the nearby villages and are counting all of the Poles," the woman went on.

Immediately, Jadwiga feared the worst. The last time the "authorities" came for her family, it was in Poland and it forever changed their lives, but the Uzbeki woman was convincing. In the short distance ahead, two men in uniform were already walking toward her. At first, Jadwiga thought it might be members of the Polish Army, but the woman informed her it was The Red Cross and the organization had come to offer assistance.

Could it possibly be true? For many months there had been talk that the Polish Army in Exile or some other form of relief would arrive near Tashkent, and for so many months they had all waited, praying to God that it would become a reality, all the while living like peasants on the woman's land. Without her, what would have become of them?

The tiny seedling of hope pulled Jadwiga out into the middle of the road. When the men arrived, she immediately noticed their armbands with the insignia of a cross emblazoned into them. A quick introduction and then one of the men informed her they were there to collect information on how many Polish refugees were in the area; they were also instructing the Poles on where to go to receive assistance.

So, it was true. Help had finally arrived.

When the man asked how many people were in Jadwiga's family, the question sent a shiver down her spine as Jacenty and Mary and Ted flashed before her eyes.

"There were nine of us," she began, struggling to find the words. "My husband died. My son … I don't know where he is. My older daughter—gone. I just found my other daughter. Now, it is just me and my five children."

"How old are they?"

"Fifteen, twelve, ten, eight, five."

The agent lowered his register.

"Lady, you have no husband and your oldest child is fifteen? You do not have a chance to stay alive with five kids. You have to send the four youngest ones to the orphanage."

"I do not understand. What about my older daughter? I cannot leave her behind. I cannot leave any of my children."

The man was about the respond, but she would not have it.

"Forget the orphanage. We all stay together until we find the army."

"Lady, you must take proper action now. There are thousands of refugees in the area. Your best hope for your younger children is to turn them over to the orphanage."

And there it was—the final nail in the coffin.

First Jacenty. Then Mary. And now … her four youngest children.

Everything that had been precious to her—her home, her family, *everything!*—had slowly and painfully been ripped away from her. What in God's good name had she done to deserve such a terror? Was she being punished for going against her mother's wishes? For moving out of colony, farther east and to the edges of the Russian border?

Was this her penance—to be completely robbed of her entire family?

Several days later, Jadwiga and the two other families that had been traveling together, made a decision. They packed up what little they had and began the long walk to Tashkent with their children in tow. Widowed, fatherless and distraught, the sight of the homeless caravan traveling on the road between the Uzbeki farms and fields must have formed a lasting imprint in the hearts and minds of some of the locals who had come to know them well. But it would be the Uzbeki woman who first discovered the Miguts on that fateful morning so many months prior who must have realized the true implication of what was taking place; that her guests were leaving for good.

One glance back and the children would see their comrade, arm high in the air. A quick wave goodbye and, perhaps, a brief reflection on the unlikely occurrences that brought them all together, and then … off she went, returning to her land and the cows for which the boys had cared … and the mud hut that had become the temporary refuge for the Polish family she befriended.

In that instant, their brief moments in time together began to fade away.

Jadwiga would not turn around, for she barely had the strength to face what lie ahead; handing over her children to strangers, never to see any of them again.

The Red Cross agent had provided her with the location of an orphanage, located beyond the town of Tashkent to the west. There was also a camp nearby in which Jadwiga and Janina could possibly sleep. For two nights as they travelled, they slept in open fields and then continued the long trek by foot during the days, occasionally sighting a passenger train in the distance, envying the people inside it. If only they, themselves, had the resources to afford such a luxury.

When at last they neared the point at which there would be no turning back—for who knew what would happen after they turned over their children—the weary procession seemed to slow its pace temporarily as if to postpone the inevitable. And then, without warning, the younger children, excited to spot white tents in the distance, rushed off to explore. The mothers didn't stop them. Why hinder their joy?

Greeted by nurses and other orphanage workers, the adults told them their names, and the names of their youngest children.

"You are fortunate you arrived when you did," one of the workers said. "The Polish Army is overseeing our evacuation from Russia."

The weight of the news crushed Jadwiga's soul. Her children would be leaving Russia without her.

"How long?" Jadwiga forced herself to ask.

The worker shrugged. "One week, two? A month? Nothing is certain these days."

A month?

Jadwiga held onto the smallest bit of hope that it was true. She would have that much more time to visit the children in their new home. Quickly gathering the children together, she knelt down and tightly embraced them.

Ten seconds … A few more and then … Everyone was in tears.

"But where will you and Janina go?" young John inquired.

A nurse stood nearby. This wasn't the first time she'd witnessed such a scene.

"There is a train station and a scouting camp nearby," she offered warmly, a tinge of pity in her voice. "Some of the other mothers stay there or in the village nearby. You can visit the children every day until…"

Jadwiga nodded, but dared not let go her grip—on John, on Stanley, on Joe, on little Bronia. When she finally rose to her feet, Janina was right at her side—shaken, unsure what was truly happening. Together, they stood there in silence and watched as the orphanage attendant escorted the children through the main gate.

No dialogue could salvage the hole burning deep into Jadwiga's heart. Slowly, she reached for the rosary around her neck and forced herself to pray— something, anything. But deep down, the miserable panic held its claw-like grip.

Her worst fear had arrived—that the family had just run out of miracles.

~ ~ ~ ~

CHAPTER FOURTEEN

JANINA:

After we left my brothers and younger sister at the orphanage, we slept at the train station nearby. Every night we slept there on the bench outside, using only the large coat we had as a blanket to cover ourselves. We had not bathed. We were hungry. We were homeless. Who was going to take us in?

My mother decided we could visit the children every day, at least until they left Russia. But instead of giving them something, the children gave to us. My brothers and sister stole food for us so my mother and I wouldn't starve.

My mother hoped we could also leave Russia with them; perhaps go along with the orphanage with the other refugees, but there was too much confusion at the time and we didn't know what to do or what papers we needed to get out of Russia, or who to see about it. It felt as if there was no one to help us.

More help arrived—army personnel, the Red Cross. They came to help the orphans. There were so many children and so many of them were sick after their ordeals. My mother and I ... we just wanted to be with our family.

I never cried so much in my life—such a helpless feeling.

After everything that happened: My father—dead! My sister—dead!

And me ... somehow I found my mother on the road that one day, but now I felt as if we all would be separated forever. What could we do? We did what we knew how to do. We turned to God in Heaven and we prayed.

♦ ♦ ♦

"HOBOES! GYPSIES! Polish bums!"

The piercing remarks made by the locals after they had been set free from the Siberian camp played out in Jadwiga's mind. How could they not? She and Janina had actually *become* hoboes.

For several weeks, the train station was their refuge. At times, when a friendly guard was on duty, they were fortunate enough to sleep in the depot, but the majority of the time they spent restless nights outside on a bench on the platform or in a nearby field.

They could not go on like this. They simply could not take any more food from the children and tramp around, and what with the orphanage preparing to leave Russia, forever separating her from the children, Jadwiga and Janina had to find more enterprising ways to survive on their own.

One morning, Jadwiga folded the coat she and Janina had been using as a blanket and handed it to her daughter.

"Take it," she said, her voice somber. "Go to the bizarre nearby, sell the coat and bring back the money. We could give some of it to the children and use the rest for food."

Janina ran her hand over the coat, feeling the soft wool. "Sell it? But what will we use to keep us warm at night?"

A shrug. And then Jadwiga stood up and began to walk away, down the station platform. "It is getting warmer. We will make do until fall or winter."

"But, Mamma!"

"Enough. Just do as I say and bring back the money from the coat!"

The bizarre was a kilometer away, perhaps more. Janina had been separated from her family before. How could her mother allow her to go off on her own now?

Mother Mary, please allow your son Jesus to guide me and take care of me.

An hour later, as Janina wandered through the crowded bizarre, her heartbeat quickened and her body flooded with both fear and excitement. The last time she felt so vibrant was back on the farm in Poland; back when everybody was happy and safe and her father and sister were alive.

What glorious sights surrounded her now—vendors with animated gestures selling colorful scarves and jewelry, elderly women offering warm biscuits that smelled so tasty, musicians performing their mysterious flutes and other musical instruments. A paradise.

"Won't you buy some of these, young lady? They will look so nice on you."

Janina turned to see who was talking to her and for a moment, she simply could not take her eyes off of the extraordinarily beautiful woman standing behind a small cart filled with shiny silver earrings. The Gypsy woman must have been the age of Janina's mother, but standing there, dressed in a vibrant scarf, her face decorated with attractive makeup, she was the calmest, happiest woman Janina had ever laid her eyes upon.

The Gypsy held up a pair of silver earrings.

"I am sorry, Ma'am. I must sell this coat and bring the money to my mother."

The Gypsy shrugged. "Of course, my dear child. It is a beautiful coat. I have a friend working here who will be happy to buy it from you."

Janina was beside herself.

She followed the Gypsy's instructions and located the young gentleman at another cart in the bizarre. Tall and thin with dark hair and complexion, he was more than delighted to offer Janina 250 rubles for the coat. Overcome with pride and joy, Janina thanked the man and immediately secured the money in the small pocket change purse her mother had provided for her.

She maneuvered her way through the bizarre again, but could not resist stopping at several other vendors along the way. My, would it not be nice to have a colorful new outfit, she wondered, pining over a dozen on display.

New clothes? That would be wonderful, indeed.

"I see that my friend helped you, after all?" said the Gypsy woman as Janina once again passed by her cart.

"He was very generous," Janina replied.

"It was a lovely coat, my dear child and surely worth quite a bit of money."

Janina nodded and kept on but the Gypsy woman added, "Why don't you take a quick look at my earrings?" She handed Janina a pair of shiny jewelry and a small mirror.

There was nothing wrong with looking, Janina reasoned, and soon, she was completely enchanted by her own reflection in the mirror, holding up one pair of earrings after another. Oh, how she wished she could have even just one pair. But she dare not purchase them. Her mother would show no mercy and punish her for indulging in such an extravagance. And then, just the thought of her mother, rattled her nerves. How long had she been fawning over the earrings? She had to leave. When she turned to hand the mirror back to the Gypsy, the woman was gone. She had been replaced by a young boy.

Confused, Janina immediately set down the mirror and ran off. But instinct forced her to reach for the change purse she had been carrying around her shoulder. She stopped dead in tracks. Something did not feel right.

She pressed her hand against the change purse. It felt empty.

She opened it. Nothing. The rubles were gone.

Heart pounding, Janina stared back into the bizarre—a flowing river of strangers. How could she have been so foolish? How could she have lost the money?

Suddenly, it all became so very clear. She did not lose the money. It was stolen.

The Gypsy!

This was more than she could bear. Wandering out of the bizarre, heartbroken, the tears rolling off of her cheeks, Janina found a stoop to rest on. She must have been sitting there nearly an hour before it occurred to her that Mother was still waiting for her back at the station. But now Janina couldn't recall from which direction she had come.

"Young lady, why are you crying?"

Janina looked up. A soldier on a horse gazed down upon her, his face etched with concern.

"Are you here all alone here?" he spoke Polish. "Do you need some help?"

Help? The very thought ripped through Janina's heart. Her head fell into the palms of her hands and she began sobbing uncontrollably.

"I am afraid to go back to my mother. I sold the coat … the money … it was stolen … we have nothing left now! We will never be able to be with my brothers and sister in the orphanage!"

"Perhaps I can help… "

"Nobody can help us now! Nobody!"

The piercing declaration was a catalyst. One moment, Janina was sobbing like a hysterical child and the next, the soldier was escorting her to a nearby military club where he introduced her to his comrades.

"This young girl needs to get back to her mother. She lost 250 rubles," the soldier informed the uniformed men sitting around a table. He tossed several coins onto the table. "Everybody pitch in."

Awestruck, Janina stared at the man in disbelief.

Fifteen minutes later, she walked out of the club with more rubles than she had acquired for the coat as well as bread for the family. The soldier remained directly by her side.

"Now then, young lady. Let us we find your mother."

Upon spotting Janina with a soldier, Jadwiga's heart dropped. What trouble had her daughter caused? The soldier got off of his horse and approached her with Janina in tow. He handed Jadwiga a small sachet of money.

"Lady, do not let your daughter out of your sight. There are bums and bandits around here. It's not safe for a young girl."

Janina could not bear to look at her mother. There was no telling how badly the woman would punish her.

"Where is your family?" the man inquired.

Jadwiga reached for the rosary around her neck. "My husband and elderst daughter died. I have four younger children in the orphanage. We tried to get in but…" She paused. "It appears they will be leaving soon. I do not know how my daughter here and I can go with them; to leave Russia, together, as a family. So … this is our fate now."

The soldier nodded knowingly, for surely he had heard such tales with all the chaos the deportations and amnesty had fashioned over the months. A glimmer appeared in his gray-blue eyes. He leaned down, looked directly at Jadwiga, and said something she would have never expected to ever hear.

"I know how. I know how you can all be together."

~ ~ ~ ~

CHAPTER FIFTEEN

STANLEY:

There was a Catholic priest in the orphanage and we all began to feel safe. At the daily masses, my brothers and younger sister would pray that our mother and older sister could be with us. We had fun, played with the other children, but I missed my mother and sister. For several weeks they visited us every day and sometimes we saved a little bit of food—scraps of biscuits or fruit—hidden in our pockets for them. I remember my mother crying and looking so upset. She wanted to be with us.

I could not make sense of what was really happening around us—there were so many kids coming into the orphanage and many workers to take care of them. Many of the kids were sick and exhausted from everything they'd been through—they had been left in the hands of strangers because their parents died. I thought: But my Mamma is still alive. Why can't she be with us?

One day when my mother and sister visited us, my mother was in tears. There was something serious she wanted to tell us and I was afraid to hear it—that maybe she could not come back to us and we would never see her again. Suddenly, the thought of losing her forever upset me. I had butterflies in my stomach and I felt like crying.

And then mother said: "We can all be together! I will not be leaving you any more." She told us a military officer had made arrangements to adopt our family so we could all be together in the orphanage and my mother and my sister Janina could get a job there. I didn't know how or why the officer adopted our family. Nobody really ever spoke of it. Because of that man, we were able to stay together.

The day came when the entire orphanage was to be moved. We traveled for some time in big trucks and we were uncomfortable from how crowded it was inside and the temperatures in the desert were very hot. We never knew where we were going; we thought it was a big adventure and whenever we stopped, we ran and played and sometimes the Polish soldiers traveling with us, played with us.

But some of the kids and the adults were still getting sick and the nurses had to tend to them. My mother wanted us to stay close to her, so we did.

◆ ◆ ◆

IN A TORRID DESERT in a faraway, mysterious land, a caravan of displaced souls moved along for many days. The rows of trucks transporting them stopped only in the late afternoon or early evening to set up small camps.

Jadwiga and the other mothers could not fathom the sheer scope of how far they had traveled; how far they had traveled from their homeland. A year ago, the Poles had all been freezing, clinging for dear life in the bitter depths of Siberia and now, fate had given them another brutal monster to endure: heat. The temperatures had risen well over 110 degrees. The euphoria that swept through the traveling brigade at the beginning of their journey—how contagious and vibrant it was—began to fade. Illness spread. Lethargy set in, dragging out the already painfully long days. But seemingly all at once, everything changed once the group reached a massive seaport. There, in the crowded port, they stared in disbelief at a mammoth coal ship that emitted the foulest of stenches. Was this the angel of mercy that would take them out of Russia once and for all?

Few complained.

"We're leaving Russia. Praise Poland!"

"Down with the enemy."

"They can not get us out of here fast enough!"

Russian soldiers and Polish military personnel instructed the masses to wait in lines until their names were called, and once they were, eager Poles hurried up the planks as if their lives were still in peril back in Siberia. The anticipation of leaving Russia reached a fever pitch. Nothing could hold back the stampede.

Jadwiga kept the children close to her as the family walked up the plank, but one wrong move and surely they would all be trampled. Janina and Joe were in front of her, then Stanley, John and little Bronia in her arms. They managed to arrive on deck without incident, and immediately the enclave was led down below to the ship's lower regions and directly into an empty cargo area.

One step inside and Jadwiga's stomach turned, for what human could endure an odor so foul and wretched? But they would have to. In they went, by the hundreds. Packed tightly within the filthy compartment, Jadwiga recalled the crowded boxcars that had taken them to Siberia.

Confined entering Russia … and confined would they leave.

Any hope that the journey through the night would deliver even a speck of solace quickly faded. Braving a sudden storm on the sea, the ship rocked so aggressively it spawned an onslaught of seasickness. Cramped, surrounded by the masses, Jadwiga peered out into the dark abyss and was grateful she could not clearly see the misery before her. One by one, she found the children's shoulders or arms, touching them reassuringly and returned to the rosary around her neck. The following morning, the ship docked and the euphoria returned. Doors opened and the exposed hive swarmed out of the hell in which they had been placed. With unwavering determination, they reached the deck, hands covering their eyes to shield the blinding blast of daylight.

From the deck, Jadwiga and the others awkwardly moved forward, fervent to get off of the ship with the others, as the masses rushed down the plank. What a sight to behold. There, on the shores below, some of their fellow Poles dropped to their knees on the hot sand and cheered. Others loudly praised God, crying through any lingering anguish and their desperation to finally be rid of the Russian beast once and for all.

As this new reality unfolded before their eyes—that, at long last, they were free—Jadwiga remained unsettled.

"My dear Lord in Heaven … where on Earth are we?"

~ ~ ~ ~

Photographs

The Matriarch: Jadwiga Migut in Chicago, circa 1955, fifteen years after Stalin's mass deportation of Polish citizens into the frozen abyss of Siberia.

Tainted Destiny: Jacenty Migut during the 1920s, prior to Stalin's mass deportations.

Where It All Began: (L-R) Jacenty, Jadwiga and son Ted Migut, along with Jadwiga's parents and sister in Łukawiec, Poland, in the early 1920s, prior to a move east near Tarnopol, closer to the Russian border.

Taken By Force: This painting offers a glimpse of the horrors that befell nearly 2 million Polish people during Stalin's mass deportation of Polish citizens in Eastern Poland that began February 10, 1940.
Photo: Artist unknown, courtesy The Sikorski Polish Club, Glasgow, Scotland

Ride Of Terror: A Russian soldier forces a Polish family to meet a bitter fate inside of a crowded boxcar. Photo: courtesy of the Kresy-Siberia Foundation

Into The Abyss: Conditions inside the boxcars were deplorable. Days, sometimes weeks, passed with barely a scrap of food or sufficient water supply.
Drawing: Telesfor Sobierajski, courtesy of the Kresy-Siberia Foundation

Exiled: Taken from their homes and stripped of their dignity, the Poles braved the frigid depths of Siberian slave labor. Nearly half of them perished during their lengthy confinement, either due to hard labor, the miserable living conditions and/or the illnesses the circumstances spawned.
Photo: Circa 1941, courtesy of the Kresy-Siberia Foundation

Slave Labor: Most Siberian labor workers spent nearly twelve hours a day in the forests cutting down and tending to trees and logging.
Drawing: Telesfor Sobierajski, courtesy of the Kresy-Siberia Foundation

Birth Of An Amnesty: In summer 1941, after Hitler's military attack on the USSR, the events spurred the signing of the Sikorski-Maisky Agreement, which found Stalin freeing the deported Poles. They were granted an "amnesty." Above, Basia and Farynka Sgrunowska, seen here on a train from Lugova, Ukraine, to Krasnowodzk (now Türkmenbaşy) on March 23, 1942—the busy seaport transported Polish refugees across the Caspian Sea into Pahveli in Iran.
Photo: From the private archives of Zofiz Jordanowska, courtesy of VideoFact

Escape From Russia: By the end of 1943, approximately 33,000 Polish civilians had passed through Persia (Iran).
Photo: Ted Morawski, courtesy Kresy-Siberia Foundation

Renewal In Persia: When a move from Pahlavi, on the shores of the Caspian Sea, to Tehran became necessary in 1942, the Polish Army in Exile and the Red Cross oversaw efforts to transport tens of thousands of Polish orphans and refugees.
Photo: Irena Kus, courtesy of Kresy-Siberia Foundation

Refuge In Africa: The Miguts, (Clockwise) Jadwiga, Joe, Stanley, Janina, Bronia, and John, circa 1943, outside of a Polish orphanage in Tengeru, Tanzania, Africa. Nearly 18,000 Polish people, including orphans and refugees, were sent to Eastern Africa for safety during the 1940s.

A New Life: Jawidga Migut and her children circa 1944.

Unlikely Haven: The
Miguts outside the two huts
they shared in the Polish
orphanage circa 1946.

Raised In Africa: John
Migut, circa 1949, outside
of the African orphanage.
He was 15 years old.

At Work: A native Masai woman
takes a break from work duties in
the Polish orphanage in Tanzania.

Rites of Passage: This image showcases Polish refugee children in Tengeru, Africa, taking part in choir practice in front of a dormitory.
Photo: Courtesy of Jadwiga Dzwiniel (front row, ninth from the right), from the book "NZ First Refugees—Pahiatua's Polish Children.".

Hollywood Glitz: Joan Rivers with Greg Archer (L) and Jeff Dinnell, covering the Red Carpet at the Comedy Central Roast of Joan Rivers in 2009.

Forgotten Odyssey: A monument honoring the nearly 2 million deported Polish citizens during the 1940s rests on a busy thoroughfare in Warsaw, Poland.

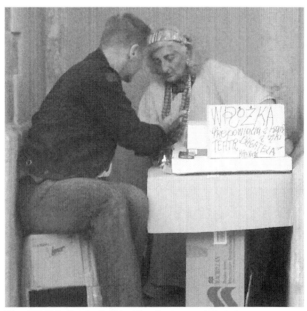

You Will Inherit A Big, Fat Legacy: A Polish fortuneteller unearths mysteries for the author in Krakow's Market Square in 2012.

Grave Situations: Discoveries in a remote cemetery in Eastern Poland spark more questions for the author.

Legacy Lives On: The Migut Family and extended family at an annual gathering in summer 2013. At that time, four surviving members of the original clan—Janina, Stanley, John (far left) and Bernice (center)—continued to pass along tales of endurance and survival.

Part Three

The Grace

CHAPTER SIXTEEN

SPRING 2012 WAS IN FULL BLOOM in Santa Cruz, California, but the rising temperatures did little to alleviate the chill in my bones. A week had passed since I plunged deeply into the material about my Polish family and I could not shake a lingering funk. One day I found myself sitting on the terrace of the Mediterranean-esque villa on which I rented a cottage house. I was deeply involved in Google maps on my laptop, retracing my family's journey...

Łukawiec, Poland to...

A slave labor camp in the Novosibirsk region of Siberia to...

Uzbekistan to...

Iran to...

The image in my mind: a relentless mobile of suffering.

Poles being shoved into boxcars...

Polish children hopping over corpses in a labor camp...

Jadwiga digging into the soil as she frantically searched for her dead Beloved.

When I finally looked up from the laptop, my attention fell upon several dragonflies and hummingbirds frolicking near a palm tree. I was unnerved by the dichotomy of the two worlds in which I was living—my family's grim past and the tranquil California garden setting.

True, I had allowed my family's story to play out inside of my mind. But now I could not get it *out* of mind. What little mind I had left.

Losing your mind is hardly an elegant affair. When the mind goes, it is best to wear some kind of bib. Spiritual spit-up happens. It just does. The messy endeavor seems to thrust you into a deeply profound soulful excursion from which there can be no turning back. To that end, it is pointless to hang on to the You that you always knew yourself to be. Hence, life becomes much more eventful with spiritual dribble running off of the chin.

Simply put: My mammoth serving of Bad Things Happened When Stalin Sent My Polish Family To A Labor Camp did not go down well—at all. Lexapro, Wellbutrin, Paxil, Abilify and everybody's favorite emotion-numbing pal, Prozac, well, *they* might help.

Oh, how tempting it was, but in lieu of popping pills I opted to park my ass back into a therapist's office. Besides, why thwart a perfectly good, and can I just say, vigorous, mood swing with man-made mood enhancers? Let's face it, professional mood swingers all know that the wind pressing against your back on the way down may be devastating, but the breeze rushing across your face on the way UP—that's what we all live for.

I had seen counselors and therapists, off and on, for more than twenty years, mostly to deal with the circus act that is my emotions. The majority of my posse of therapists seemed to be entertained by me. Perhaps I was able to articulate what I was feeling and chase it back with a flair for the dramatic. Who knows? Overall, therapy helped—with myriad issues and that endless, tiring tenure of Somebody Please Love Me So I Know I Am Significant. However, once, in the late 1990s—yet another time when I felt shaken and downtrodden—my eightysomething Jungian therapist fell asleep during our sessions.

Three times to be exact!

I would have been more devastated—I mean, really, the nerve; boring I am not! But I kept going back to him because it seemed as if The Universe was handing me delicious writing material. Still, watching your therapist nod off while you're in the throes of telling your "story" does not send your self-esteem skyrocketing north.

I went to another therapist to recover.

My latest therapy comeback had a purpose—to spark a deeper understanding of my current bout with depression, perhaps the worst I had experienced in years. My new therapist—I'll call her Dee—was a fiftysomething Zen Buddhist lesbian who looked undernourished. Thin and pale with short, cropped graying hair, I wondered if the poor creature—she of plaid shirt and blue jeans from the '90s—had the strength to deal with me. Dee with wire-framed eyeglasses. Dee whose lips never parted when she smiled. Not that Dee had much to smile about, mind you. I was not the best company. But the woman gave it her all as she sat calmly across from my refuge on her salmon-toned sofa.

I considered for a brief moment—because Brief was all I could muster with my mood swinging at 111 miles per hour—what it must be like to be *her*.

All calm.

And Buddhist.

And lesbian.

Soothing, I concluded.

But I wasn't there to understand her. I was confused about my family's history, yes, but also troubled by other life circumstances. I no longer enjoyed my job as an editor, I was losing even more interest in interviewing celebrities, and I did not love living in Santa Cruz.

Lost, trapped, and confined—such a winning trifecta.

"You know, looking back, all those daddy issues I processed during the 1980s and 1990s seem so delightful by comparison to how I feel now."

The sides of Dee's mouth lifted ever so slightly. "You believe you had Daddy issues?"

"Don't we all?" I retorted with vigor, thinking of Stalin. Did *he* have Daddy issues? Mommy issues? Well, clearly, he had *issues*.

Dee leaned forward in her chair. "Stay with that; stay with what you're feeling about the..." She lifted her hands and gave me her best quote fingers... "'daddy' issues. Take a big, deep breath."

Buddhists love deep breaths but sometimes I wonder if it's just to avoid what they are really feeling. Or worse—to anesthetize what's being felt.

As if feelings are a bad thing.

As if feelings should be tossed aside!

What is so wrong with *FEELING YOUR FEELINGS?*

I released an exhaustive, frustrated sigh and scanned my current surroundings—a therapist's office, for God's sake! Ha. Look where all of my *feelings* had taken me.

Fine. Time to surrender.

"Oftentimes when intense feelings arise, we can use them as clues," Dee offered compassionately.

"Do they mind?"

"Mind what?"

"Being used like that?"

Her head tilted. "Do you think they mind?"

"I think my mind needs minding."

"If you're willing to explore some of these feelings and actually sit with them, rather than react to them, you may better understand *what* they are trying to communicate with you. They may be asking for your attention in an effort to heal something."

I chuckled. Clearly, she did not mean *heel* something. Or maybe she did.

Whatever. Perhaps one way to temper some of my reactions was to accept my new reality. I had grabbed the carrot—the big one dangling in front of my prominent nose; the one that was Polish family's history—and taken a free fall down an emotional rabbit hole. But there wasn't a Wonderland waiting for me on the other side. Far from it. Rather, only a lurid assortment of unimaginable scenes playing out in the forefront of my mind on repeated loop.

The Russians at the door...

Young John licking the ice off of the nails in the boxcar...

The nurses poking Janina with needles...

I had thought that by simply looking at what had happened to my family, that it would alleviate my restlessness. But had it only stoked its fires even more?

As I sat across from Dee, the seedlings for the epiphany emerged: Was there something else I needed to do with all of my family stuff—the drama, the history, *their* story, which had infiltrated my own psyche?

"Perhaps these waves of emotions and confusion will lift or, at the very least, become more manageable, if you allow yourself to simply step through the new portal that had been opened up for you."

I sighed. "You mean?"

"Go deeper."

"Deeper?"

"You're a journalist. Could there be something more to gain by investigating both the historic events of the past and the emotions that come up for you as they relate to your family?"

I sat back and thought about it: A crash course in history chased back with Genealogical Soul Scraping? My, that sure did not sound like it was for sissies. Was I truly up for it?

Dee just sat there in silence. She smiled. Her lips did not part.

"I'm afraid our time is up."

"Of course it is," I wanted to say. Instead, I peered out of the window just as the sunlight broke through several clouds—they were heading east.

Fitting. All of the signs kept luring me back to Russia.

Back to the past…

~ ~ ~ ~

CHAPTER SEVENTEEN

SEVENTY-FIVE YEARS AGO, Stalin came pounding on my family's door. Now it was time for me to do the knocking. However, my new excursion was book-ended by reluctance and loud complaints. Ewan McGregor? Bruce Willis? John Travolta? I take it all back—Bored with the entertainment business? Please, bring those celebs back. Suddenly, the idea of researching why a superstar decided to get into acting seemed like the best job in the entire world.

Probing into Stalin and the mass deportation of Poles? Not fun.

Volumes have been written about Stalin, and much of it is sobering. Simply put: A Russian cobbler and a peasant woman have three sons. Two of them die in childhood. The third son survives ... and the ripple effects change the world.

Joseph Stalin was born Iosif Vissarionovich Dzhugashvili (also noted as Jughashvili) on December 18, 1878 in Gori, in Eastern Georgia. However, some reports list his date of birth as December 6 and it's well known he created a new birthdate for himself—December 21, 1879. His father Besarion Jughashvili was a cobbler, and reportedly an alcoholic who abused his son. Stalin's mother, Ketevan Geladze, was born a peasant.

When Iosif was fifteen, upon the urging of his mother, he obtained a scholarship to a Russian Orthodox seminary in Georgia, but he rebelled against the religious order and the imperialist leanings of the day. Some accounts note that he may have been expelled in 1899 rather than leave on his own accord—

his political views opposed Russian emperor Nicholas II's tsarist regime at the time. Not long afterward, he fully embraced the writings of Vladimir Lenin, the revolutionary politician and political theorist who began serving as the leader of the Russian Soviet Federative Socialist Republic in 1917.

Early on, Iosif was so captivated by Lenin's work that it literally transformed him into a full-fledged Marxist revolutionary. In 1903, he joined Lenin's Bolsheviks, the division of the Marxist Russian Social Democratic Labour Party that would eventually split from its core and transform into the Communist Party of the Soviet Union. In the three decades that followed, Iosif's pursuit of power became relentless if not disquieting. He would go down in history as one of the world's most oppressive tyrants.

The writing may have been on the proverbial wall early on. Iosif helped organize the infamous 1907 Tiflis Bank robbery, the cash shipment that would help fund the Bolsheviks' revolutionary activities. The robbery resulted in forty deaths and nearly fifty injuries—and also found Iosif et al walking off with the equivalent of more than 3 million American dollars. He was sent into Siberian exile numerous times, but managed to escape most of these incarcerations. During that era he officially took on the name Stalin, an amalgam of the Russian word for steel—*stal'*—and Lenin's moniker.

After numerous rounds of political hopscotch—and a countrywide identity shift when Russia officially became the Soviet Union in 1922—a dramatic change occurred in the 1930s. Communist Party leader Sergey Kirov (also noted as Sergei) was shot to death on December 1, 1934, at his Leningrad office by beleaguered Communist Party member Leonid Nikolaev (Also spelled as Nikolayev). Most politicos speculated that Stalin instigated the effort. By this time, Stalin had secured himself in the political arena as General Secretary of the Central Committee of the Communist Party. Initially the position was administrative, but upon Kirov's death, Stalin used the role as a springboard to become leader of the entire country. His notorious purge against "internal enemies" was launched, and morphed into The Great Purge between 1934 and 1939. This involved the large-scale elimination of The Communist Party, especially the Old Bolsheviks and a variety of other government officials. It also included massive police surveillance and repression of peasants. A significant number of rigged trials ensued and Stalin's "internal enemies" were either executed or imprisoned in the Gulags. In 1936, when Stalin made Nikolai Yezhov the head of the People's Commissariat for Internal Affairs (NKVD), which oversaw state security and police forces, the remaining Bolshevik veterans were killed off.

By 1938, Stalin had few internal enemies left. His unparalleled reign fueled another dramatic life-altering event: the signing of The Molotov–Ribbentrop Pact.

Soviet foreign minister Vyacheslav Molotov and Germany's foreign minister Joachim von Ribbentrop crafted and signed the accord, which became the official Treaty of Non-Aggression between Germany and the Soviet Union. Also known as the Nazi-Soviet Pact, the documents were signed in Moscow on August 23, 1939. This agreement allowed Hitler to invade Poland at will. But only one week after the Soviets rampaged areas in the Far East in The Battles of Khalkhin Gol (or the Nomonhan Incident), which saw the fall of The Japanese Sixth Army. The best part of the agreement, at least for Germany and Russia, was the stipulation that Nazi Germany would not engage in combat with the USSR, which gave the USSR temporary non-involvement in the mounting European war. The agreement also prevented Germany from forming any kind of military alliance with Japan.

On September 16, 1939, when Russia declared victory in the Nomonhan Incident, Stalin ordered Soviet forces to invade Poland on September 17.

Earlier that year, in the spring, my family had settled into their farmhouse in bucolic Liczkowce (today known as Lychkivtsi in Ukraine), approximately seventy kilometers southeast of Tarnopol (now Ternopil), which rests 125 kilometers southeast of Lwów. The region was officially part of the recognized Second Polish Republic (1918-1939), which rose from the border-shifting ashes of World War I (1914-1918) and the Polish-Soviet War (1919-1921).

However, these reorganized Polish boundaries along Ukraine in the east were plagued with a questionable inheritance. Political unrest was rampant at the time. However few Polish families in the area could have predicted the full extent of this cobbler's son's wrath. Like a dragon descending over a medieval village, Stalin's invasion of Poland turned into a bona fide reign of terror, followed by Sovietization. Stalin's strategy was to occupy the Eastern Borderlands (today western Ukraine, western Belarus and eastern Lithuania), also referred to as The Kresy, with a population of more than 13 million people that included Belorussians, Czechs, Jews, Poles, Ukrainians, and other citizens. Sovietization had one purpose: To liquidate the entire Polish state. The mass arrests of civil leaders, priests, policeman, and judges began almost immediately—on

September 18, 1939—and continued until June 1941. In all, approximately 200,000 Polish POWs were captured by the Soviets. The majority of them, like my family and other Polish citizens, were sent to the Gulags.

By this time, Lavrentiy Beria had become head of the NKVD. A well-known political official at the time, Beria succeeded Yezhov as NKVD head in late 1938 and Yezhov was blamed for, among other things, the economic ramifications spawned by The Great Purge. Yezhov would meet his fate in 1940, when orders were given for his execution. It was common at the time for Stalin and the government to swiftly change course and condemn former officials for circumstances they themselves set in motion. Yezhov's execution was par for the course.

In the meantime, Beria took the political baton that was handed to him and oversaw the execution of thousands of prisoners. He did more than become part of Stalin's elite inner circle. He crawled into the strategic bed with the man and produced a sinister offspring: The mass deportation of Polish citizens.

Under Beria's supervision, the first of several grand-scale deportations of Polish citizens took place on February 10, 1940, a day of infamy that will be forever engrained in Poland's history and my family's psychological makeup. More than 100 trains, each carrying an estimated 1,000 to 2,000 Poles, transported nearly 220,000 souls—military veterans, settlers, foresters and farmers—into the glacial abyss of Siberian slave labor.

Several months later, on April 13, 1940, 320,000 Polish individuals—so-called "family system of enemies," mostly women and children—were also removed from their homes and forcibly resettled in Kazakhstan. In the summer of that year, another 240,000 Poles were deported from Polish territories occupied by the Germans. A fourth round of deportations, this time in the Lithuanian Soviet Socialist Republic, took place in June 1941. Those people were sent to POW camps or the Gulags, adding another 200,000 souls to the deportation tally.

The estimated total number of Polish people deported: between one and two million.

The slave labor camps were scattered throughout Russia: Archangel, Vologda, Smolensk and Moscow in the north; Krasnoyarsk, Tomsk, Omsk in the east; and Bernaul, Karaganda and Novosibirsk in the south, among others.

At the time, the USSR covered more than 17 million square kilometers (nearly 6.5 million square miles). Tallying the long list of those penitentiaries is not a simple feat. Back in the 1940s, Stalin and his henchmen had already established camps for "criminals and military prisoners," as well as women's and children's camps, and countless others. The majority of them housed Stalin's own countrymen.

In Magdalena Maciejowska's thesis, "Deportation of Polish People," penned at the Jagiellonian University in Kraków in 2002, the author reports, as many other have, that Stalin had already been sending his own people to these concentration camps "en-masse since 1929." The cobbler's son had milked his own people for, as Maciejowska points out, "cheap and obedient slave labor" for quite some time.

In his revealing and revered book, *Stolen Childhood*, Lucjan Krolikowski, a prominent Polish priest, himself a deported Pole, wrote about the initial boxcar transports, noting that sanitary conditions "mocked even the most elementary human requirements. Two-and three-week treks were completed in unheated cattle cars through the severe cold … Hunger, disease, dirt, and exhaustion decimated the exiles along the way."

◆ ◆ ◆

So, my new therapist was correct. Exploring the backstory of my family's odyssey was opening my eyes to a world I never knew existed—and a world I feared knowing more about. I might have stopped exploring right there—take a breather and all that—but then I received an email from the Kresy-Siberia Foundation.

Back in 2004, I had, somewhat "by accident," connected via the Internet with a man named Stefan Wisniowski, based in Sydney, Australia. Our first emails took place after I published the newspaper article chronicling my family's journey. Stefan reached out to me in hopes of linking that article to the website for the Kresy-Siberia Foundation, which he helped launch and was at the helm as its president. At the time, I was more than happy to share the story. However, after exploring what was actually on the foundation's website—real-life accounts from deported Poles and other historic facts—my chest tightened. I resisted exploring what had been documented on the foundation's site.

Staring at Stefan's email, I now wondered if that resistance had sent me screaming into the night, searching for an emotional rescue party—fame, fortune, and the bright lights of Hollywood. I had thought that interviewing stars like Patricia Heaton, David Duchovney and countless other celebrities had something to do with growing up a pop culture freak. And maybe it did, to some degree. I was quasi-obsessed with television shows and motion pictures. But suddenly one question haunted me: Had I been running toward a fantasy to avoid dealing with something much darker—in my family's life, and in mine?

Stefan's message, which arrived in an old email account I rarely used, detailed an update about the Kresy-Siberia site. The timing of its arrival piqued my interest. How was it that the president and founder of an organization that first made a name online as a Yahoo group—and since the early 2000s had become an ever-evolving virtual museum designed to bring the lost and untold stories of Poles during World War II to greater light—would email me at the time I truly began probing my family's past?

It's a sign, Greg.

Well, any mood-swinger who believes God and The Universe communicated with him through blinking streetlamps would have known that.

And what of the Kresy-Siberia Foundation? Its purpose was "to inspire, promote and support the worldwide research, remembrance and recognition of Polish citizens' struggles under occupation and in exile in connection with the Second World War and in doing so to … record the experiences of Polish citizens living in Poland before and during the Second World War and their life in exile during and after the war," among other things.

Perhaps I was being led to do something similar.

After emailing Stefan, with his help, I located vast amounts of historic documents and records related to the mass deportations. One of those documents stood out. It was a list of trains that transported the Poles into the miserable depths of Siberia. I sat at my desk and contemplated the computer screen, my hand hovering over the mouse. Fate dared me to click that damn document because there was a strong chance I would discover more clues to what actually happened to my family. And didn't I owe it to myself—and my relatives—to uncover as much information as I possibly could?

I manned up and clicked away. A few moments later, my eyes scanned a list of dates and other data. The left-hand side of the document itemized counties and villages from which the Poles were plucked.

No. 1: Augustow

No. 66: Lwów

No. 116: Kalusz.

On it went.

No. 134: Tarnopol.

I stopped there. Tarnopol (now Ternopil) was located near rural Liczkowce (now Lychkivtsi), the village from which my family had originally been taken. Based on my family's recollections of the duration of their ominous sleigh ride—an hour, perhaps two—it seemed likely they would were taken to the trains at the nearby departure station listed on the document: Chodaczkow, near Tarnopol.

As I scrolled further, scanning the entire list of 236 entries recorded there— entries of all the deportation trains—Column H stood out. It listed the number of people forced into each of the "escorts"/boxcars.

My eyes traveled south:

1,859 people.

1,111.

1,158.

1,669.

1,716.

1,493.

Thousands of human beings taken by force.

Up top again, one of the dates, February 5, 1940, stood out. Oftentimes the Russians prepped the trains several days before the actual deportations. The February 5 date aligned with February 10, the Saturday the NKVD took my family. But to what station in Siberia were they taken?

From the Tarnopol listing, my eyes ventured right. I was looking for Novosibirsk. My family told me they were taken there. When I finally located the region, in the column below it I saw the name of the arriving station: Czerepanowo (also known today as Cherepanovo).

I had struck gold.

My family had been taken from Tarnopol to Cherepanovo in the Novosibirsk region. Next, I located the number of people in their train transport: 1,241. That is approximately the amount of people you could pack into a large movie theater. I kept on, the word "escort" standing out. What a horrible term. To "escort" suggests a safe passage—much like a Boy Scout escorting an elderly woman across the street.

"Hello Ma'am. May I escort you to the other side?"

"Why, yes," the woman would reply thankfully. "Please."

The Poles were *not* escorted. They were carted off like cattle.

My family's "escort" was the 13th Division in the 233rd Regiment. There were twenty-three guards overseeing the transport. The name of the officer in charge: Kozlow.

Oh my, I wondered. Would it not be fascinating to locate *that* man, or his family? Oh, how I envisioned the scene: There I am standing on the porch of a modest-sized farmhouse in Eastern Russia. A young girl opens the door and greets me.

"Come to the door, great grand-daddy," she calls out. "There's somebody here from America. And he wants to see *you!*"

Moments later, a frail man in his late nineties slowly makes his way to the door, aided by his cherished cane. Hunched over, bald, liver spots on his forehead, he looks up and contemplates my presence.

"Do I know you, young man?"

"Not really. But you were in charge of the train that took my family and thousands of other Polish citizens to a slave labor camp. I just wanted to know: Have you given it much thought, lately?"

What a scene *that* would be indeed. But I had to let it go—for now. I had no way of knowing if the man was still alive—*yet.* However meeting him face to face would certainly be a phenomenal opportunity. Not to punish him, but to grasp another vantage point from that era, perhaps that of a young soldier forced to do things he didn't care to do—or, that he didn't mind doing at all.

Either way, I had to know. But not now. There were other dots to connect.

The First Guidebook to Prison and Concentration Camps of the Soviet Union, written by the late-Avraham Shifrin in the early 1980s, lists more than ten camps in the Cherepanovo area in the region of Novosibirsk. But I was concerned. The book lists only the camps that were in operation at the time the author wrote it—a sobering reminder that even thirty years ago, human injustices were still occurring in prison camps throughout Russia. But there was a strong chance most of the camps listed in Shifrin's book could have been in operation during the mass deportations, especially the one to which my family was taken.

More importantly, was it, or remnants of it, still around today? Could I locate the exact whereabouts of my family's labor camp? It seemed, well, reasonable, considering the insanity I was facing. A jaunt to Stalin Land? Sure. Why bother with the Pirates of the Caribbean in Disneyland when you can experience real-life terror?

I pressed Pause on the idea and proceeded to review my notes.

According to my Uncle John's accounts, sent to me a decade ago, there were approximately twelve barracks in the labor camp where the family was held. Each barrack housed a number of bunks, three levels high, enough to pack in anywhere from fifty to seventy people. For mattresses, the prisoners slept on sawdust, six inches deep, which posed a particularly vexing problem during the summer months: Lice and other bedbugs made sleeping conditions challenging. Oftentimes, by morning, a significant portion of the body was covered with bug bites.

There were no pillows to sleep on, no sheets or blankets for the Poles to cover themselves with during the harsh Siberian winters, when the temperature plummeted well below zero. Were it not for the large wood-fired stove that emanated modest heat in each of the barracks, most of the people confined there would have perished from the pitiless cold.

The Polish labor workers in these camps had their daily *norma* to fill. In most of the camps, men, women without children, and older teenaged boys and girls, were sent to cut down trees in the forest, or assist in clearing the snow for the workers so they could cut down timber. Typically, two main workers were assigned to a tree. Meanwhile, several other workers would saw the fallen tree into smaller portions. Most of the wood was used for stoves in the camps—primarily in officials' quarters—and the larger pieces were placed on tractors and hauled off to trains, where they would then be sent to other areas for storage and used to create lodging or future railways.

The workers rose for work at five in the morning and returned to the barracks at six or seven in the evening. For their efforts, they would receive modest food rations—600 grams of bread each day—and, according to some reports, several rubles, hardly enough to sustain one person, not to mention an entire family. The majority of the camps housed some kind of cafeteria—although others had none at all. The food—often boiled water with vegetable roots—had to be paid for.

Imagine the heart-wrenching conundrum for the workers when the soldiers had not bothered to pay them. In most instances, the workers bartered with each other or, if they were lucky, with the occasional passer-by from a nearby village. Clothing items were often exchanged for rubles with these villagers, but the short-term fix to obtain food did little good in the long-term. Lack of protective clothing would be the death of many people in the camps.

The entire system was designed to crush the souls of those working within it. And if they did not perish from the punishing work conditions or ongoing hunger, eventually, the onslaught of illness or diseases generated from living in such conditions and braving the grueling weather, drained the life from their weakened bodies.

~ ~ ~ ~

CHAPTER EIGHTEEN

TWISTS OF FATE DEFY LOGIC. They collide at the intersections of Serendipity and Synchronicity and have that uncanny ability to dramatically change things—for better, for worse, forever. Such was the case in the summer of 1941 when an unlikely hope found its way to the enslaved Poles in Siberia. An unexpected ally-by-default emerged in the form of Adolf Hitler.

Yes, Hitler.

It was improbable that the world's infamous Nazi devil and commander, the man who orchestrated the genocide of nearly 6 million Jewish people, was fully aware that he would be partially responsible for forever altering the lives of the nearly 2 million Poles who were deported in the aftermath of the Molotov-Ribbentrop Pact set into motion in 1939. Hitler's massive attack on Russia on June 22, 1941, dubbed Operation Barbarossa, sent more than 3 million German troops into the USSR across a nearly 2,900-kilometer front. Named after Frederick Barbarossa, a medieval Holy Roman Emperor no less, Hitler signed off on the operation months earlier, in December 1940. The attack was considered one of history's largest military operations in casualties—more than 5 million from both sides—and yet it offered Hitler another coup, primarily in Ukraine. However, his military forces were never able to take over Moscow, and that mission's unraveling would forever change Hitler's Third Reich.

That initial German attack was a blessing in disguise for the deported Poles, but to a number of historians it was just another political chess move. In fact,

Heinz Magenheimer, one of Austria's most respected military historians, noted that Operation Barbarossa was launched in anticipation of a Soviet strike against Germany and that the operation beat Stalin to the punch by just a few weeks. Furthermore, other historical analyses reported that Stalin intended to attack Hitler and Germany shortly after signing their infamous non-aggression pact in 1939.

Regardless, Hitler's attack rattled Stalin, and the Russian leader turned to and joined forces with the Allied powers of World War II, which at the time consisted of France, Poland, Great Britain and the British Commonwealth—Canada, Australia, New Zealand, Newfoundland and South Africa. The United States, of course, would not enter the Allies fold until after Japan bombed Pearl Harbor in December 1941. One man, Britain's former Foreign Secretary Anthony Eden, a close confident of British Prime Minister Winston Churchill and a man who'd been lauded as a peacemaker, factored into the unusual series of events that unfolded next.

Eden had retained his diplomatic ties after stepping down as Foreign Secretary in 1938. He strongly encouraged Polish Prime Minister Władysław Sikorski to open negotiations with Ivan Maisky (also spelled Maysky and Mayski), the Soviet ambassador to London, with the idea of strengthening diplomatic relations between Poland and Russia. Sikorski spearheaded an agreement between the two governments and the Sikorski-Mayski Agreement was signed on July 30, 1941. In it, Stalin declared all previous ties and pacts Russia had with Germany, particularly the Molotov-Ribbentrop Pact, "null and void," thereby dismantling the 1939 Soviet-German partition of Poland. For suffering Poles, the agreement stipulated the release of Polish prisoners of war who were deported and held in labor camps. It granted them immediate amnesty—yet few officials knew at the time that of the estimated 2 million Poles who had been deported, nearly half of them had perished.

However, the Sikorski-Mayski Agreement was riddled with obstacles. Initially, Sikorski would not sign a treaty designed to strengthen diplomatic relations between Russia and Poland unless the Soviets adhered to the Polish position and freed her prisoners from the Gulags. Stalin was not swayed. There was also some pushback, primarily from the Soviets, regarding the number of Polish prisoners being held in the USSR. British officials at the time claimed the number hovered near 200,000 while the Soviets considered it to be as low as 20,000.

Were it not for the efforts of Britain's Ambassador to the Soviet Union, Sir Richard Stafford Cripps, the future of the imprisoned Poles would have been dramatically different. Cripps was considered a chief negotiator with Stalin and chronicled the events in his diary. According to his journal, he met with Stalin in late July of 1941—a time when negotiations had stalled—and persuaded the Soviet leader to "grant immediate amnesty to every Polish citizen detained in his country."

This time Stalin agreed to free the Poles. It sparked debate, however, and there was a catch—Stalin wanted to use the Poles for his own purposes elsewhere. Regardless, Sikorski reversed his stance on the matter and ultimately signed the treaty.

The term "amnesty" was, and perhaps still is, considered controversial. Many Poles at the time believed it implied the Soviet Union actually had legal rights to imprison Polish citizens during the deportations. Of the questionable terminology, Polish political advisor Józef Retinger wrote in his memoir that another Polish diplomat was responsible for coining the phrase—a Mr. Potulicki, the man who drafted the actual document. Retinger claimed that Potulicki, eager to set something positive in motion, mistakenly used the term "amnesty" instead of "release" in the treaty's text. By the time of its signing, it was too late to alter the phrasing—a more appropriate term would have been "manumission" or even "emancipation."

As the Polish Government in Exile continued to operate out of Great Britain, on August 12, the Presidium of the Supreme Council of the USSR—basically a body of supreme parliaments—issued a formal decree that stipulated, in part, that an "amnesty is granted to all Polish citizens on Soviet territory at present deprived of their freedom as prisoners of war."

A few days later, on August 14, Polish general Zygmunt Bohusz-Szyszko and Russian general Alexander Vasilevsky signed a pact that gave birth to a Polish army within the USSR.

Enter Władysław Anders.

The once-cherished general in the Polish Army had earlier been imprisoned and often tortured in Lubyanka Prison in Moscow. However after the signing of The Sikorski–Mayski Agreement, Anders was released and arrangements were made for him to work with the Red Army to defeat Hitler. Allies with the Russians? Working alongside the enemy that took your homeland, sent you to the Gulags and seemed to have little regard whether you lived or died?

What did Anders think of this situation? No doubt he understood it was a political maneuver. Regardless, it opened the gates of the camps and allowed the deportees to, at last, take their first fragile steps toward freedom.

As news of Anders' formation of the Polish Army in Exile, also known as Anders' Army, spread throughout Russia and in and around the labor camps, spirits began to rise. But fear and distrust still maintained a fierce grip. How could the Poles rely on trustworthy news from the Russian government?

More than seventy kilometers southeast of the city of Novosibirsk, on the outskirts of the village of Cheraponovo, in an isolated labor camp where many Poles had been imprisoned for nearly eighteen months, the summer of 1941 was momentous. On a late-August morning, eight members of The Migut Family, most of them wearing the same clothes in which they arrived, collected the few belongings they possessed and tottered toward the open gates of the camp. Two other families were by their side, one of them a family of five with the surname of Chorociej; the other family's name not preserved for history.

That scene remained vivid in my mind as I returned to my notes.

The three families, sluggish, weary, and distraught, approach the open gates. Heartbeats quickening over the uncertainty of the situation, the mothers grab the hands of their beloveds and hold on for dear life. Could it actually be true, they wonder. Were they actually being set free? The gesture—the locking of hands—triggers something. A moment later, a member from one family takes the hand of the comrade next to them. A member from the other family does the same thing. One by one, hands connect and a human link is formed and the creation of a moving human wall is gently pulled by the inertia of the freedom that awaits on the other side of the gates.

When asked about that fateful day, my Uncle John, who was seven years old at the time, looked off in the distance and said: "We walked through the open gates and did not look back. We were afraid to; afraid they would come after us; afraid that it was a big joke. Nobody trusted the Russians. So we kept moving. We went into the forest; we walked and walked and walked—for hours maybe. Finally, we found some train tracks near the forest and snuck into a boxcar that would take us far away."

◆ ◆ ◆

The amnesty was a cosmic Catch-22. The Poles may have been freed, but free to do what? To go where? Returning to Poland was not an option as the war was still playing itself out there. The most logical choice was to head south.

After spending many months braving harsh weather conditions—temperatures in winter often plummeted to forty to sixty below zero (Celsius)—the warmth of the sun would soothe their tattered bodies before the return of a chilling fall and winter.

Not all of the camps released their Polish labor force, however. Some of them, in regions farther east, had norma to fill and the Russian officials there completely disregarded the release orders for a time. For other camps, news of the amnesty arrived sporadically and oftentimes freedom became vexing and the refugees were suddenly faced with an entirely new battle for survival.

Yet these fractured souls who were freed endured, wandering like Gypsies, stealing occasional rides in freight trains whenever the opportunity arose. For those who were fortunate enough to sneak aboard a passenger train, hiding in the public toilet sufficed. Others kept moving throughout the cars to avoid being caught by officials. The majority of these refugees, however, found themselves heading south by foot for long stretches at a time, to destinations unknown to them. Oftentimes, many days passed without a meal, but, as they had discovered back in the camps, they could rely on nature for occasional nourishment—berries and other small fruits from the forest, however sparse. Still, these moments of sustenance did little to curb the fact that for the most part, the deportees suffered from exhaustion, starvation, and malnutrition. Many people, after several days of travel, returned to larger villages or cities where they had greater opportunity to find discarded food—small slices of bread perhaps and other remnants disposed of in the garbage.

It was common to travel in packs at night, resting in the forests during the daylight hours. Unwashed, their stench sparked more than questionable glares from the locals. What a sight to behold, though, when, in the depths of their uncertainty, these wanderers met fellow refugees along the path. Perhaps the faint glint of optimism in their eyes revealed their true identities. Guards down, they exchanged information in hopes of obtaining proper food or locating medical care.

Initially, the NKVD had encouraged the young Polish male refugees to join the Red regiments, at least temporarily until Anders' Army was officially formed. Leery of this option, for who could fully trust the Russians after what they subjected onto the Poles, many of the men persevered and continued traveling until they could locate the Polish Army in Exile themselves and fight alongside their own comrades.

The first main Polish army headquarters was created in early September 1941 in Buzuluk, located in the Orenburg District of the Ural Mountains. Military recruitment centers were established in Koltubanka, Kuibyshev (also spelled Kuybushev), Tatischevo, and Totskoye. However, locating the Polish Army was a daunting task, especially for those who'd been sent into hard labor in the farthest northern and eastern stretches of Russia, places such as Archangelsk (also spelled Arkhangelsk) or Tomsk. In addition, the majority of the refugees had already become gravely ill—most of the men lacked the physical strength to go into combat—but the drive to keep moving trumped everything.

The mass exodus of the Poles evolved into an immense but slow-moving tsunami of misery spreading toward southern Russia—from the plains and low plateaus in the western regions to the mountains in eastern areas. From the farthest regions north, thousands of deportees, the vast clusters of whom were the size of a Chicago suburb, collected themselves in Orenburg and at the Orenburg Gates, along the Ural River and near the border of Kazakhstan—just over 1,400 kilometers southeast of Moscow. At this juncture, the men, hoping to make a difference through military action, continued on, heading to Kuibyshev. The others—women, children, the elderly and the sick—continued on the journey south, with nothing more than their prayers and a determined grip on hope.

Farther east, the Poles who had been imprisoned in areas as remote as Baikal, charted a course along the most southern end of Russia, close to the Mongolian border. Their goal: To reach Alma-Ata (now Almaty) in southeast Kazakhstan. These are but two examples. The number of refugees wandering across Russia at the time was staggering.

In addition to the Poles having been granted amnesty, the NKVD had begun relocating thousands of Soviet citizens from various regions threatened by war to areas farther east and into Asia Russia. Matters were further complicated when the NKVD, fueled by a mix of paranoia and the need to control, began monitoring the Polish refugees, thwarting their plans. At times, trains did not stop at various stations—a well-devised ploy that prevented Poles from either boarding or disembarking trains. Other reports indicated the NKVD secretly hoped to direct several groups to resettle into the poorest, westernmost part of Turkestan along the Aral Sea where life-threatening diseases were rampant—the epidemics of the day: enteric fever, dysentery, malaria, and typhoid.

As the fractured folly moved on, several outposts, particularly a branch office of the Polish Embassy, were formed and representatives began offering aid and direction to the freed deportees. But what route had my family taken?

A baffled detective, I studied numerous Russian maps. If my family embarked on a course for Uzbekistan, I wondered if they initially wandered southeast, through the Russian plains and forests, beyond Barnaul, and then into Kazakhstan. Then west, into the Almaty region, where other deportees had been heading at the time—those who were imprisoned farther east had begun traveling just north of the Mongolian border. I phoned home. Surviving family members had no recollection of their path toward freedom or any significant land markers.

Uncle John was particularly candid: "Mother of God! How in the world am I supposed to know for sure, Greg? Listen—our mother only had one thought in mind: Take care of the children; take care of the family!"

"Yes," I pressed him, "but didn't you talk about it later?"

"Talk about it? Are you nuts? Nobody talked about it. It's not like today where everybody has to *share* everything."

Guilty as charged.

I often prided myself for being a *feeling person*. In fact, sometimes it took months to get through a funk. Oh, how I loved to brag about that. But as I attempted to wrap my mind around the complicated task the Polish deportees faced in finding proper refuge and possibly locating the Polish Army in Exile in the latter half of 1941, I had to ask myself something vital: What truly aided these people in their survival?

Tenacity?

Hope?

Miracles?

All of those things? Or was it, quite simply, basic survival—at any cost?

I could not help but wonder: What is it that keeps us going during the direst of circumstances?

Something much greater than ourselves, I suspected.

~ ~ ~ ~

CHAPTER NINETEEN

A MOCKING PARADOX PRESENTED itself in 1941 when Russia allowed the Polish military to join its ranks to defeat Hitler. More than a year before this "amnesty," in April and May of 1940, Stalin had signed off on orders permitting the NKVD to execute members of the Polish Officer Corps in what became known as the notorious Katyn Massacre.

The German government discovered the mass graves of Polish officers in the Katyn Forest, twenty kilometers west of Smolensk, Russia, in 1943. Initially, the Soviets dismissed the findings, diverting blame onto the Germans. The number of victims of these denied assassinations was approximately 22,000. Regardless, suspicions began circulating among the Polish Government in Exile that the Russians dirtied their hands with this mass disappearance and thought nothing of it—or of using the Polish military for its own benefit after the amnesty.

In fall 1941, the Polish deportees were not yet aware of the Katyn Massacre. They continued to flee south while Anders collected his resources and strategized. There were misgivings at the time that Russia would not surrender the seized Polish territories and that Soviets were not offering proper assistance to the Polish Army In Exile. Reportedly, out of all the infantry divisions that had formed, only one—the 5th, under General Mieczysław Boruta-Spiechowicz's command—had been given adequate supplies. Other Polish military divisions were left to their own devices. And yet, Anders prevailed.

In describing General Anders, Stanislaw Kot, the new Polish Ambassador in the Soviet Union, said the general's appearance was "wretched"—Anders had endured the Gulags, after all. Kot also noted that Anders, in an attempt to rescue the young Polish men who had been freed, began issuing call-up notices for men from the age of seventeen.

Other accounts from Kot, and Russian and Polish officials captured the gravity of the situation for both the military and the refugees. In a dialogue on September 8, 1941, with Vyacheslav Molotov, the Russian Commissar for Foreign Affairs who was instrumental in the notorious Molotov-Ribbentrop Pact in 1939, Kot wanted to confirm that Russia would, as promised, supply arms for the Polish Army in Exile. To which Molotov shot back, in part, "We cannot supply arms ... Great Britain and America must realise that we are shedding our blood for them. They must provide us with arms."

Speaking of the Polish refugees, Kot told the American Red Cross in Moscow on October 2, 1941, that, "the situation of the Polish citizens so far released is wretched. Their debility, total lack of clothing and footwear, and the complete lack of funds make their desperate position still worse. The Soviet government has stated that it is unable to give any help at all ... the Ambassador appeals to the American Red Cross for help."

In a cable from Kuibishev to the Polish Embassy in Washington dated October 27, 1941, Kot reported: "For some time now transports of Polish people have been routed to Uzbekistan and they are being employed on the cotton plantations and on irrigation and construction works ... People are dying of hunger *en route*."

Even more revealing was a conversation Kot had with Stalin himself in the Kremlin on November 14, 1941: Kot confirmed the Soviet leader would allow the Polish military to form as many divisions as they had people for, on condition they obtain equipment and food supplies from abroad.

"All that remains is to indicate the place where we can proceed with the formation of detachments," Kot added.

To which Stalin hotly retorted: "It will not be Uzbekistan, to which place Polish citizens are travelling illegally."

Kot's rebuttal? "Uzbekistan was not our idea, but was indicated ... by the Soviet military authorities."

Deciphering the Soviets' madness was beyond taxing, but on some level their unpredictability made sense. Stalin was paranoid that in the Soviet's new alliance with the Polish Army in Exile, the Poles would be given arms. He felt strongly that each Polish military division should immediately be sent into battle, something Polish officials vehemently opposed, preferring the more sane approach: being prepared.

Stalin's modus operandi implied one thing: Eradicating the existence of the Poles was still in the forefront of his mind. Had the Polish military divisions leapt too quickly into battle, it would have been their ruin. Were it not for Great Britain, who offered remarkable support, the Polish military would not have acquired proper clothing and other supplies.

As winter 1941 began, the sheer volume of Polish deportees on the move was unfathomable. Train stations became a common gathering ground throughout southern Russia. The refugees were able to receive cups of boiled water and often begged for food or money from other travelers. At the stations they found it easier to hop back into another open boxcar on a slowly moving train. At night, groups huddled together at the outer edges of the station's platforms to sleep, until authorities discovered them and demanded they keep moving along. While passing through villages within the areas of Kazakhstan, Kyrgyzstan and Uzbekistan, many of these "Polish tramps," as they were often called, scoured trash bins outside cafeterias, homes or businesses, or collected fruit that dropped from trees. In frantic attempts to feed their children, mothers divided these near-rotten findings among the family, but often, days passed without even a crumb of food. Many wanderers took to sleeping under trees in the forests, in fields off the roadways, or in parks or public squares, their soiled clothing now loosely hanging off them, their bones protruding through their skin—living skeletons surviving, somehow, on the sheer force of their prayers and the unpredictable winds of fate.

Still more strange alliances formed. Imagine the wicked irony when some Polish refugees began working alongside Uzbeks and Kirghizians, a group of people who considered themselves heirs of the Genghis Khan era, spawned in 1226. After the Mongolian Empire was established, stretching from Korea to the Persian Gulf, and north toward Poland, a great majority of Russia was under Mongolian dominance. In fact, until the latter part of the 18th century, Russians were often considered "objects of commerce" in Mongolian Turkestan. Approximately 10,000 Russians and Persians were sold. Time, of course, changed everything, and Russian politicos eradicated the region's religion and closed thousands of mosques. When the Uzbeks and Kirghizians understood the full scope of what the Polish refugees' endured, these natives, far from forgiving the Russians, did more than simply befriend the Poles. They expressed deep empathy and concern for the deportees' well-being and care.

In late 1941, news spread that the Polish Army in Exile would, in fact, be redirected to Uzbekistan. Anders had finally become so frustrated by the lack of supplies, food, and other military aid from the Soviets that he opted for this move. The deportees followed, hoping to gain assistance from the Polish military.

In January 1942, the new army headquarters was set up in Jangi-Jul (also known as Yangi-Yul, Yangiyo'l or Yangiyul) about twenty-five kilometers southwest from the city of Tashkent in Uzbekistan. Other units were stationed in Kirgisia, Kazakhstan, and Tadzykistan. Recruitment centers were based in Kermine, Samarkand, Bishkek, Almaty.

The distance from regions such as Novosibirsk, where my family was imprisoned, to these areas in southern Russia is more than 2,400 kilometers (1,500 miles). Today, it would take several days of travel via rail to go that distance. In 1941, by foot, an occasional train ride, or hitching a ride on another motor vehicle or arba, the trek spanned many months and was plagued with complications. The NKVD's curious habit of shifting train schedules at random prevented proper transportation further south. Other obstacles, such as illness and disease, delayed progress. The refugee population continued to shrink, with the dead left behind and buried in unmarked graves in the soil of their enemy.

Meanwhile people who were too sick to continue traveling were, by the sheer grace of God, accepted into various hospitals with open beds. The others kept on. Exhausted, often distraught, they relied on their prayers as a compass during this massive descent into southern Russia.

~ ~ ~ ~

CHAPTER TWENTY

IN JANUARY OF 1942, NKVD head Lavrentiy Beria wrote in a note to Stalin saying the amnesty had freed 389,041 Polish citizens, which included:

* 200,828 ethnic Poles,
* 90,662 Jews,
* 31,392 Ukrainians,
* 27,418 Belorussians,
* 3,421 Russians, and
* 2,291 persons of varying nationalities.

I picture this as a perverse exchange between the two men. Stalin didn't really care about the well-being of the freed deportees and the Soviet authorities did little to assist them. Most of the deported souls who were freed relied on word of mouth from their own comrades on where to go and what to do.

Russian officials encouraged these refugees to work in nearby villages on collective farms. Some of them did. They settled into various villages in Kazakhstan, Uzbekistan and Turkmenistan—to note but three regions. Mothers, many of them widowed, enrolled their children in local schools and accepted random acts of kindness from strangers in the area. They found shelter wherever they could—in villages or in mud huts on local farms.

Many others, who decided to leave, waited for the occasional, floating feather of information to reach them on the erratic political winds.

"The Polish military is gathering for maneuvers nearby! Surely they can help!"

"Word is that Anders will be in Tashkent."

"God shines down his favor on us. Tomorrow we go!"

And off the refugees went, searching for the military and the remote chance that they could be fed and given shelter. For how much longer could they endure the endless wandering?

As thousands of refugees continued to funnel into southern Russia and Polish men attempted to enlist in the military, Polish embassy officials from Kuibyshev began coordinating with other agencies and organized posts in various cities, towns, and villages in Uzbekistan and Kazakhstan. In early 1942, members of the Red Cross began tallying the refugees in a number of Uzbeki villages and shared vital information with other refugees. News went out that several orphanages were being formed in Uzbekistan—from Tashkent to Bukhara—to care the thousands of Polish children who had lost their families. News of theses orphanages brought hope, but concerned mothers, like my own grandmother, feared that after handing over their children they would never be able to see them again.

When a Polish settlement in Bombay, India, discovered Polish children were suffering and dying in Asiatic Russia, the country became one of the first to offer aid to the Poles. The fact that the Russian government did little to assist them during the ominous "amnesty" motivated Poles in the Indian settlement to rally together. They felt there must be a way to help the children. Thomas Roberts, a Jesuit priest who served as archbishop of Bombay since 1937, took immediate notice. Others, such as Sir Archibald Webb, deputy minister of internal affairs for India, also stepped up. With assistance from the Council of Indian Princes, a custodial council was formed in New Delhi in early 1942.

Political turmoil raged elsewhere and blood was still being shed on the German-Russian front. Hitler's Operation Barbarossa had, at that point, taken over Kiev but failed to capture Moscow, which thwarted his entire enterprise. The events did little to lessen anxieties for the Poles, especially those overseeing the orphaned children in Uzbekistan. However, as their lives dangled like broken twigs on a fragile vine, a new sprout of hope emerged. The Polish Red Cross organized a relief expedition from Bombay to Tashkent, where General Anders had been stationed. With it came medicine, clothing and food—in a caravan of several trucks driven by Hindus.

Britain fully aligning itself with Poland?

Uzbekis coming to the aid of Poles?

Hindus offering a big hand to Polish orphans?

These seemingly random unions became a saving grace. However, as expected, the Russians did not welcome aid for the refugees. How could the government justify such things as gifts and medical supplies to the Poles on Russian soil when the vast majority Russia's own citizens were suffering in poverty?

Meanwhile, Polish officials continued imploring adults to take their children to the nearest orphanages because this would be the only chance for the children to survive. Mothers, fathers, uncles, aunts, older sisters, and brothers—broken families suffering the loss of their loved ones who had perished along their journey—obeyed, tearfully depositing their little creatures into the hands of strangers. That their own fates remained uncertain did not matter. At least the children would find a way to have better lives.

At the time—March 1942—the Polish military comprised more than 80,000 officers and 35,000 civilians, yet they were surviving on rations for 30,000 because the Russian military was no longer able to properly feed and service them. And then startling news emerged: Stalin approved evacuations of the Polish military along with 10,000 members of their families. He must have still been calculating in his mind how to keep the Polish territories he had seized. With a significant number of troops diverted elsewhere, he could keep his political paws on Poland. No doubt suspecting the evacuations would create more problems with an already unmanageable refugee population, the Soviets insisted they take place within a week's time. One week.

The news generated additional pandemonium, especially among Polish refugees who had been freed from labor camps and had wound up on collective farms or in factories. They desperately searched for the proper military units, hoping they could evacuate Russia with the military. At last, they had a real chance for freedom.

The mind-bending events of that time placed General Anders in yet another quandary. He decided to disobey Stanisław Kot's orders, since Kot reportedly leaned toward leaving Polish families behind in Russia. Anders began overseeing evacuation of the Polish military and, in an effort to offset growing panic among the refugees, he began enlisting Poles into the military at will, regardless of age or sex. In the forefront of Anders' mind: Safe refuge for his fellow Poles.

On March 19, 1942, this Polish general orchestrated the evacuation of Polish soldiers and civilians who had found shelter near the Polish military camps. Between March 24 and April 4, more than 33,000 soldiers and nearly 11,000 civilians, including 3,100 children, said goodbye to Russia.

The dates of this evacuation are noteworthy: It happened during Lent and Holy Week. And what of the other Polish refugees? Many more months passed before a significant new chapter began for them, and for my family.

During the summer of 1942, tensions between Russia and the Polish Government in Exile escalated. Stalin's decisions became more unpredictable and Polish officials were even more distrustful of the dictator's true motives. For instance, Stalin assured Britain that Polish forces would assist the country in the south following British setbacks in Africa, which fanned lingering suspicions that Stalin simply wanted to eradicate any existence of the Poles in Russia and create a more cohesive Communist force. Stalin's prime objective was to mobilize all forces to combat Germany, not to protect the refugees whose lives he had impoverished.

With the fates of the Polish forces in southern Russia, and the countless refugees still seeking aid there, at the forefront of his mind, General Anders oversaw another set of evacuations from Russia. Once again, this included military, their families, civilians, and children. The second evacuation of Poles, which took place in late August and early September of 1942, was notably larger than the first—nearly 45,000 military personnel and more than 25,000 civilians, including my family. Between the March/April and August/September evacuations, in all, approximately 116,000 Polish military and civilians left Russia for Persia.

Anders' devotion to the Polish people spared many lives. But one fleeting decision could have dramatically and permanently altered life events at that time.

What if my grandmother, Jadwiga, had *not* deposited her children in the Polish orphanage? What if she had *not* sent her daughter Janina to sell one of their coats at a nearby bizarre? What if the Gypsy had *not* stolen the 250 rubles my aunt collected from selling the coat? What if my aunt had *not* broken down into tears only to be discovered by a Polish soldier? That soldier was one of the family's many miracles.

Or was it my aunt's tears?

Or the shifty Gypsy?

Or my grandmother's decision to sell the coat?

As the significant sea change played out in southern Russia, caravans escorting the orphans and refugees out of the country traveled west from areas near and around Tashkent, all the way to the port in Krasnovodsk (now Türkmenbaşy) on the Caspian Sea—a journey of nearly 1,200 kilometers.

The destination from the Krasnovodsk port: the Persian harbor of Pahlavi.

At times, the plans for reaching Krasnovodsk were carried out without much refinement. The Russians did little to make the transition simple. Shoddy communication from the Soviets forced refugees to endure additional hardship—in this case, waiting in Krasnovodsk for a proper transport to arrive. When it finally did, transportation came in the form of a dank coal ship with wretched interior bowels that reeked of fuel fumes. Thousands of these Poles, including my family, scrambled toward the deck and as the NKVD kept a watching eye on the planks, they prayed to their Heavenly Father that their names had been properly placed on the transport list.

And if their names were not listed? The NKVD showed no mercy. The refugees were not allowed to pass. People already on board were led down into the ship's lower deck and placed in a cargo area designated for coal. There, the Poles huddled together, packed, once again, like cattle in fusty quarters. Already weak or ill, they endured, braving seasickness or passing out from lack of air in this chamber of the macabre as the ship sailed through the night.

The following morning, after the ship had docked and the Poles found their way onto the shores of Pahlavi, there, for the first time in more than two years, these tormented mortals were free.

They wept. They sobbed with joy. Some fell to their knees. Bonded by the desolation they suffered together, strangers tightly embraced for oh, how God had blessed them. They had survived their ordeal.

For now.

~ ~ ~ ~

CHAPTER TWENTY-ONE

A BAND OF HOMELESS POLES finding refuge in Persia (now Iran) was about as likely as Stalin hosting a Polka Party for General Anders. This was yet another incident with Polish deportees that was greatly under-reported in 1942 and thereafter. Seventy-five years after the first major wave of Polish civilian deportations began in February of 1940, most accounts of World War II still focus on Hitler's barbarism, not Stalin's shocking disregard for humanity. Especially his wrath on the Poles.

In the face of, or, maybe, in spite of Stalin's abhorrent actions, numerous tales of unlikely survival and brotherhood reveal a universal truth: The inclination to offer a hand often outweighs the inclination to chop it off. This became especially evident to my family and the other Polish refugees during late summer of 1942, for on the Persian beaches of the Caspian Sea, in Pahlavi, a bona fide white tent city bloomed. This city became the new home for the refugees, many of them walking skeletons, about a third of them children. In this surreal asylum, a place void of terror and turmoil, for the first time in months, the Polish refugees were properly bathed and almost all of them checked for lice—many of the children had their heads shaved.

A much-needed quarantine area was created within the tent city as illnesses were still rampant. That was the only way the authorities, predominantly the Red Cross, could initiate proper protocol to aid in recovery efforts despite being overwhelmed by the growing demand to treat the ailments—dysentery, horrendous exhaustion, malaria, a variety of skin infections, and typhus, which plagued the majority of those individuals sent to the infirmary.

Not all of these souls survived. One report, for instance, noted a Polish Pastoral Service Abroad approximation that 600 children perished in Pahlavi.

When a move south to Tehran became necessary in an effort to care for the Poles near a larger city with better resources, the process was perplexing to execute. Transporting thousands of displaced Polish refugees was a grand challenge, but other dangers were involved. The route to Tehran required moving through the Elburz Mountains (also known as Alburz or Elburs), the significant mountain range in northern Iran that is roughly 900 kilometers long and boasts ridiculously steep, dangerous roads. As precarious as it was, the military caravan cautiously travelled over the menacing, narrow thoroughfares where drivers never knew for sure if another vehicle would be heading toward them in the opposite direction. Would there ever be an end to harrowing events for these refugees?

Once in Tehran, officials there, primarily the International Refugee Organization—which would become an official United Nations entity in 1946—began mass efforts to assist the refugees, my family among them. But again, they were not prepared for the massive number of people in need of aid. Five transit camps were erected in the region with one designated for just the military, another, just for the orphans. One camp in particular was established in the most surprising locale: The lush gardens of the newly appointed Shah, Mohammad Reza Pahlavi—the same Shah who was overthrown in the Iranian Revolution in 1979. Mohammad was the son of Reza Shah Pahlavi, who had been ousted in September 1941 after British-Soviet pressures, mainly because he refused to remove all German nationals in the area and fully join forces with the Allies. Regardless, the Shah's palace would go down in history as one of the more unusual refuges for these displaced Polish people.

Meanwhile, in the nearby city, a hospital, a hostel for the elderly, and a home for sick children were also established. As the Polish refugees acclimated to the region and the warmer climate, neighboring communities continued to offer assistance. When space became limited within the tent city, refugees were redirected to shelters in nearby schools, boarding houses, churches, and additional warehouses. Meals were offered, but while lamb or hearty soups appeared inviting, few of these poor souls could properly digest their richness.

After eating nothing more than scraps of bread for nearly two years, their bodies were not equipped for such treats and they endured digestive disorders.

Other, more fascinating developments, occurred 340 kilometers south of Tehran in Isfahan where a large number of Polish orphans were moved. The presence of these Polish children touched the hearts of local people who bonded with them, so much so that even when the Polish Army had to leave the area, many families and children chose to stay behind. In fact, from 1942 to 1945, approximately 2,590 Polish children in Isfahan below the age of seven resided there. The area became a socially and ethnically vibrant community and would go down in history as one of the most interesting, and under-noticed, factoids about Iranian culture.

Nearly twenty boarding schools were established for the children in Isfahan and it would eventually take the title of "The City of Polish Children" (or *Isfahan—Miasto Dzieci Polskich* in Polish). Some seventy years later, in 2008, the Polish Postal Service issued a stamp commemorating Ifahan's significant role in the lives of the Polish children.

During that time in 1942, moods softened, but potential threats lingered. The Russians still occupied Northern Persia. The new Shah agreed to lend Persia as a gateway for supplies to aid the military allies, but specifically signed off on a six-month arrangement of the Russian presence. Needless to say, the mere sight of Russian soldiers triggered fear among the refugees and they were given specific instructions by the Polish military and orphanage officials not to mention anything about their ordeals to the Russians. For who could predict how these soldiers would respond?

Even here, the Russian menace was lurking in the periphery.

Around this time, in a desperate attempt to save face, the Russian government had the audacity to deflect much of the blame for the Poles' predicament— primarily their deportations and imprisonment—onto the Germans. The fact that the Germans were nowhere near many of the deportation areas in eastern Poland in 1940 apparently didn't matter to the Russians. If they were going to rewrite history, why not deny culpability?

In Tehran, the Poles were temporarily shielded to some extent from political dilemmas, but other worries surfaced: Where to bury the dead? Saint Lazarus Order of the Monks offered a cemetery for the growing number of deceased, but it quickly filled to capacity. Another cemetery was created near the city and would eventually assume the name Dulab Polish Cemetery. To this day, it still rests in an eastern suburb of Tehran and comprises Catholic souls, including the graves of English, Czechs, French, Germans, Armenians and Italians. The Polish section of the cemetery is now overseen by the Embassy of the Republic of Poland in Tehran. It remains the largest burial spot of Polish refugees in Iran during World War II and includes nearly 2,000 tombs, including soldiers and civilians, most of which were Polish refugees who perished in hospitals and evacuation camps. On a monumental statue bearing an iron cross rests a commemorative stone plate with an engraved emblem of the Republic of Poland. The inscription reads: "In remembrance of Polish expatriates having stayed here in God forever on their way to Fatherland. 1942-1944."

In all, there are two Polish cemeteries in Iran, and six Polish sections and several single Polish graves at various cemeteries for a total of approximately 2,806 graves. The Kresy-Siberia Foundation states that 2,119 Polish refugees died in Iran. It is interesting to note that of the approximately 650 military graves in Iran, none of the Polish soldiers laid to rest there were killed in action. Rather, they died from disease and/or physical exhaustion.

In fall of 1942, when Great Britain notified the Polish government-in-exile of the next phase of the refugees' journey—primarily that Britain was now ready to grant the refugees hospitality in several of her colonies in various parts of the world—there was another surge of hope.

The first step in this new development would be to transport the Poles from Tehran to Baghdad. Departures from Tehran were carried out in intervals. The military set the course first along yet another hazardous roadway, one on which they, as soldiers, may have been equipped to travel. However few personnel ever imagined they would be transporting children, especially during wartime.

After a respite in Baghdad, the caravan continued on with occasional stops. Large groups of refugees were taken to Ahwaz (also spelled Ahvaz), near the Persian Gulf, while a significant number of others moved on to Karachi, which, at the time, was run by British India. Today, as the capital of Pakistan, Karachi boasts a population of 23 million. It is the third largest city in the world among populations within city limits, but back in 1942, it served as yet another springboard toward a new life for the Poles. Bombay (now Mumbai) also figured prominently in some resettlements.

To this day the world is mostly oblivious to the prominent role the Middle East and India played in the lives of the Polish refugees. By the end of 1943:

- approximately 33,000 civilians had passed through Iran,
- 3,933 refugees remained in Tehran,
- 2,388 were in Isfahan,
- 2,834 in Ahwaz,
- and 66 in Mashhad.

The remaining 4,300 refugees were evacuated to Baghdad and Beirut at the end of 1945. India first began accepting Polish orphans in January 1942, and HH Jam Saheb Digvijay Sinhjii, the Maharaja of Nawanagar, accepted 500 children into his territories.

In March 1942, the Polish Consulate in Bombay embarked on a Red Cross expedition from Ashkhabad to India with roughly 160 to 175 Polish children. More than 600 children were spared imminent death, thanks to three more overland transports. By April 1942, when Polish orphans arrived in Bombay, they were taken to the transitory camp, Bandra. And then in June 1942, the government of India accepted 10,000 Polish children with the Polish government-in-exile co-funding their stay. In July 1942, the children from Bandra finally arrived in Balachadi, Nawanagar.

By the time the refugees in the second wave of evacuations, including my family, reached India in the fall of 1942, many weeks passed before final arrangements were secured to transport them to safer destinations from the ports of Karachi. Meanwhile, with the orphans now in safe hands, the Polish military were diverted elsewhere.

Once again, a twisted providence intervened. With their thoughts still turned to God, thousands of refugees found themselves boarding three ships, one of them transporting them to safety to the most unlikely destination of all: Eastern Africa. Approximately 18,000 Polish refugees were sent there. Other groups, smaller in size and mostly consisting of orphans, were taken to Mexico and New Zealand.

The International Refugee Organization was instrumental in helping coordinate many of these transports. In fall 1942, because of dangerous circumstances—primarily Japanese aircraft—three ships filled with thousands of Polish orphans and civilians departed Karachi with a convoy of British naval units. My family was on one of those ships. True, these were better conditions than the transport across the Caspian Sea, but the quarters below deck were hot, cramped, and musty. There was also a sense of danger in the air.

Polish refugees traveling through the Arabian Sea in 1942? Another wild card history books do not always notice.

The ship on which my family traveled held approximately 5,000 people, mostly orphans. Nearly all of the adult women had been hired to work for the orphanage; very few Polish men were present. They had either died or enlisted in the Polish Army to fight alongside their former oppressors—Stalin's military—and the Allies to defeat Hitler. Seasickness, while rampant, became manageable, but on that journey near the equator another blow came—literally.

My Uncle John recalled that officials on his ship reported that a German submarine maneuvered through the refugees' convoy undetected by the ships' radars. It launched a torpedo toward one of the ships carrying civilians and orphans—the third ship, which was directly behind the boat on which my family traveled. My research uncovered that the cargo ship Empire Guidon was torpedoed and sunk in the Indian Ocean, east of Africa on October 31, 1942, by the German sub U-504. Was that sunken freighter the ship my uncle recalled?

In my uncle's words:

> I was terrified to death as I watched that ship go under. The screams from children in the water were unbearable. Desperate, drowning kids tried to hang on to the sailors who were trying to save themselves, too. Some of the sailors had knifes in their teeth and I wondered why. And then I saw the biggest horror in my life. The sailors began knifing the kids who were trying to hang onto them. They did it to save themselves. None of the other ships came to their aid. All they did was blow their steam off and move in zigzagging patterns to avoid being hit by another torpedo.

~ ~ ~ ~

CHAPTER TWENTY-TWO

SO MUCH FOR ERADICATING my depression. Who in God's name encouraged me to probe my family's past? Me? My friends?

Your therapist, Greg. Blame it all on that woman who does not part her lips!

Oh course—*her!*

The more I investigated Back Then, the more I felt downright awful in the Here and Now.

Furthermore—and this was just *cruel, cruel, cruel*—all of my vices suddenly failed me. Food, alcohol, sex, television shows—once the go-to for avoiding uncomfortable feelings—offered absolutely no comfort or levity whatsoever. Something unsettling stirred deep within my inner world and would not allow me to rest until I uncovered as many details as I could about my family's deportation and the deportations of millions of Polish people in the 1940s. I had to make some sense of it—if that was even possible—and, somehow, grow personally in the process.

But while growth is a wonderful thing at times, it is rarely comfortable. Yeah, nobody remembers to mention that clause in the fine print on The Growth Contract.

When I received news that the major cable TV magazine for which I had long been penning celebrity features unexpectedly folded and would not pay my outstanding invoices, which hovered near $5,000, I briefly considered packing it in, running away to a Carmelite Monastery down in Carmel to splash holy water all over myself and hide out with the nuns for the next decade. I simply did not have the mental and emotional bandwidth to deal—with anything.

Had I brought this new turn of events on myself? I'd spent years New Aging myself into a corner with all that "be careful what you think and feel, for you are bound to manifest it" ideology. After all, I had become disillusioned writing about "showbiz." Perhaps that lingering indifference fueled my current situation. However I never anticipated a significant, and much needed, extra source of income would completely vanish, thereby leaving me financially stranded and, well, getting what I had been craving— to not write about the entertainment world as frequently as I once had.

Well, the entire Where's The Money? thing felt like sandpaper scraping across the thin skin of my years of financial mismanagement. What can I say? I took the Pollyanna Course in Finances 101. Did I have to be reminded that I was thousands of dollars in debt with no additional income or any real motivation to pull myself through it?

Apparently I did. Moods swung and that *family story* kept lurking in the periphery.

Haunting me.

Hunting me.

For respite, I turned back to the works of Florence Scovel Shinn, Penny Pearce, Michael Drury, Wayne Dwyer, Deepak Chopra and Louise L. Hay. I meditated. Well, I tried. Quieting my mind seemed an impossible task. I practiced Bikram yoga. I prayed. I chanted on mountaintops. I grunted, groaned, and cried like Holly Hunter on the end of a dock in *Broadcast News*. The first half of 2012—a bona fide Rodeo of Rumination! But again, what you resist persists. You can ignore it if you wish, but really, once you begin walking along any spiritual path, no matter how many detours you wish to take when things begin to feel uncomfortable, ultimately The Universe will lead you right back to the very thing to which you are destined to pay attention.

I wondered: Why had I become so enchanted with Hollywood and celebrities in the first place? Was it an escape? Did I want to be like those celebrities? Did I feel special writing about them? And by writing about them—over and over again—had I lost sight of myself? My family? Had I made a career out of hanging out in a star-cluttered world and telling everyone else's story because…

What?

I was apprehensive to tell my own?

We all arrive here on Earth full of potential—clean slates, fresh newbies—but either we forget, or are rarely told, that unless we're willing to look back and fully assess where and from whom we came, we're likely to create a life that is not fully our own.

Could it be true—that we can never become who we are meant to be until we're willing to let go of who we *think* we have to be? Who the hell was I—*now*?

Ever since I decided to confront the past head on, I felt as though I, too, had been tossed onto a Russian sled with my family on that cold February morning in eastern Poland. I rode along with them in the boxcars. I shivered in the sawdust in the barrack. I stood knee-deep in snow underneath a birch tree, my feet, my calves chilled to the bone as I awkwardly attempted to saw through the thick, frozen bark with a large saw I did not know how to use.

I could no longer distinguish whether I was impacted by my family's story or just plain impregnated with it. Silly me. I had to ask my therapist.

"Impregnated?" mused Dee the Therapist. "So, you're calling yourself a surrogate of sorts? A host?"

"Am I?" I countered.

"Are you?"

"I dunno."

"Well, dear Greg, now, I'm confused!"

Lovely. My therapist was confused. Not a good sign. On the plus side: Unlike the Jungian therapist, she wasn't falling asleep.

Lexapro, Wellbutrin, Zoloft—maybe it time to become part of the 20 Milligrams Club after all. But I resisted. There must be another way. There had to be a natural elixir for my depression. After all, how much longer could I walk around feeling like I was traveling with thousands of Polish refugees in 1942?

I must have Googled "Help Me, My Family Survived Stalin's Wrath, And I Feel the Funk, Brother" to answer that question, and I immediately wished I had not. I soon discovered information about the impact of the Holocaust and World War II on the children of its survivors. A term in *The International Handbook of Multigenerational Legacies of Trauma*, edited by Yael Danieli, stood out: The Echo Effect.

The Echo Effect could apply to almost *any* child of war survivors. It revolves around the idea that children of parents and/or close family members who survived a war are also affected on an emotional and/or psychological level by the family's traumatic experiences. The child is said to echo what exists in the parents' inner worlds and, on another level, a child's psychic reality reveals the significant marks of trauma that their war-torn parents experienced—experiences that their parents and family members may or may not have had the proper psychological tools to deal with, fully integrate, and transform. As a result, these children are left to carry on working through of the trauma—regardless of whether or not they know this is unfolding within them.

Transference phenomena, to which the traumatic legacy is lived out as one's inevitable fate, also comes into play here.

The handbook revealed that a vast majority of children of war survivors have attempted to repair their parents' and family's lives by "eliciting testimonies or writing down the parents' histories." Well, I did need a laugh, even though it sprouted from a kind of sickening irony. It also noted that many of those children are therapists and—for the love of God, really?—*journalists* "engaged in professions that valorize the spoken word, knowing and the telling of stories as a way to impact others and/or heal."

I felt as if I'd just been bitchslapped by Victoria Grayson on an episode of *Revenge*.

The child is said to echo what exists in the parents' inner world...

Left to carry on the trauma...

The traumatic legacy is lived out as one's inevitable fate.

What was my family's traumatic legacy? More importantly, was it my inevitable fate to live it out? A game of mental tennis began.

First volley: *Greg, your family survived life-and-death circumstances during the 1940s, but they came out the other side—stronger, self-assured, and determined. They arrived in America with nothing and worked extremely hard. They bought homes. They got married. They raised children. They acquired what every immigrant hopes to achieve: The American Dream.*

Second volley: *Yeah, but have you ever asked yourself if they ever really—like, really—dealt with what happened to them on a psychological or emotional level?*

Third volley: *Please! Did they have time? All they knew how to do was to survive—at any cost.*

Fourth volley: *Nice try, but all the emotional and psychological stuff they may not have been dealt with—and you may never know what the hell that is, by the way—guess what? There's a strong possibility that you—yeah, you and your cousins—could be carrying all that around. You know, underneath the surface and all.*

Game. Set. Match.

But another mind game began.

What are the emotional after effects of being shoved into a crowded boxcar and sent to Siberia?

How is somebody affected psychologically after eighteen months of slave labor?

What happens to you internally when you're left to wander as a homeless refugee in unfamiliar parts of the world with no assurance of, well, anything?

I was on a roll—and unraveling at the same time.

How does the past—our family's, our own—materialize in our everyday lives? How had it materialized in my own life? The popular Polish saying, "Not my circus, not my monkey," suddenly came to mind. But had I been living that saying in reverse? The whole Stalin Did Something To My Family thing now felt as if it was my circus *and* my monkey. And the convivial ringmaster was having a field day in the spotlight:

"Step right up, step right up. Now appearing on Center Stage: Chubby Polish Kid with Fluctuating Self-Esteem sheds weight and wanders thousands of miles away from home—yes, thousands and thousands of miles, just as his family did. Watch how he seeks guidance from The Powers That Be in faraway lands—that's right, just as his family did. Look with wonder at how well he breeds financial instability and fuels a fabulous kind of Lack and Insufficiency (cue: sad accordion chords) —a feeling of lack and insufficiency his own family probably experienced. Witness how he often feels empty, confined, and trapped, believing there is absolutely no way out of his self-created imprisonment."

I knew there was a good reason I never liked the circus.

How had I not seen any of this before? There were many times in my life when I became engaged in and/or remained in situations I didn't truly desire to experience in the first place. More often than not, I tended to remain in those situations longer than necessary, which made me feel trapped, without a "way out," all the while searching for a "sign" that would help me untangle myself from it and miraculously survive against all odds Read: escape.

Wasn't that the theme of my family's odyssey—albeit not as dramatic as theirs? Had they not searched for some type of rescue?

That curious couple of years I had shared an apartment with a so-called psychic who insisted the two of us had many lifetimes together; someone who believed that thousands of years ago she had my baby, and that a couple thousand prior to that, I could have died in her arms?

Check.

Serial dating and that three-year relationship with the over-critical, work-a-holic Capricorn who wanted to change me?

Check.

All those years of perpetuating a cycle on financial insufficiency?

Ka-ching!

The list was long. And what of my current predicament?

I no longer wanted to live in Santa Cruz. Yet there I was—for more than a decade—searching for a financial and practical way out of there. I had never truly longed to become the editor of an entire newspaper—a writer, yes, but an editor, not so much. Yet there I was—an editor and I seemed to always want out of the job, yet never knew how to be set free from it.

True, many of those experiences added tremendous value to my life and ushered in other meaningful times, for which I was grateful. However, the fact that I could, in present day, to some degree, be mirroring my family's past melodramas—lost and uncertain refugees surviving against all odds—was beyond unsettling and did little to alleviate that very loud "okay, now what?" blaring from the radio speakers inside my mind.

I questioned other life events, such as the fact that as a teenager, I moved from Chicago to Phoenix, which was nearly the same distance in miles between Novosibirsk—where my family had been imprisoned—to Uzbekistan, the portal in which they were finally led toward freedom.

Perhaps I was making too large a symbolic leap.

Or maybe not. The emotional vault door had been opened. In a short span of time, I discovered other material, beyond *The International Handbook of Multigenerational Legacies of Trauma*—

- 1973's *Manifestations of Concentration Camp Effects on the Second Generation,*

- 1980's *Separation-Individuation Conflicts in Children of Holocaust Survivors* and

• 2002's *"Enactment" in the Lives and Treatment of Holocaust Survivors; Offspring*, which reported findings that children of camp survivors had a compulsion "to recreate their parents' experiences in their own lives through concrete acts."

Fine. What was I supposed to do? Sit on my therapist's couch and confess: "Hi, my name is Greg and I think I have a really bad case of Help Me, The Grass Is Always Greener On The Other Side Of The Slave Labor Camp?"

Was it possible that, in some way, I became a storehouse for emotional energy that did not originate from me—at all? Unbeknownst to me, had I become the recipient of a plethora of memories, intense emotions, and, to some extent, unresolved issues invisibly handed down to me from a group of World War II survivors with whom I shared DNA—emotional and otherwise? Like a sponge, had I absorbed that energy deep into the very fiber of my being—my cells, even? Did that energy gestate there? Were their energetic vibrations requesting an outlet to be released now? Was my current discomfort a Big Clue to either investigate who I really was and what came before me on a deeper level or, simply move on in another direction entirely?

I could not be the only human experiencing such a thing—if, in fact, I was actually experiencing it. Christ—everything was beginning to feel like that reality-shifting movie *Inception*, where every dream-like layer the protagonist explored only provoked more uncertainty. I had to face one truth: I had arrived at another fork in the road. Embracing my family's story—and, to some degree, reliving it—was one thing. Fully understanding what it wanted to teach me and finding a way to transform and excavate it from the very walls of my soul?

Well, suddenly, that required a jackhammer.

～ ～ ～ ～

CHAPTER TWENTY-THREE

"SO, WHAT DOES YOUR THERAPIST SAY about all this stuff you're feeling?" asked my chipper friend, comrade and colleague Christine, she of vibrant redheaded flair, crystal blue eyes, and powerful cigarette inhale. She was also an associate professor at a very alternative psychology graduate institute in Northern California so our talks often delved deep. We were seated across from each other at a black metal table on the deck of her Santa Cruz townhouse.

"I dumped my therapist," I announced.

"The lesbian Buddhist?"

"Yep. No surprise—she barely reacted."

"How could you let her go at a time like this?"

"Trust me, *she'll* be fine!"

Head tilting back, Christine knocked back the rest of an expensive pale ale and shot me a concerned look. "But what about you, sweetie?"

"I'm fine."

"You're a mess."

"You're right—I *am* a mess."

"Go back to therapy!"

"Really? Pay somebody a hundred bucks to watch me play out my Lifetime Movie Channel drama? Why do I get the feeling I have become the best damn entertainment a therapist doesn't have to pay for?"

Christine inched a newly opened bottle of Rock Bottom ale closer toward me from across the patio table.

"Well," she offered. "The alternative ain't pretty."

"Thanks. I'll use different face cream. You know, to eliminate the puffy bags of defeat forming underneath my eyes."

We left it at that. However, in the days that followed, I turned to the goddess of mood swings—Carrie Fisher. Not personally—literally. And not literally but *literally!* As in reading some of the Divine F's books. Although, I think La Fisher and I could have a marvelous conversation.

"My parents were Hollywood Unusual and I am really bipolar!" Carrie would tell me over a diet coke and a cigarette.

I would toss my head back and chortle. "I see you your bipolar and raise you with My Family Barely Escaped Stalin's Wrath And The Untold Story Of Nearly Two Million Poles Seems To Be Living On Inside Me! So there!"

No matter. Long-term happiness is so pedestrian, anyway. Depression—now that's juicy. It must be—21 million Americans suffer from it. In that respect, I was dreadfully "normal." (Side note: I do not take depression or mental illness lightly. It's just that humor—one of my self-defense mechanisms and certainly the least caloric of the bunch—loves to kick in whenever I feel something really intense.)

By early June 2012, everything felt intense.

My mood wasn't the only thing that plummeted south. My finances continued sliding that way, too. Freelance writing—still scarce. Sure, there were blogsites that wanted my celebrity interviews—for free. Celebrity interviews, once a rare thing to nab, were now being coordinated by a new breed of plucky PR pros. Some of these clever titans were more than happy to spoon-feed the public's escalating obsession with the stars, no matter who had the proper credentials to write the story.

I decided to pick and choose what and whom I wanted to write about and post the articles on my *Huffington Post* blog. I ventured forth, desperately clinging to the belief that my thinking would lean toward something, well, *rational,* again, and at that moment everything would start to make more sense.

That is, when the thousands of Polish refugees craving safety and desperately searching for a place to call home weren't wandering around in the nether regions of my mind.

One Sunday morning, as I drove along California's Highway 1, heading to the Carmelite Monastery in Carmel—look, what could go wrong with splashing holy water all over myself?—I glanced at myself in the rearview mirror. *You're done, Greg. Done.*

To which I responded—to myself: "I'm not *done*. I can't give up on the family thing now."

Why not?

I did have a point. Why not indeed. Perhaps there was nothing more for me to do. I explored the past—looked into my family's odyssey more thoroughly. Did I need to do anything more? It wasn't as if I *had* to understand *everything* that happened and *everything* I was feeling. Did I?

The Television Critics Tour in Pasadena was nearly a month away. Perhaps it was best to leave the past where it needed to be—back in the past. There would be countless new television shows to write about and a gaggle of celebrities to interview if I attended the tour.

Yes. That would be a fine plan.

I detoured and parked my Miata near Carmel Beach. Every bench along the pedestrian path was occupied. Left to wander down toward the beach, I slipped off my sneakers, hid them beside a boulder, and plodded across the sand for several minutes until I discovered a log that had been washed up. I sat my ass down in front of it, leaned back, and watched three surfers ride a decent crest toward the aquamarine shore.

"Screw The Echo Effect," I blurted out loud. "And screw history. Get me some chocolate and bring on the celebrities!"

A giggle.

Three seconds later, I dissolved into a puddle of tears.

~ ~ ~ ~

CHAPTER TWENTY-FOUR

A FEW DAYS LATER, I WAS SORTING through emails on my laptop at my desk during a brief break from overseeing the editorial management of producing our weekly publication. I had to decide which celebrities and television shows to feature on my *Huffington Post* blog. The stars come out en masse at the biannual Television Critics Tour, which spans several weeks and I had already registered for. The main networks and cable channels unload their talent at these affairs and the nation's television writers all convene at a posh hotel to attend a number of noteworthy panel discussions and to also nab one-on-one interviews with various actors, actresses, producers, and directors. The last time I attended the event, months earlier, I interviewed Jeffrey Dean Morgan, headliner of the series *Magic City* on the Starz channel. There was my half-hour Wilson Phillips interview, too, at which Carnie Wilson kept apologizing to me for bumping into the cup of Starbucks tea I was holding, thereby sending half of it onto the plush carpeting of Pasadena's Ritz Carlton Hotel. Some of that splash found my pants, too, and it looked as if I had a minor bathroom accident. Nothing a napkin over the lap didn't fix. I focused on the positive—that the musical trio was back in action with a new reality show to boot.

Afterward, the pop singing sensation's chart-topping '80s song *Hold On* continued to play on in my brain.

A lot of good that did!

As I scrolled through Fall 2012's TV offerings, the lingering indifference I felt before sitting opposite Ewan McGregor was present. Regardless, I pushed myself to make a decision. Would I write about the new Fox sitcom starring Mindy Kaling, *The Mindy Project*, NBC's quirky but heartfelt family comedy, *The New Normal*, or the oddball ABC outing called *The Neighbors*, which co-starred Jaime Gertz and revolved around a family that moves into a neighborhood occupied by disguised aliens from another planet?

Step one: email publicists about acquiring interviews.

Step two: wait for a response.

I never got to step one. An email from a stranger diverted my attention:

> Dear Mr. Archer,
>
> My name is David Migut. I grew up in Chicago, but now live in St. Augustine, Florida. I'm 36 years old.
>
> A few years back, I came across your article, "The Family Gift" on the web.
>
> I found it interesting not only because I have the same rare last name—Migut—and because I grew up in Chicago, but also because … my grandfather, Stanley, may have been the cousin of the seven Migut children (your mom and aunt and uncles) that you wrote about in your story … I am going by the memory of my oldest aunt, Rita.
>
> Rita was born in 1938 in Chicago, and has memories of cousins who had relocated from Poland to Chicago … and that they visited her family around 1953. She says she was about 15 at the time.
>
> She recalls three brothers and a sister, and stories about Africa and…

Well, the man had me at Migut, but *Africa*? This person had to be referring to my family. I kept reading:

> I'm looking at notes I wrote over three years ago when I talked to my aunt, so this is not fresh in my mind. My great grandfather was Peter Migut. My notes indicate that, at least based upon my Aunt Rita's belief, your grandfather may have been my great grandfather Peter's brother. If this were true, my grandpa and your aunts and uncles would be cousins. That would make you and I second cousins, once removed…

The absurdity of it all provoked a laugh—out loud—which startled the hell out of me. I could not recall the last time I laughed that kind of happy laugh. I contemplated the two family pictures resting on the high shelf opposite my desk, my eyes falling upon my grandmother, Jadwiga.

What were the odds that a stranger with possible blood ties to me would suddenly appear out of thin air and email me at the exact moment in time when I became fully unraveled by my family's legacy?

I sat back in my chair, closed my laptop, and immediately looked up.

Really, God? A long-lost Polish cousin?

~ ~ ~ ~

CHAPTER TWENTY-FIVE

"MOTHER, YOU'RE NEVER GOING to believe this but I think The Universe located a cousin I never knew we had."

"The Universe did what?"

I pulled the phone away from my ear. My dear Polish mother, Bernice, has always been cautiously practical to the core—in the best way. Once, not long after I moved to California in the late-'80s, I happened to share with her that I had temporarily taken to placing crystals and gemstones underneath my pillows. (To my defense: It *was* the era of the Harmonic Convergence.) To which she hotly responded:

"Crystals? Are you crazy? What is California doing to you? I didn't raise you to sleep with crystals! I'm sending you a rosary!"

Needless to say, the woman had grown accustomed to my tendency to explore things on the fringe, walk new spiritual frontiers, and utter phrases that sounded, for lack of better terminology, Russian to her.

I relayed the facts to my mother: the alleged cousin's name; that he was born in Illinois; that he has an aunt named Rita who remembered my mother and her siblings.

"He's going back to Poland for a visit," I told my mother. "Do you recall anybody from your father's side of the family named Pete?"

"Wait a second. Uncle Pete? Oh yes. He was a barber in Chicago. Of course I remember him."

"You're kidding?"

A few hours later, after retrieving another email reply from my Uncle John, the dots were connected. David's great-grandfather Pete was one of my grandfather's five brothers. Pete also had a twin sister, Kasia. Four Migut brothers, along with Kasia, came to the United States in 1906—another brother, along with my grandfather Jacenty, remained back in Poland, only to suffer a much more brutal fate.

The bottom line: David and I we were indeed second cousins.

Quickly I emailed my cousin, informing him we were most definitely related and I would love to connect with him via a phone call. And then, for no apparent reason, my mother phoned me back that very same day—less than fifteen minutes after my message was sent to David.

"You should go to Poland. You should go with this David ... this cousin."

I didn't know how to respond. Poland? I'd always dreamed of going to Poland but...

My stomach performed somersaults as I mentally scanned the thing that used to be a viable bank account with my name on it—not a comma located in any of the numbers there. And my credit cards—all maxed.

I sighed, overcome with a mix of confusion and scarcity. Perhaps my alleged psycho-emotional inheritance—that "There is not enough," "We are lost," and "There is no way out"—was not alleged, after all. I wondered: To what degree were my money management skills—or lack thereof—directly linked to a lack of sufficiency in my generational past?

The Echo Effect...

Here's the thing about the psyche: It's challenging to always be certain which side of it is bullshitting you. Wasn't I done with all this scab picking? Now, suddenly, I wanted to dive back into the emotional abyss?

Go to Poland? How? Thousands of dollars owed to me were still being held hostage by that cable TV magazine for which I had been writing. New writing opportunities were scarce. Furthermore, I had no additional income coming in. Even with my full-time job as an editor, I was just getting by. Besides, this long-lost cousin of mine was apparently heading back to Poland for a trip at the end of June. There was just no way...

I stopped thinking for a moment.

Suddenly just the idea of going to Poland opened another realm of possibility. Of course. Why hadn't I thought of it before? I am a writer. I am an investigator. If I was to fully acknowledge the fractured fairy tale my family and I had been living and transform even a fraction of it, then heading back to the source—to the land where it all began—made perfect sense.

"Mother, that's a fantastic idea."

I hung up the phone. "Now then," I mused out loud. "What about the money?"

Asking for a sign and on some occasions, simply just screaming for help, had worked for me before, so there was no need to stop doing it now. As revered author and lecturer, the late-Florence Scovel Shin, often reminded her readers: "All ships come to me on a calm sea."

In other words: Don't freak out.

If something is meant to be, it's meant to be, and it will most likely present itself calmly—not on the heels of chaos or anxiety. Staring at the seeds you just planted in your garden might be a terrific exercise in focus, but I doubt it makes anything bloom faster. Sometimes it's best to fertilize the metaphysical soil by simply letting it be.

I said one simple thing and repeated it a few times: "God, Universe, the dog down the street—if you want me to go to Poland, show me the way to make it happen."

Meanwhile, Hollywood could wait. Time to return to the Polish refugees sailing across the sea—the ones heading to Africa and other points southward.

◆ ◆ ◆

After the surprise attack of the German ship and the loss of so many lives, two ships remained in the convoy transporting the Poles. Often, the sailors aboard these ships brightened the spirits of the refugees. The men had become sympathetic to their plight, especially the children. On the ship's sun-drenched decks, they, like the men in the Polish Army before them, became surrogate father figures to the children. After all, so many of those children no longer had fathers. The sailors found time to keep the young ones occupied with play or pointing out the wonders of the sea.

The emotions of these tattered individuals, so many of whom had lost their families or parents, softened as the sea breeze kissed their cheeks or a random flock of seagulls diverted their attention to the horizon. What mysteries and adventures awaited them now, more than 10,000 miles from their homeland?

They had survived the harsh Taigas of Siberia and the hot breath of the deserts only to be thrust into a journey through a rich and fascinating aquatic paradise. And what of this place called Africa, with its jungle paradise? What would life be life for them there?

My family's ship docked just south of Mombasa's Kilindini Harbor, in the Port of Tanga, the second largest port in Tanganyika (now Tanzania), Africa. The other vessel continued further south. And so began the dispersing of thousands of Polish refugees into the lush regions of Eastern Africa in November of 1942, an event that remains one of the most fascinating, quirkiest, and under-reported moments in catalogued 20th century history.

In total, 33,000 Polish refugees were transferred to various parts of the world and more than half of them, some 18,000, were sent via British ships to Africa in 1942 and 1943. They were dispersed to settlements in several British colonies—Tanzania, Uganda, Kenya, and South Africa, and North and South Rhodesia. There were nineteen camps in total. Tanganyika held the largest settlement with 4,000 refugees in Tengeru, near Mt. Kilimanjaro and Mt. Meru. In Uganda, the camps were located in Masindi and Koja on Lake Victoria; In Kenya, they were situated in Rongai, Manira, Makindu, Nairobi and Nyali near Mombasa. In every settlement, Polish churches, community centers, hospitals, and schools were created. Because scouting—boy scouts and girl scouts—became such an integral part of life for the children, General Anders sent instructors to the camps.

And how was that first train ride through the African jungles and towns in Tanzania?

From my Uncle John:

> As we traveled to Camp Tengeru, we could see Mt. Meru, its top peeking out of the clouds, but there was no snow. We went through the town of Arusha, which was very clean and full of flowers in the parks. At that time, the native Africans were not allowed to live in towns. They were allowed to work in towns but for the night they had to leave for their villages. Arusha had many different stores with merchants from all different countries but mostly from England and India. Arabs, Greeks, Irish and Turks were also visible. Me? On that train ride in, at first I could not take my eyes off of the natives. We didn't know there was such a thing as a black man! I grabbed my mother's hand and was fascinated by it all.

Into the unknown they went—yet again. But sometimes not "knowing" turns out to be a fruitful thing.

Less than a week after David Migut entered my life and I was presented with the possibility of heading to Poland, as unlikely as it seemed that I could go at the time, "the impossible became possible," as revered Hollywood studio chief Robert Evans often noted. Seemingly from nowhere, I was suddenly on the receiving end of some of my own green.

Cash—and a significant amount of it, in fact.

In a strange—or not so strange, depending on the way one looked at it—turn of events, I received several thousands of dollars from an unexpected source that wanted to remain anonymous. They wanted me to explore my family origins. I never asked for a thing—at least not from an actual human being. There was one caveat: "Have fun in Poland," read the note. Completely overcome with gratitude, I eagerly booked my trip to Warsaw.

Later that same week, I opened a card my mother sent me. She had found a picture from the 1950s of my grandmother, Jadwiga, standing in the backyard next to Uncle Pete, my grandfather's brother. I immediately snapped a picture of it and emailed it to my long-lost cousin, David, in Florida. After all, unbeknownst to him, his inquiry into our family—that one simple email at a random moment in time—had given birth to the entire series of events I was now experiencing.

Within a week's time, I went from being a broke, navel gazing, confused, blond to being on the receiving end of a trip to Poland in the fall—and one that came with a guarantee of enough funding while I was there.

Meant to be?

It sure felt that way.

~ ~ ~ ~

CHAPTER TWENTY-SIX

"IT IS A LONG FLIGHT TO WARSAW my friend, please—eat your pork sandwich!"

I glanced at the tall, middle-aged Polish man with brown bangs sitting beside me on the airplane. His name was Mark, but it could have been Strong Like Bull with his broad shoulders and stocky build.

I held up a hand. "Please. I'm still full from the *other* pork sandwich they gave us two hours ago."

At least that's what I thought I said in Polish. Whatever I said made Strong Like Bull laugh.

Well, I didn't think I was being *that* funny. I understood most of the native language. I'd spent time at countless Polish family gatherings absorbing my family's lyrical banter—and all of those loud car rides with my uncles and aunt certainly helped—but I did not speak fluent Polish. Besides, what sort of "strength" did I need to sit there and wait for Lot Polish Airline Flight 004 to land in Warsaw, Poland? Did I really need to "stock up?"

And then I thought about it. When an entire culture has long been plagued with lack, why wouldn't they "stock up?" That idea must be ingrained in the mass consciousness to some degree.

Alas, why psychoanalyze it? My mood swing had finally swung the opposite direction and I wasn't about to jinx it. I was on a flight to Poland—a miracle.

I asked Mark where he was from.

"North of Rzeszów," he replied.

Now I was chucking. "You don't say? Really? My family originally lived around that area." At least that's what I thought I said in Polish.

Strong Like Bull nodded. I smiled. I must have said it correctly.

Several hours later, after a failed attempt to acquire some decent REM sleep, I decided to check on another Mark. My fortysomething cousin was sitting near the back of the plane with his father, my Uncle John.

I was still baffled by how *he* wound up on my trip to Poland.

Hours earlier, I had met my uncle and cousin at Chicago's O'Hare Airport for my connecting flight from California, which somehow became *their* flight to Poland through yet another series of serendipitous events. My uncle was to help settle the estate of another family member, related by marriage, back in Poland. He decided, unbeknownst to me, to arrange his travel in conjunction with my trip.

"How the hell did we end up on this trip together?" was the first thing I said to my cousin and uncle when I entered the waiting area at O'Hare's International terminal. I chased it back with an "it's a sign," and then I asked if my Uncle Stanley, my uncle's brother, was still planning on picking us up in Warsaw.

"Call your mother!" Uncle John cut me off. "She's worried."

"About what?"

My cousin Mark, tall, stocky and linebacker-esque himself, shook his head. "She doesn't want you to go into Ukraine. You know, back to where the Russians took the family from the farm."

"Oh, that."

Mark shrugged. "Might not be a good idea. Crime. You know?"

"Crime shime. It will be an adventure." I sat down in the terminal chair and turned to face my uncle. "Don't you want to go back to the exact spot on the planet where it all happened for you and the family?"

Uncle John—he of animated facial expressions that never failed to provoke a chuckle—purposely swallowed hard and forced his blue-gray eyes to widen in mock terror.

"Have you lost your mind? I don't want to go into Russia ever again!"

'It's not Russia. It's Ukraine."

"Well, it was our home. There's nothing there but empty fields and mud."

"I'm not going there to sightsee. It's a pilgrimage."

My uncle waved a dismissive hand. "You Californians! What are they feeding you there? The tofu has gotten to you. You've lost your mind!"

But had I?

The Echo Effect...

From the deepest part of my soul, was I attempting to heal something I did not fully understand? Sitting there in the terminal with my uncle and cousin, I followed the thread to the genesis of my idea to actually head into Ukraine. It was a summer day when my cousin Mark informed me over the phone that he and his father would be traveling with me to Poland in September. What were the chances, I thought, that the uncle who had originally shared most of the family story with me, would be going to Poland at exactly the same time I was? From that fertile soil sprouted another idea. As long as I was traveling back to the motherland, anyway, why not head farther east and dip into Ukraine, the western points of which, back in 1940, was still part of Poland? I would head through Lwów, make a wide right toward Ternopil, and then locate the exact spot from which my family had been taken—actually rest my hand on the soil from which they were plucked by the Russians. It was the perfect opportunity, I reasoned with myself—and my panicky mother over the phone. But arranging proper train transport into Ukraine online proved to be challenging, and now, with so much resistance from my mother, I wasn't sure the excursion would actually happen.

My Gotta Get To Ukraine Plan was still on my mind as I approached my cousin and uncle in the back of the airplane.

"How can I convince you to go back to your home?" I asked Uncle John.

"Greg—no! It's mud."

"It's history."

"It's time for you go back to your seat."

He chuckled about it, but as I stood there, I peered into his hazel eyes. What lurked beyond them? This was a happy-go-lucky fellow. But how—how could he be after being ripped out of his home? How could he be after playing a labor camp game that found him hopping over dead, frozen bodies? How could he be after stealing food placed on corpses in an open grave in Uzbekistan? How?

In what compartment of his psyche had my uncle stored the emotional after effects of what happened to him? Had he fully dealt with those emotions? Had anybody in my family? Why did it feel as if I had been placed underneath some sort of cosmic funnel and all my family's experiences surrounding the mass deportations had poured through that funnel and, in effect, right into my psyche? I still could not make sense of it all.

Back at my seat, I retrieved my laptop and sat down. Strong Like Bull was vigorously wiping his mouth with a napkin. What? Did he eat the entire pig?

"And what are you reading there, my friend?" That Mark inquired.

"It's about my family. They lived in Africa for a while."

At least that's what I thought I said in Polish.

Mark appeared genuinely interested with the story—for about five minutes. He passed out from a food hangover shortly thereafter. Me? I continued reading what my Uncle John had written so many years ago, when I first asked him to recount his tales:

> When we first arrived in Africa, the Masai tribespeople were walking along the dirt road of Camp Tengeru. Most of them gave us strange looks. We looked at them very strangely, too. Some of them had never seen a white man before and I had never seen a black man. The Masai had long ponytails and their faces were painted white. They carried a spear in one hand and a Fimbo—a special club made out of wood—in the other. Long shiny knives hung on ropes from the sides of their bodies. No shoes—and some of them were hardly wearing any clothes at all. But they did not harm any of us. They were just going to their villages because the dirt road in Camp Tengeru was the only road there at that time...

The scene: That dirt road; a small village in a jungle setting. Through the clouds of dust of a passing truck, a half-dozen Masai tribesmen see a caravan of young Polish children, each and every one captivated by the new exotic world they had just entered. The Masai take a step back, their gawking filled with fascination. A Polish boy raises his hand. He waves. A broad grin completely enlivens the face of one Masai. This interchange foreshadows the temperance and ease about to unravel in the next chapter in the lives of these Polish refugees...

> Because my mother was an orphanage worker, we were given two huts to live in just on the other side of the wall of the camp—one hut for the boys and the other for the girls, which included my mother. There were six of us now—Ma, Jenny, Joe, Stanley, me and Bernice.

The roofs of our huts were covered with palm tree leafs but other huts had banana leaf roofs. The huts were designed to house three people and each of us had a sleeping bunk roped to hold a sisal mattress with mosquito netting over the bed. A rectangular table with three chairs rested in the middle of the hut and there was one food cabinet. The dirt floors had to be wiped with water daily to minimize the dust.

There was a door and one window, but it was very dark inside the hut so the door and the window always had to be opened when we were inside, at least during the day. In the evening, we had naphtha lamps that emitted a foul odor—there was no ventilation in the hut. But when that lamp was turned down during the evening, from my bunk I could see through the roof and on a clear night I lost myself in all the many, many stars up there.

One evening, while we were all asleep, some monkeys found their way into our hut through the roof. They ate our daily ration of bread. We couldn't believe it! Monkeys!

Outside, was a banana tree with little bananas growing on it and the rest of our garden consisted of six papaya trees and many beautiful flowers all around. My mother loved flowers so she tended them year round. I had to water the flowers every day with my brother Stanley. Eventually, he and I raised pigeons, chickens, and rabbits for food. We had a hound dog, too. We called him Norciu and he was lots of fun.

Using bamboo sticks and a small metal rooftop to reflect the sunrays, my brother Joe designed an outdoor kitchen for my mother, and she loved to cook in her new kitchen. All of us kids attended Polish School in Camp Tengeru. There were grammar schools, high schools, trade schools, and a general education lyceum for the older kids. My mother worked for the orphanage of Mrs. Grosicka, and cooked, washed, and ironed clothes for the orphans. We had no washing machines or electric irons—no electricity at all—so all of the washing had to be done by hand, including sheets and blankets. Ironing was done with an iron using charcoals and the charcoals had to be changed every half-hour. Our camp was truly self-sufficient. We had outdoor toilets, outdoor water faucets, and a small farm. Fresh meat from cows and pigs was rationed daily, because we had no refrigerators.

About a year or so after we arrived, an American missionary priest arrived to Camp Tengeru from New York—Father Jan Sliwowski. He mobilized the people to help build a Catholic church. I helped build that church and I became an altar boy in that church. After everything that had happened to us, everybody seemed to be much happier and we were grateful to finally have a proper place to pray.

~ ~ ~ ~

CHAPTER TWENTY-SEVEN

CROSSES. MY EYES WOULD NOT stray from them. More than two dozen metal emblems of varying height and design lay awkwardly in a roofless train car nearly twenty-five meters away from me as part of a public monument sandwiched between two busy one-way Warsaw thoroughfares. Several of the spiritual symbols stood erect while others lay in disorganized intention as if to insinuate that, like the deported Poles they represented, they had been tossed aside without thought or care.

At my feet—a charcoal-colored plaque. The inscription in Polish read: "In the East; Victims of Soviet Aggression." Directly in front of me—one long, ominous railroad track leading up to the train car filled with the crosses. The monument was dedicated to the Polish people who were directly affected by, or lost their lives, as a result of Stalin's invasion of Poland and the mass deportations.

Time to stroll alongside the track.

Inscribed on each makeshift railway plank were the names of the Polish towns or villages and the regions from which the Polish citizens were taken before enduring their treacherous route to Siberia via crowded boxcars.

Grodno + Kodziowoe.

Luniniec + Pinsk.

Lwów + Brygidki.

I paused. Lwów? That was near the region from which my family was taken. I continued walking and a few moments later I spotted it—Tarnopol + Husiatyn. There it was, right at the base of my foot; the marker honoring the thousands of Poles taken from the area in which my family once dwelled. I bent down and slowly traced the thick lettering of Tarnopol with my finger.

Grandmother, grandfather ... you are remembered right here.

Well, tears would follow soon, especially if I allowed the images of hundreds of thousands of Polish citizens being carted off in boxcars and into the horrid depths of Siberia to continue projecting in my mind with 3D/high-def images. What kind of human allows something as horrific as these deportations to happen?

Stalin—and Beria of the NKVD.

I offered a silent prayer for the deceased—and one of thanks for the souls who survived. I stood up and moved on.

Up close, the car filled with the crosses was far more menacing than one could predict from a distance. Perched on an incline, its rough texture and mix of leaden gray and deep charcoal black mimicked the essence of Rodin's famous sculpture, "Gates of Hell." I stepped closer and ran my hands along the side of this monument, its skin jagged if not mysterious and its hodge-podge design of distorted shapes suggesting the appearance of skull fragments.

The deceased. I was aware that reports varied on the actual number of dead as a direct result of the Soviet repression. According to Polish historian, Professor Andrzej Paczkowski, 90,000–100,000 perished (based on a figure of 1 million deportations and 30,000 executed by the Soviets). However, the documentary, *A Forgotten Odyssey—The Untold Story of 1,700,000 Poles Deported to Siberia in 1940*, which was released in 2000, writer/director Jagna Wright paints a more startling picture—based on a total 1.7 million deported Poles, approximately 400,000 survived the ordeal. And The Kresy-Siberia Foundation reports that of the 1 to 2 million Poles deported, at least half perished.

I looked away from the monument—to compose myself, to breathe—but in the process, suddenly realized where I was actually standing and wondered why the monument was in the middle of several busy streets. There was no easy access to it—cars sped down one avenue; others along another street that ran parallel. Why, I thought, was there not a physical building, a museum in Warsaw, to honor millions of Poles whose lives were directly impacted by Stalin's mass deportations?

I had by this time come to realize that what happened to those Poles warranted more than a passing mention in the history books, or a history class taught in schools. A few days earlier I had visited the Warsaw Uprising Museum, a significant enclave housing a vast array of artifacts and historic records about the Nazi's terror in Poland; and it honored the millions of Jewish people who perished during the Holocaust. But as I stood at the top of this monument, remarkable as it was, I was consumed with a mix of anger and disappointment.

What would it take to finally create an even more viable tribute to the Polish deportees; something more than a small block on the outskirts of town? The millions of souls who endured Stalin's madness deserved more.

My mind leapt to the Kresy-Siberia Foundation. The organization seemed to share a similar belief—that there should indeed be a physical museum. (Weeks later I learned of a vacation spot in Northern Poland in the village of Szymbark, located within Kartuzy County, near Gdansk. Within a small park rests a boxcar used in the original deportations as well as a replica of a Siberian barrack. I questioned the location of this "vacation spot," which was nearly 800 kilometers away from where the actual deportations took place. Why was no official museum erected in Warsaw or another location in central or eastern Poland?)

Two beeps of a car horn forced me to bend down and peer through the openings between the crosses on the monument. My Uncle Stanley had returned to pick me up across the street in his compact Suburu.

Time to go. But I was not about to let the issue drop.

~ ~ ~ ~

CHAPTER TWENTY-EIGHT

"HOW THE HELL ARE WE GOING TO eat all of this food? There's only four of us!"

Cousin Mark shook his head and placed one finger over his lips as his eyes suggested if I was going to open my mouth, it ought to be only to consume the food we were going to have to eat. When a Polish matriarch wants to feed you, resistance is futile.

The dining room table had become precious real estate for a culinary mob and new neighbors were moving in—quickly. A white platter filled with cut and peppered beefsteak tomatoes and onions, two full plates of fresh potato and meat pierogi, and a bountiful bowl of succulent pea salad begged for our attention. Meanwhile, a basket of fresh sliced rye bread, a large plate of sliced ham, a dish of hard-boiled eggs and a rectangular plate that had become the bed for plump, heated polish sausage, each began making the rounds.

"Sit down and eat," commanded my aunt Donna.

Uncle Stanley—eighty and stout with robust cheeks and combed back gray and black hair—rolled up his shirtsleeves as if he was about to do hard labor. He knew the drill and he was more than happy to please his wife. My cousin Mark and I exchanged looks again. We were not leaving that table without consuming at least 10,000 calories—each!

Uncle John had left us for a quick trip up north to help settle estate matters. We planned on meeting him there in a few days when he, Mark, and I would embark on an excursion to Kraków. From there, my uncle and Mark would head to other points north, which was fine by me. I desperately wanted to explore Kraków on my own and, if fate would allow, head east from there into Ukraine. But thus far, making arrangements by train still proved vexing. And with my mother still fretting about it back in Chicago, the uncertainty lingered.

But to touch that land…

Uncle Stanley handed me a large dish filled with warmed, plump pierogi doused with melted butter. I took four. Aunt Donna—she of blond finesse and diminutive yet spitfire twirl—passed by and with a serving fork, quickly slid three more onto my plate.

"Eat!" she crowed in Polish. "Build up your strength. I hope you like. It is my pleasure."

I consumed every one of those tasty, succulent creatures and seemingly within minutes, and when a platter Polish sausage made it's around the table and a few of those juicy meats landed on my plate, I asked forgiveness from my digestive system for the pieces I was about to gobble up.

Uncle Stanley had four children with his first wife back in the states. He moved back to Poland more than fifteen years ago with Donna and they have been enjoying their two-bedroom condo and a spacious balcony filled with well-tended, colorful flowers ever since. Over the last few days, they were a dynamic duo of sorts, playing tour guide for Mark and me. We had taken in the charm of Old Town Warsaw—*Stare Miasto* in Polish—and its numerous, fascinating cobblestone streets, each filled with a cultural bounty of old-world restaurants, specialty and ice cream shops and colorful locals. Oh, how we cavorted around the breathtaking Wilanów Palace, which miraculously survived the Polish partitions of World Wars I and II. And my heart melted one evening during a brilliant laser-light show at the thoroughly modern named Multimedia Fountain Park. Afterward, I walked right up to Aunt Donna and startled her with a tight embrace—all because the sophisticated water-and-laser light presentation in the park was so unlike anything I had ever seen. I was overcome by it; I actually shed a few tears. The Warsaw Uprising Museum had been on our to-see list as well. It was a haunting gallery of survival, of triumph, of death, and the thought of it now, as my memories stirred at the table, forced me to consider the monument for the deported Polish people, which I had visited earlier in the day. I asked my uncle if he, too, felt there should be a museum erected for the deported Poles.

"But of course," he replied, still chewing his food from across the table. "But will it ever happen?"

Aunt Donna returned from the kitchen with a bowl of warm Borscht and placed it on the table in front of me.

God in heaven ... how much more food was there?

When another half-dozen pierogi were sent my way, my troubled eyes found Aunt Donna. She shrugged.

"You don't *have* to eat them."

I recognized her emphasis on the word "have." I was going to eat those pierogi—or else! I handed the few that remained back to my uncle.

"Your mother made these when you were in Africa, right?"

Uncle Stanley swallowed a small piece of buttered rye bread and nodded. "All the time. Potato pierogi."

"Even in Africa? Amazing."

"We had a good life there ... after everything that happened," he added softly, looking off into the distance. "Listen, Greg, did John tell you about the time finding Christmas trees in the jungle?"

Mark and I exchanged looks. We had both heard the story from my other uncle, but I couldn't resist hearing it from Uncle Stanley. And so, buttering yet another piece of rye bread, my uncle brought the story to life.

The family had been living in Africa for several years. Jadwiga's repeated attempts to contact family members back in Poland fell short. She had a sister, Catherine, in Chicago, but there had been no significant movement made to assist any of the Miguts to get out of Africa. One year, during Christmastime, John, nearly ten years old at the time, convinced the slightly older Stanley to help him find a Christmas tree.

"You're crazy, brother? Out here? Where?"

"In the jungle," John quipped.

Off they went, sneaking out of the camp and through the trails in the jungle nearby. Some fifteen minutes later, after crossing a small creek, John pointed to a pine tree in the distance.

"I'll go up there and cut off the top."

At this point I interjected. "Uncle Stanley, wait a second. There are pine trees in Africa?"

My uncle shrugged. "I think so. It looked like a pine tree. You know—tall!"

"I see."

And so … Stanley fretted about the height of the tree, however John wasn't concerned. He immediately began climbing the tree, wrapping his legs around the trunk. He pulled himself up higher and higher. He must have been twenty-five feet in the air when he peered down at his brother, but Stanley was shaking his head.

"Fool," John chuckled. "Live a little." And then he climbed a bit higher, reached for the small machete in a holder attached to his waist and proceeded to fiercely strike the bark.

"Move away!" John shouted. "She's about to come down."

But it was too late. The top of the tree was already sailing down toward Stanley like a well-directed torpedo. It nearly fell right on top of him.

John's head fell back in laughter.

"Alright. That's enough. Let's go," Stanley urged.

"But I'm just getting started brother." Down the tree John went … and right back up another one he climbed.

"Let me get a few more," John announced, figuring he could donate a few trees to the church and save one for the family.

"Well, hurry. We have to get back soon."

"Relax. We'll be fine."

John secured himself another top-level branch and went at it again. He repeated the pattern—down one tree and up another—several more times until he had acquired three, five-foot-tall trees.

"How are we going to explain this to mother?"

"Who cares? It's Christmas trees, brother!"

But Stanley was been correct about one thing. It was getting late, and they did have to get back. Scrambling to collect the trees, they carried them down the path and stopped at the creek. John took off his shoes, tied the shoelaces together, and flung them over one of the trees. Stanley did the same. The shin-deep creek's robust current forced the brothers to maintain proper balance but they managed to hold a steady pace, carrying one tree at a time over their shoulders.

After they crossed the creek the final time, with all of the trees in tow, the brothers, breathless but invigorated, dragged their cargo beyond the bank.

"We'll be home in no time," John cheered.

Just then, six members of a Masai tribe suddenly emerged from the brush. Glaring at the brothers with the fierce intensity hunters typically assign to prey, the men kept a tight grip on their spears. A tall, thin man stepped forward, glanced the three treetops, and frowned, his eyes narrowing slightly as he studied John and Stanley with stern admonition. No one moved.

"We're going to die over your stupid idea!" Stanley muttered under his breath.

"Hush!" John spat. He needed to concentrate. He noticed several coins on the leader's necklace. Immediately, John spat out a phrase in Swahili, but the Masais were an entirely different tribe. The men just glared back at him. When the leader raised one arm and pointed to the trees on the ground, immediately, John used his foot and nudged one of the trees closer to him.

"Take it."

The leader shook his head and pointed to what had been flung over the pine.

"Oh my goodness," Stanley remarked. "They want our shoes!"

"I know what they want, brother! Let's just give it to them and be free!"

The brothers handed over the shoes, but now the leader was stroking the edges of his long necklace and fiddled with the coins there.

John poked Stanley with his elbow. "Money! He wants money!"

John plunged his hand deeply into his shorts' pocket and he retrieved several shillings. Stanley did the same, but not before adding: "They're going to rip off our heads next!"

John smacked his brother on the arm. "Fool. Don't give them any ideas."

As my uncle's colorful tale unraveled again around the Warsaw dining room table, I sat back and added, "But they didn't rip off your heads, Uncle Stanley. Did they?"

My uncle's blue-gray eyes brightened as the memory played out inside of his mind. "They let us pass—with just *two* of the trees."

"And what happened when you got back home?"

Uncle Stanley's smacked the tabletop, forcing it to rattle a bit. "Goodness! Our mother was so mad at us for not having our shoes that she grabbed us by the ears and began swearing!"

Laughter erupted around the table. Even though I'd heard the story before, it never failed to capture my deep interest. Young boys in Africa. Priceless. Later, as Donna began clearing the table, my uncle, Mark and I picked at what food remained—nearly everything had been devoured save, perhaps, for a few slices of rye bread. Uncle Stanley handed me the breadbasket.

I held up a hand. "God, no!"

We talked more about Kraków and how much I was looking forward to seeing the vibrant city.

"Goodness, Greg. You will love it," my uncle assured me, reaching for the butter dish. He sliced off a generous wad with his knife, smoothed it over another piece of bread, and began chewing away. His hand returned to the butter dish, gently straddling it.

"Did you know, Greg, that due east of Kraków, near Rzeszów, is very close to where we're from originally?"

"Yes. I did know."

My uncle slid the butter dish toward me and pointed to it.

"My mother was from the village of Łaka."

He found the brown mustard jar and placed it a few inches away from the butter dish. "And my father was from the village of Łukawiec."

Entertained, my eyes remained glued to the objects and what they represented. Lifting the thin triangle-shaped glass saltshaker with two fingers, my uncle positioned it between the butter dish and the mustard jar. He tapped the top of the saltshaker.

"And between these two towns was a church," he went on, "my parents met at that church when they were kids and then got married in that church. All of us kids were baptized in that church…"

I didn't need a light to go off—or on—above my head. I scrutinized the saltshaker for several seconds, my heartbeat quickening.

Forget Ukraine!

"Uncle Stanley! You're brilliant! That's where I need to go. I need to go back to *your* home—where your mother and father met. Where they fell in love. *That* church! That's where it all began!"

~ ~ ~ ~

CHAPTER TWENTY-NINE

MY PENCHANT FOR SPIRITUAL GOODIES—incense, tarot cards, the I Ching, Dionne Warwick's Psychic Hotline. and that "Lamb of God" hymn from Catholic mass—peaked in the late 1980s. I was a journalism student at the Walter Cronkite School of Journalism at Arizona State University and had become the Arts & Entertainment Editor of the University paper, *The State Press*.

I thrived, writing about plays and movies. I even created a Where Are They Now? spread about the cast of *The Brady Bunch* and *The Partridge Family*—Come on, get happy, and all that. And I was—very happy.

Until my breakup with the newsroom's artist sent me spiraling down an emotional rabbit hole. Oh, how I wanted our love, and our love affair, to last. What bliss it was. Deep talks, a stellar connection, secrets from our co-workers. It was delicious. And, this was college, after all. I was young. I felt—*so much*!

But it was not in the cards. Hearts were broken—mine—and so, for solace, I turned to what, at the time, felt like a comrade. Fiona—a fortysomething, thickset woman of average height with short, thin chestnut hair. Fiona was one of the few adults hired by the university to work in the production arm of the newspaper. She quickly noticed my mood had plummeted.

"I'm sorry you're hurting. Would you like to come over for a tarot reading?"

I looked up from the large IBM computer screen. "Is it that obvious? That I'm sad?"

"Yes, dear."

"Crap."

She gave my right shoulder an affectionate squeeze. "Just come over and we'll see what we can do."

Later that night, I was greeted at the door of Fiona's modest apartment near the university by her teenage son, Henry. He stood there, wearing nothing but a pair of extra-large gray cotton shorts typically found on athletes. But Henry was no athlete. Well over six feet tall, he must have been at least a hundred pounds overweight and apparently loved to walk around shirtless, his rolls of flesh enjoying the open air.

"Hey, Ma," he hollered as he held the door open. "*He's* here."

Slightly shaken by the disdain in his tone—the way he uttered *he* had some punch—I walked in just as Fiona was coming down the staircase from the bedrooms upstairs. She hugged me and turned to Henry.

"We're going upstairs now."

I swallowed hard. "We are?"

She took my hand and smiled. "For privacy.

Henry landed into a nearby leather recliner and huffed. "What about the pizza?"

"We'll order it later," Fiona mused. "Have some Cheetos in the meantime."

Henry wasn't pleased about that, for he'd already consumed them. How many bags, I wondered suspiciously, but stopped myself from further judgment. I, too, had been an overweight teen. I, too, had found solace in food—bags of Doritos, gallons of ice cream. I knew the routine. The only difference? I did it with clothes on.

Upstairs in the bedroom, several vanilla-scented candles flickered.

"Now, sit down," Fiona sighed, shutting the bedroom door behind her.

I swiftly scanned the room—crowded and a bit unkempt with several dressers and a pile of unfolded clothes. Several "spiritual" paintings—dreamcatchers, Native American Indians, Lemuria—hung on the walls. I sat down on the edge of the only place available—the queen-sized bed—just as Fiona lit another votive candle and then a stick of frankincense incense, before placing them atop the dresser.

"Where's your desk—you know, for the reading?"

"Oh, that! Turn around. Just face me on the bed. We're doing it here."

"Excuse me?"

"The reading."

My heart was beating so fast I could not think straight. Suddenly I wanted out of there. What the hell was I, a Catholic-raised Polish guy, doing in this stranger's dimly lit bedroom that reeked of vanilla?

Seeking solace?

Sure, but suddenly it smacked of a scene from *The Graduate*. Was I that desperate for comfort? Was I that far gone emotionally that I couldn't dust off the remnants of my ill-fated college romance without turning to an older woman who, my instincts told me, wanted to offer me more than just a tarot reading?

Yes. I absolutely was that far gone.

Fiona did not seduce me on the queen-sized bed that evening … however, the Queen of Cups figured prominently in the reading from her Mother Earth tarot cards. Another seduction attempt occurred several weeks later in Sedona—after Fiona had, apparently, channeled some wise, ancient Native-American Indian soul as the two of us sat atop a mountain underneath the moonlight on a vortex overlooking a canyon. Clueless was I—apparently channeling of this sort was, like oysters, a good aphrodisiac? Fiona wanted me. Later that evening, on yet another queen bed, Fiona told me we had shared several past lives together. I decided that perhaps, in my effort to "heal" from my broken relationship, my repeated viewings of Shirley MacLaine's mini-series *Out on a Limb* might have gotten the better of me. Suddenly, I missed Catholic mass.

And yet a sign-seeker I was destined to become.

My Escaping Fiona memories were with me in Kraków as I sat atop an unstable cardboard box. And not just any cardboard box either. This portable container rested in a concrete cubbyhole on one side of Draper Hall in Kraków's Main Square. The hall is one of the signature markers in the square, a behemoth mercantile exchange crowded with vendors within its lengthy rectangular sanctum, with a seemingly endless sea of people parading through. As for the cardboard box on which my Polish ass was planted? Simply a makeshift chair in the cramped "office" of an elderly woman whose delicate but weathered features recalled the old crone from Disney's *Snow White and the Seven Dwarves*.

A bona fide palm reader. To which my Uncle John cautioned me earlier: "Greg, if you're really going to see her, you better not tell your mother."

"And why not?"

"Oh, boy! After she finds out you went to see a Gypsy lady, she may never make you pierogi ever again!" And then he laughed. "Be careful. That lady might cast a Gypsy spell on you!"

"Please. I'm not four. I'm in my forty! *Ish.* What's the big deal?"

And then I thought about it. How in the world would anybody in my Polish- Catholic family ever fully grasp that my spiritual awakenings somehow began on the frowzy bed of a lusty tarot reader in Scottsdale while her teenage Baby Huey devoured his second full bag of Cheetos in the living room, only to end up with my ass sinking into a cardboard box as I sat opposite a timeworn Polish palm reader in the heart of Kraków?

My uncle, cousin Mark, and I had arrived in Kraków a few days earlier and they were about to depart again for more adventures north, while I remained in the area. We kept ourselves occupied in the thriving historic gateway, a blessed destination in that it was one of the few cities in Eastern Europe not structurally demolished during World War II—remarkable considering all that transpired in Warsaw in the north, Germany in the west, and Russia in the east. The Nazi General government had stationed themselves in Kraków and Auschwitz was just several kilometers away. History—everywhere.

From our hotel near the main train station, we found the resilient Wawel Castle, which sits on the Vistula River and was originally built in the 14th century. We wandered the city's numerous historic corridors and inevitably found our way right back into Kraków's breathtaking Market Square, the largest medieval town square in all of Europe. Anchoring the square is St. Mary's Basilica (Church of Our Lady Assumed Into Heaven). A glorious and gothic spectacle, it was erected in the 13th century and rebuilt in the 14th. Every hour, a trumpet signal plays Kraków's anthem—also known as Hejnal Mariacki—atop the taller tower of the basilica's two turrets. A noontime hejnał can be heard as well. In fact, it is broadcast live on Polish national radio and plays throughout Poland and abroad for the diaspora.

As the story goes, in the 13th century, a trumpeter played the hejnal, which consists of five notes, from the basilica's tower. Every hour, he reportedly played it four times—to the four winds (north, south, east, west). There came a day when, during such an excursion, the trumpeter saw in the distance a rising cloud of smoke; an army of Tatars heading toward Kraków. Fearing that the city was about to be attacked, he fretted over what he could do to warn the citizens. Surely, if he fled back into the city, it would waste precious time. Instead, he remained where he was and proceeded to play the hejnal—and did not stop. Louder and louder he played until, at last, the citizens and the military realized the man must be signaling danger. Apprentices, artisans, soldiers and citizens rushed to the walls of the city and a major attack was thwarted.

But legend reveals that the trumpeter's triumph was also his tremendous sacrifice. According to the story, the Tatars had come close enough to the city to hear the trumpeter and, upon spotting him in the tower, one of the men grabbed a bow and arrow and released a deadly shaft that lodged in the trumpeter's throat.

This story plays out in present day in a unique way: the hejnal abruptly stops each time it is played, every day.

Kraków's entire Market Square boasts many other luminous treats. Every cobblestone corridor leading into it offers other passageways to various streets, each one filled with shops and sights and happy passersby. The area seems immune to sorrow, to heartache. More than seventy years after Hitler and Stalin besieged Poland—and just over twenty years after the end of Communism in Poland—the atmosphere overflows with possibility. History has proven that there are people who revel in their attempt to crush the human spirit, but inevitably you cannot exterminate that which you cannot see. Try as one might, there is no way to extract what resides in the human heart—love, honor, devotion. All of that is present in Kraków.

And so it came to be that in the triumphant square, my relatives and I delved into hearty Polish culinary wonders—plates full of stuffed cabbage or bowls of delicious borscht. After one meal, just several meters away from an enormous yet marvelous bust by sculpture Igor Mitoraj, I happened upon the Polish palm reader. But the moment I sat atop a cardboard box across from the woman—she, too, sat atop of her own cardboard chair—I wondered if I had crawled into a litter box that hadn't been changed in weeks. Was it urine? Body odor? Both?

How old was the woman—seventy-five, eighty-five? Hard to say. Posed there like a staged prop, her loose-fitting emerald green schemata blanketed her diminutive frame. Two large, beaded, dark green necklaces hung heavily over her chest. Meanwhile, a folded babushka with splashes of jade and amber loosely pulled her thin yet frizzy grayish blonde hair away from her forehead.

I forked over a few zloty and Scent Of A Woman instructed me to turn over my left hand with the palm facing up on another cardboard box she used as a table—a clever portable office, I'll give her that. She briefly considered the lines on my left hand and then her dark eyes lifted, falling upon something in the distance, beyond my right soldier. She exerted about as much life force as an old horse in its last days wandering out to pasture.

She spoke softly, and in Polish. No matter. I recorded the entire conversation on my iPhone, thinking I would have my uncle, or my dear childhood Polish friend, Renee, in Minnesota, translate the reading. At that moment, however, I prayed for a light breeze—anything to alleviate the stench.

"Pan pracuje?"

My brain unraveled the Polish: "Do you work, sir?" I nodded.

"Do you have any kids?"

"I don't have any children."

When she asked me what I did for a living, I nearly fell through the cardboard box. Wasn't *she* supposed to be telling me about my life?

"I am a writer."

On she went. I heard words I understood—work, working hard, people, family, life, living. And then...

"You will tell a story..."

Or something like that.

"...others have needed you and you will have a story to tell."

Yes. It really must have been something like that.

Later, as I hoisted myself up from the sunken cardboard box, I tossed everything she told me into the blender of my mind, pressed puree and consumed the cosmic smoothie she had given me. *A story to tell.* Indeed.

My uncle, eagerly waiting nearby, grabbed my forearm. "Well, don't keep us in suspense. What did that old Gypsy say?"

"Not really sure. But I think it had something to do with me living a very long, long life."

He shook his head. "Fool. She cast a spell on you!"

Maybe so, I thought. And with any luck, it was a very good spell. I could use as much good juju as possible for what I was about to do next.

~ ~ ~ ~

CHAPTER THIRTY

A PLEASANT, SPIRITED BREEZE flowed across the platform of the Rzeszów train station on Saturday, the first day of fall. I had just travelled approximately 177 kilometers east from Kraków to come here. Noticing the small market, which was accessible from the main platform, I made a beeline inside and grabbed the first bottled water available off of the rack—Nałęczowianka Mineral Water. I smiled, remembering the last time I'd grabbed a bottled water with such urgency—and ended up moving to Hawaii.

What? I asked myself. *Are you going to move to Poland now?*

Not a bad thought, actually. But at the moment, I had to tend to other matters. My Uncle Stanley's butter dish/mustard jar/saltshaker presentation sparked my eagerness to locate the church in which my grandparents met, fell in love, and were later married. After all, it was the same church in which my aunts, uncles, and my mother were baptized in the village of Łaka, about six kilometers northeast of Rzeszów. So inspired was I by the thought of finding that haven that I practically pushed my Uncle John and my cousin Mark onto their train from Kraków so they could continue on with their own adventures—and I could go on with mine. I had transformed into a Polish Dick Tracy and I needed room to explore.

On the middle shelf, behind the twentysomethng female cashier at the market counter sat an inviting blue and gold rectangular box of Polish cookies. *Sugar!* How could I pass up such an opportunity? Especially since there was nary a pint of Ben & Jerry's ice cream within a 200 kilometers.

Soul searching—it works up an appetite.

"Please, miss. May I have those cookies?"

The clerk—her long hair a deep obsidian, her thick eyelashes even darker—stood there a moment, inspecting me. I suspected she really wanted to laugh—*at* me! Good God. Had I butchered the Polish language again?

"Please?" I offered timidly.

A smile, but I could tell she wanted to bust out a giggle. Amid the rising shame, I resorted to my default line, which I knew how to pronounce—backward and forward and in my sleep: "I understand Polish but I do not speak it very well…"

"Oh, no no, sir. You speak Polish just fine. Very well."

She was too kind, especially with the "sir" part, and when I flashed myself a look in the store window on my way out, I realized how ill-used that remark actually was. Clad in jeans, a black button-down Banana Republic shirt and a chic, form-fitting gray and black European jacket that sported an unusually odd amount of shoulder pad action à la the late-'80s—not to mention my oversized reflector sunglasses—I didn't *look* like a "sir." I looked like an aging New Age sugar junkie about to board the Mothership.

I ripped open the box, reached inside, grabbed three little cookies, and immediately shoved each and every one of them into my mouth.

"Okay, Rzeszów," I mumbled in between bites. "Here I am!"

Rzeszów was not immune to war. During World War I, a number of battles took place here and it became home to a large military base for the Austro-Hungarian Army. A significant fortress sat nearby. Deeper investigation on my part suggested the area could have been where my grandfather first became involved with the military efforts of the Austro-Hungarian Army.

It may have been during that time, too, when Grandfather Jacenty became more leery of the Russians.

In the summer of 1914, at the beginning of World War I, Russian troops headed toward Rzeszów, and by September 21 of that year, they had it in its grasp. I found it particularly interesting that I arrived in the town almost 98 years to the day of that event. That initial Russian occupation spanned about sixteen days, finally halted in the aftermath of an Austrian attack in early October. The Russian forces persisted, however, and the Austrians were only able to hold the town for about a month. To the dismay of the military and locals, the Russians eventually created a frontline between the nearby cities of Tarnów and Gorlice, hence Rzeszów suddenly became the epicenter of the Imperial Russian Army.

The Russian occupation reigned until May of 1915, when they were finally pushed out of Rzeszów and Eastern Europe. The Austrians may have been back, but other wartime dramas and destructions in and around the town impacted life there. The population dwindled. Several years later, Rzeszów officials announced their loyalty—and, in turn, the town's—to the independent Polish government. By November 1, 1918, Rzeszów was a free town and began to expand. It became the capital of a county in the Lwów district—the city of Lwów itself rests 168 kilometers east—and transformed into a significant facet of the Central Industrial Region, a powerfully effective four-year endeavor later initiated by Eugeniusz Kwiatkowski, a prominent Polish economist and Deputy Prime Minister. A downright enterprising goal, the four-year plan's thrust was to create a solid industrial center in the middle of Poland and strengthen the economy—and as far away from any borders whatsoever. Set to begin in the fall of 1936, with an end date in summer of 1940, it would have fully succeeded, but the political ramifications of Hitler and Stalin's union and the initiation of the Nazi-Soviet Pact halted everything.

In September of 1939, the Germans bombed Rzeszów and within a short time, renamed the town Reichshof. By then, my immediate family had already moved east to Liczkowce near the town of Tarnopol in what was still eastern Poland.

The Miguts may have relocated to the east—and eventually into the clutches of the Russians—but in their original home of Łukawiec, near Rzeszów, the remaining citizens also faced significant challenges. By 1941, a ghetto had formed in Rzeszów and labor camps were established. During World War II, approximately 20,000 Jews were murdered in Rzeszów. More haunting: about 123 kilometers east was the Bełżec Extermination Camp, the site of the first Nazi German extermination camp in German-occupied Poland. Approximately 500,000 Jewish people were believed to be murdered at Bełżec.

There appeared to be no part of Poland, or much of Eastern Europe, that was immune to the dark cloud of terror during the 1940s.

◆ ◆ ◆

From the steps of the main platform of the Rzeszów train station, box of cookies in tow, I considered the town before me. The curved thoroughfare that ran parallel to the station, housed several three-story hotels, plus apartments and eateries. Two perpendicular streets on either side of the road led travelers away from the station and hinted at a bit of mystery down each of their paths. On the roundabout, several hundred yards away from me, a half-dozen taxis of varying green, white and yellow color schemes, rested curbside.

As a stream of travelers hurried by me and down the steps, I tossed another raspberry-filled cookie into my mouth and pondered the taxis, wondering which lucky cab driver was going to listen to me explain the curious mission I was on—and in massacred Polish no less.

I approached the first cab in the roundabout. A pleasingly plump, sixtysomething gray-haired man with a bulbous nose, thick eyeglasses, and a face to which gravity had not been kind, sat behind the wheel. He reminded me of some of the souls I encountered at the Chicago South Side Saturday Night Polkas to which I had been dragged by my parents when I was a tween— The older, Eastern European, guy who'd seen it all, was tired of seeing it all, and just wanted to remain hunched over a bar, chasing back shots of Polish vodka and taking long drags off of a Kent cigarette.

"Please sir, hello. Do you speak English? Could you…?"

Bulbous Nose shot me an indignant look. And then his exhausted steel-blue eyes fell, stopped at my feet, and slowly made a judgmental pan upward. He paused at my neck when a veer to the right, and then left, suggested that, yes, the shoulder pads on my jacket must have looked positively ridiculous. Either that, or he became frightened by his reflection in my aviator shades.

A grunt. A shrug. A roll of the eyes. He indicated the cab directly behind him with his thumb. I took the hint.

On to Cab Driver No. 2, who was thoroughly involved in a newspaper. I gently tapped the window. The driver nodded, folded his paper and indicated I should get inside. I breathed a sigh of relief. For a moment, I feared I was becoming a Traveling Goldilocks, searching for the cab driver that was "just right." I slid into the backseat from the driver's side, my bottled water and box of cookies coming along for the ride.

"*Jak się masz?*" I offered warmly, taking off my shades. "How are you?"

We locked eyes in the rearview mirror.

"Good, *good*," he responded in Polish, singing it more than speaking it, the second "good" rising an octave.

Fiftyish, his cheeks—so full, so plump—were the type that would turn beet red from uproarious laughter or from an ungodly amount of liquor consumption. A cheery chap was he—with his bushy, unkempt, gray eyebrows and snug-fitting pale blue driver's cap.

My heart softened. I liked this Cab Driver With The Round Happy Polish Face.

I inched forward on the edge of the seat. "Do you speak English?"

He shook his head indicating he did not. I took a big, deep breath and went at it. "Please sir, can you drive me to the towns of Łąka and Łukawiec? I am a journalist. I am looking for a church. My family used to live in the towns…"

However, I was certain it sounded more like this: "Please sir … drive you me to Łąka and Łukawiec? Journalist … church I look. Family live here … far far far away time ago!"

The man moved his hand as if he were writing with a pen. "Journalista?"

Ah. I got one word right. "Yes!"

Cab Driver With The Round Happy Polish Face smiled broadly, placed his hands on the steering wheel and immediately pulled out of the line. "Where would the fine sir like to go?"

"Are you familiar with the church, St. Onufry, in Łaka?"

"Oh, yes! I will, of course, find it for you, sir. Yes, yes!"

He sounded downright excited about it.

"I hear it's an old church. Is that right?"

"Why, yes. Old. Very very old. Yes, indeed!"

"You've been there?"

"Łaka? But of course. Live nearby. All my life, sir. I know the way!"

"Please take me there, drop me off and…"

"Drop you off? Yes. Oh yes! I will do it."

"And wait for me," I quickly added. "Please?"

A wave of a hand. "Wait at the church? But of course. It is not a problem! I will do this for you, sir. Yes, yes. Oh, yes!"

So animated were his words that it sounded as if he were reciting a fairy tale to a child. Breathing a sigh of relief, I sat back in the seat, my gaze falling upon the open cookie container, which had slid out of its packaging. What the hell. I swiped four more cookies and began slipping them into my mouth.

Several kilometers down the road, just north of Rzeszów proper, I considered sharing with my new lyrical friend/driver that I was on a kind of spiritual vision quest—all because of Stalin, a broken picture frame, severe mood swings and a long-lost Polish cousin I had never met. But who the hell knew how to say all of *that* in Polish? Besides, why complicate matters? Cab Driver With The Round Happy Polish Face did not need to think he was carting around a crazy person. No. And, really, it was much too early in our friendship to begin over-sharing. Instead, I asked him his name.

"Yes, yes! Oh yes, yes."

Perhaps I had asked incorrectly? But damn if this guy couldn't finish a sentence without making it sound like a carol.

"My name is Gregory. What's yours?"

"Oh, yes. Yes. Yes. Sure it is. A fine name for the man."

Terrific. Time to let go of Name Game. My attention drifted onto the fertile Polish countryside.

The villages of Łaka and Łukawiec have remained farm-rich and culturally under-developed for decades—long after the summer of 1920, when my grandparents had already married and Jadwiga had given birth to the first Migut child, Ted. Łaka's population is modest—only 1,700—and vast open fields, rolling green hills and sporadic clusters of birch trees, which stretch out for miles, remain its most loyal neighbors.

I recalled Uncle John's tales about my grandmother; how she had regularly walked into the town of Rzeszów for food and other supplies. She must have embarked along the road on which I was now traveling; must have walked right along the dirt paths beside the open fields passing by me.

Suddenly mystified by the realization that my grandmother had been exactly where I now found myself—that more than seventy-five years ago the woman ventured back and forth, from village to town—I wondered: Could it be possible that some of her energy, her actual energetic vibration, lingered?

Yeah—I went there.

How much of our energy do we really leave behind?

All at once, the fine hairs on my arms and the back of my neck stood on end. Through the bevy of shiver-provoking goose bumps arose in me a suspicion that something much more profound was taking place than simply returning to a family home—and one on which I had never really held much focus. As if the Gods were combing through the air, ridding it of unnecessary tangles, I sat there believing that if I reached out my hand, I could, in fact, touch another world, another dimension—that something significant was just beyond the edges of my fingertips.

I spied Cab Driver With The Round Happy Polish Face in the rearview mirror. *Hey buddy. You feelin' this? Have we just entered some quantum time bubble or something?*

But I didn't say that. Besides, to my knowledge, there was no way to actually say "quantum time bubble" in Polish. Odd, considering Copernicus and all that.

Could it be that as I got closer and closer to the villages from which my grandparents hailed, the veils of time and space—the past, the present, the future, whatever—were simply melting away? My family—their *there* and my *here* suddenly occupied the same space; the same cosmic-spiritual frequency.

Or something like that.

"You like?

"Huh?"

Cab Driver With The Round Happy Polish Face adjusted the volume on the radio. "Listen, listen!"

I nodded, shaking off the temporary trance as an upbeat Polish pop song with a catchy melody flowed from the radio speakers. The male singer recalled the Italian pop star Zucchero, somebody I had always wanted to interview, a crooner with deep yet smooth chops; somebody able to carry the listener along a jazzy backbeat. But I could only understand a few of the Polish lyrics.

"Listen … When I was a boy … my father … Listen…"

Locating the voice memo button on my iPhone, I pressed record. I would have it translated later. At the very least, the funky Polish pop song would be forever preserved.

"You understand? You understand?"

I smiled. "Yes, yes—*oh* yes!"

Now I was the one who sounded melodic.

Just then, Cab Driver with The Round Happy Polish Face—I really had to get the man's name soon—pointed one of his very thick Polish fingers and indicated the approaching landmark.

"Łaka! Łaka! Łaka!"

I looked up just as the green village sign disappeared behind us.

We found the village in which my grandmother was born. Grinning, my heart a flutter, I was on the edge of the car seat seat again.

"Now then, where the hell is that church?"

~ ~ ~ ~

CHAPTER THIRTY-ONE

SAINT ONUFRY—ONUPHRIUS/ONOUFRIOS from the Greek root—became a venerated saint in both the Roman Catholic and Eastern Orthodox churches hundreds of years ago. The name Onufry means "he is continually good."

Onufry reportedly lived as a hermit in the 4th or 5th centuries in the desert in Egypt. Some accounts list Onufry as having studied jurisprudence and philosophy prior to becoming a monk near Thebes. Most historic accounts of Onufry note that a protégé, Paphnutius the Ascetic, a 4th-century abbot, embarked on a pilgrimage to study Onufry's hermit lifestyle, primarily to decide if the lifestyle would jibe with his own. After weeks of roaming the desert, Paphnutius stumbled upon a frenzied soul who sported a loincloth made of leaves and had long, mangled hair.

Frightened and confused, Paphnutius ran away from the man, but something lured him back and he eventually befriended him. Legend foretells that Onufry conveyed to Paphnutius that he had been living as a hermit for seventy years. (With no chocolate or catering—this would have ruined most people.) The two men dialogued until sunset when, at that time, bread and water miraculously appeared near the hermit's cell-like portal. A night full of prayer later, and Paphnutius came to realize that Onufry was near death. Bemused, he inquired if he should occupy the holy man's cell after his death, but Onufry was insistent—Paphnutius was to return to Egypt and have a memorial for him there.

After Onufry perished, Paphnutius tried to dig a grave, but the ground was too hard and he just covered Onufry's body in a cloak and left him between several large boulders. Later, when Onufry's cell mysteriously collapsed, Paphnutius took that as a sign that he should move on.

Centuries passed. More details surfaced and adoration grew for Onufry. One account suggests that during his long duration in the desert, the only visitor he ever had was an angel who delivered the host to him on Sundays. And then, in 1498, a monastery in Jabłeczna, in eastern Poland, was dedicated to Onufry, and the date of June 12 is the feast day on which St. Onufry is celebrated in the Eastern Orthodox calendars.

The Church of Saint Onufry in Łaka, Poland, was built in 1744.

I wasn't aware of that at the time of my journey east. I was so intent on visiting the land from which my family had been taken in the village originally known as Liczkowce in what was now Ukraine that I hadn't even considered looking into the backstory of the original villages from which they hailed, let alone a spiritual threshold erected more than 350 years ago. Had my Uncle Stanley—he of saltshaker show—not mentioned that his parents met as children in the Church of Saint Onufry, and were later married there, and that all of the Migut children were baptized there, I would have never followed the thread.

Fortunately and quite luckily, I had guidance. Several email correspondences with my dear friend, Eric, back in California, became the pillar candles I needed as I walked closer toward the altar of my family' past. My friend had discovered the location of the church in the Rzeszów parish. This was all due to dear Eric's robust interest in my family's tale. Eric—a delightful, brilliant savant in ways words cannot capture. If I pondered something out loud or via an email such as, "I wonder how far Łaka is from Rzeszów" or "Holy mother of God: I just learned my grandmother and grandfather fell in love in an old church in Łaka and I simply have to find it!" The next thing I knew, not only did I have URL links in my inbox about the history of the Rzeszów parish, but also pictures of The Church of Saint Onufry and a Google map image showing me its exact location on planet Earth.

If angels do come in human form, Eric was one my most valiant celestial guardians—perhaps one of the few with the broadest wingspans. And apparently, I would need him as I continued to learn more about the Stalin-encoded energy that was deeply embedded within my emotional DNA.

♦ ♦ ♦

The cab stopped in front of the iron gates at the back courtyard entrance of The Church of Saint Onufry and my eyes lifted, locating the church steeple, which stretched resplendently into nature's sapphire tapestry above. At the same time, my hand anxiously burrowed deep into the box of Polish cookies and I kidnapped the final two sweeties in there. Into my mouth they went. I figured I had about eleven minutes before my water broke—before the tears flowed. Until then: *Forgive me Father, for I have binged!*

Cab Driver With The Round Happy Polish Face turned and noticed my fervent expression. "Go, go! I will wait down the road by the trees. Over there, sir."

What a guy. He deserved a drink. A Polish bear hug. *Something.*

I stepped out of the cab, slammed the door, and looked up. St. Onufry held up pretty well for an old guy, yes he did. Although, the church must have been refurbished several times over the decades, time had faded its light mustard yellow dressing and stucco-like veneer. He was no St. Mary's Basilica, the crown jewel of Kraków. In fact, St. Onufry was not grand at all, but, standing there in front it, to me, it was more than just a village church in the middle of Nowhere, Poland. It felt like home.

In the short distance ahead—the church entrance. Lovely. The open door summoned me with otherworldly invitation and I hurried toward it amid a flurry of frenetic thoughts and emotions.

I can already smell the incense, can't you?

Dip your hand in holy water. It will help later. You know, when you lose your mind again, Greg.

Really? We're out of cookies?

Inside of the chamber entryway, I briefly peered through the glass on one of the wooden doors. What the church lacked in exterior decoration, its interior was a sight to behold. A fortress. A haven. A spiritual nest where my grandparent's fairy tale began. I simply could not contain myself any longer. I had come so far. I reached for the long silver door handle and pulled—hard.

What the...?

The doors were locked.

Locked?

~ ~ ~ ~

CHAPTER THIRTY-TWO

SAINT POPE JOHN PAUL II once remarked: "The way Jesus shows you is not easy. Rather, it is like a path winding up a mountain. Do not lose heart! The steeper the road, the faster it rises toward ever wider horizons."

Yes, but surely God had to realize how much I wanted the spiritual horizons to widen here. The Supreme Being had to know exactly how I wanted things to go—*my way*, which, technically, was really *his* way, or Yahweh's. Or *the* way.

Whatever.

No time to dissect semantics. Cab Driver With The Round Happy Polish Face was not going to wait around all day under the Eastern European maple trees. I simply had to get inside of the locked church.

I grabbed the silver door handle one more time and gave it a good tug. Nothing.

In a flash, my iPhone was out of my coat pocket. I snapped several pictures of the church's stunning interior, turned around and considered the carving of the crucified Christ on the back wall of the entryway.

"Shouldn't you be up front?" I remarked, indicating the locked church behind me.

Clearly not the time to be glib. I immediately apologized, sat down on the bench underneath The Lord and allowed my spiritual beak to peck away at some other options. What I needed was a sign.

A sign!

Ha!

Precisely what got me into this predicament!

And yet ... maybe it was the only thing to get me through it. All I had to do was Let Go! After all, Pushing never makes things that much easier. Except, perhaps, when you find yourself in a revolving door, and even then you have some inertia working with you.

Get some air!

"Good idea," I told myself—or God. Whoever it was that was telling me to step outside.

As I emerged from the entryway, a warm, fall breeze cascaded through the courtyard and tickled the leaves on the trees in a grove surrounding the church. The offering evoked a mystical, otherworldly feel—soothing—and my internal spiritual barking subsided a bit.

Bark less, walk more.

A grand idea. I discovered another door on the side of the church but it, too, was locked. I kept on, however, and along the way, snapped several photographs—of another set of iron gates on the other the side of the courtyard; of the significant wooden cross firmly planted in the ground nearby; of the courtyard walls and the variety of square-shaped cutouts that were evenly spaced from each other and included a place to sit. I imagined the locals praying there and considering the images in the faded, wood-framed paintings inside, each depicting a different scene from the Stations of the Cross. I stopped in front of a painting of Christ's first fall, the large cross digging into his right shoulder as he struggled to find his balance on the ground amidst a group of angry Roman guards.

A cross to bear.

After I completed an entire loop around the church and I was right back where it all began—at the entryway—I noticed a small building about 100 yards away off to the side of the courtyard. Small house? Office? I couldn't know for sure but suddenly, the rectangular strip of buttons next to the main door instantly brightened my mood.

Doorbells!

Time to see who wanted to come out and play. I was at the door in seconds.

I pressed the first button—with the name Proboszcz—and waited. Nothing.

I pressed the second button—Wikariusz. Twice. Silence.

I pressed the third button—Kancelaria. Three times. Nope.

What did I have to do: Huff and puff and blow this spiritual house down? A quick pivot on my heels and I considered the entryway of the church again.

Think, Greg, think. What would a sane person who wasn't wearing a coat with shoulder pads do if they were in a similar situation? What actions would they take if they stumbled upon a locked church that they simply had to get into?

And then it came to me.

Pray!

Well, of course.

Back in the entryway, I settled on the bench and reminded myself that there just had to be some *thing* bigger at work here. I thanked the heavens, the stars, the powers that be. Minutes passed. And then … a few more. Much calmer, I prayed for the best result to unfold in the current situation.

And then, I just let it all go. I had to.

I stood up, glanced at the interior of the church one last time and walked outside, where, seemingly from nowhere, a blond boy in his late teens appeared in the middle of the courtyard.

I blinked.

What the hell was he? An apparition?

I squinted—just to be sure he was real.

Dear God! It's a human being!

Collecting my fallen jaw off of the concrete, I surmised the stranger must have emerged from the wooden door in the center of a long brick wall, which ran perpendicular to the Doorbell Hut. I hadn't noticed the wall or the small door before.

It didn't matter. I went in for the kill.

The slightly hefty guy stopped dead in his tracks as if he was about to be tackled by a maniacal linebacker with ridiculous-looking shoulder pads. His entire face—so very deer-in-the-headlights. I actually felt sorry for the guy.

"Excuse me. Please—help!"

He took not one, but two, significant steps back.

"Uh, hello?" was all he muster in Polish. That he said it as a question, poor thing, momentarily worried me, but what the heck—this could be my only chance to get inside of the church.

"Please, please. Can you help me? I'm not from the area, but my family used to live around here…" I stumbled for the right words. Crap. Suddenly I couldn't remember how to say anything in Polish. I began waving my hands as if I was playing a game of charades, the same way I did with Cab Driver With The Round Happy Polish Face.

"Long, *long*, time ago…" I went on, "My family … live here … they did."

The teen's eyes widened beyond his wire-rimmed glasses and a breathy titter flowed from his mouth. I couldn't tell if he wanted to laugh at me or just shoo me away.

"I don't speak Polish well," I huffed. "I understand all of it. Writer—me! Have to get into the church." I pointed to it directly behind me—using both of my hands. "*That* church! My grandparents—married in there. Yes. Married. I am a journalist and…"

The teen perked up.

"*Journalista?*"

Now, it was I who took a step back. Was there a journalist shortage in eastern Poland? Everybody seemed surprised whenever I mentioned the occupation.

"Yes. *Journalista*. My family went to mass here. Do you have a key to open the church? Is it possible to go inside for maybe…"

I held up both hands, the universal sign for "this many."

"Ten? Maybe fifteen minutes?"

He contemplated my offer, glanced the church entrance beyond my right shoulder, and studied my face, my being, my frazzled demeanor.

"*Journalista?* Really?"

I suppose I, too, would have questioned it. I was hardly emotionally grounded at the moment. I found a business card and handed it to him—as if handing somebody a business card in a small village in eastern Poland actually meant anything. If I knew how to say, "I'm on a mission from God" in Polish I would have, but clearly it didn't matter. I sensed that I was making headway with this—what the *hell* do I call him?—Baby Priest.

"A key?" I gently nudged. "Do you have one, please?"

He grinned and considered the secret wall from which he magically emerged. As we found each other's eyes, I recalled former Paramount studio chief Robert Evans yet again—Evans, the expert deal maker who could ascertain in somebody's eyes if he had them. This teen and I—we had a deal. I felt it.

Baby Priest studied my card for a moment and then he shrugged.

"Yes. I will go and get the key. One moment, please."

And he was gone.

I looked up. I smiled.

And then I freaked.

He's coming back, God. Isn't he?

~ ~ ~ ~

CHAPTER THIRTY-THREE

LIFE LESSON NO. 1,111: When one door is locked, apparently another one can be opened.

Providence arrived, and the sight of the thin shiny, antique-looking silver church key in Baby Priest's hand elevated my spirits. As he led me toward another entrance on the side of St. Onufry's, oh, how I wanted to hug the guy and just bury his slightly acne'd face into my chest and joyfully ruffle his floppy blond hair. Who was this hefty eighteen-year-old angel sporting blue jeans and a windbreaker?

Groundskeeper? Angel from above? Who?

Baby Priest—that's who. He appeared as if by magic. But even though I was fully aware of the synchronistic event in which I now found myself, I also knew I had to remain present in the moment. Or, at least, try to. After all, when The Universe answers your prayers, it's best not to dissect what's happening as if it were a frog in a high school biology lab. If you want to "go with the flow," then, for goodness sake, *go*! You can always wax Oprah about it afterward.

Baby Priest slipped the silver key into an old-fashioned keyhole, turned it, unlocked the thick, wooden door, and graciously held it open for me. For a split-second, I didn't know what to do. Guardedly, I took a step. And then another. When I was inside of the church, I could not move. Not yet. I gaped in wonder at my new surroundings. Baby Priest kept on, however, and slid inside a pew in the middle of the church. He knelt down, made the sign of the cross and began to pray.

When in Rome, after all. Or, in this case: When in Łaka…

Breathe, Greg, breathe. Move slowly.

Avid visitors of cathedrals and churches already know it to be true—that, depending on the spiritual portal, a kind of preternatural stillness lingers in the air; a soft yet prominent reverence. At times, that energy can be so evident and so activated, that its palpable grace heightens one's senses and opens one's heart. Escorted by that kind of grace now, I unhurriedly found the center aisle of the church and as the holy gateway's spiritual breath touched my skin, all at once, I was consumed by my new surroundings.

Bewitching—everything from the sheer grandness of St. Onufry's interior to its surprisingly prosperous ornamentation. What prayers had been made here? How many of them had been answered? More exploration was in order.

Billowy bouquets of red and white carnations rested ceremoniously in vases in front of the altar, which was draped with fair, white linen cloths. Catholic figures and saints, painted with such fantastic detail on the walls surrounding me, depicted ancient biblical scenes. The church's rounded ceilings held similar images and tales—of angels, of Christ, of a grace and a glory and a prophecy.

Behind the altar, St. Onufry's most dramatic showpiece, an opulent structure, protruded outward from the back wall. A magnanimous dark emerald edifice with majestic gold columns and gold accents throughout, two statues, saints perhaps, sat imperially perched on each side of it. Its centerpiece: a significant, detailed painting whose main image, upon first glance, appeared to be of a man assisting the fallen Christ figure during the time leading up to the crucifixion. But a longer observation suggested the beleaguered figure must be St. Onufry, a man in his summative years whose unkempt hair and long gray beard fell down toward his knees.

And the man assisting Onufry— he must have been Paphnutius.

I stood there and wondered: Was I to my family's dense, oftentimes hard-to-embrace history, what Paphnutius was to St. Onufry? After all, on some level, I had been called to "lend a hand" and sit with an aging soul—my family's fractured fairy tale waiting to be held, to be experienced, to be lived out loud.

Seconds away from truly tripping over my soul's soles, I strolled beyond Baby Priest—still kneeling in the pew, his forehead firmly pressed into his fists while he prayed. I followed his lead and found refuge in the front pew. The gray wooden kneeler must have been nearly a hundred years old—and angled slightly downward toward the floor. How positively Old World! Was it to make kneeling before God a memorable yet uncomfortable experience? There was only one way to find out.

I never enjoyed kneeling in church all that much when I was a kid attending Sunday mass at St. Genevieve's on Chicago's Westside. Exhausting—stand up, kneel down, sit down, kneel some more. Why couldn't we all just hold hands and croon "Kumbaya" for eleven minutes and call it a day? But I was too young to grasp the significance. Kneeling before God—however one defines God—is a kind of surrendering to a Higher Power; something grander than one's own mental prowess, which, left to its own devices, tends to wander too far away from one's true nature; from a divine truth perhaps.

The hard wood pressed deeper into my jeans and my kneecap began to burn. So, it *was* true: That old-world kneeler was designed to make kneeling before God a memorable experience. But I didn't budge. For several minutes, I silently expressed my gratitude. After all, something had led me to this church—and something (someone!)—allowed me to step inside of it.

I emerged from the pew and began to stroll the church in a clockwise pattern, first making my way toward the back. My grandparents met as children somewhere in here. *Children!* Their bond lasted their entire lives—even beyond my grandfather's death in Tashkent.

Lead me. Guide me. Show me. What do you want me to see here?

Questions. So many of them. In what part of the church had young Jacenty and Jadwiga sat with their own families? Where did my grandfather first spot my grandmother? Or vice versa? And what about the rest of the family? Where had my mother and my aunts and uncles sat when they attended mass?

I studied the baptismal font in the center of the aisle near the back of the church—the family had all been given their first spiritual rites there. Slowly, I made my way up the center aisle again and realized it was the same aisle on which my grandmother must have walked to marry her Beloved. Somehow, I had arrived at the exact spot on the planet where the genesis of my family began—where their love began. I had located their first thread—the origin of their origin. Who could have ever known what a dramatic tale of survival would unfold from the spot on which I now stood; a story that gave birth to homelessness, hard labor, ruin, imminent death, and rescued dreams as it played out across five continents before a sign-seeking descendant finally paid attention to the spiritual hints he'd been given so he could press Rewind and begin healing the past—only by boldly stepping back into it.

Such deep thoughts belonged in a place like The Church of Saint Onufry. And had I not noticed Baby Priest still engaged in prayer, several pews away from me, I would have remained standing in the center aisle much, much longer. But Cab Driver With The Round Happy Polish Face was waiting outside. And I had more to discover.

Slowly, I turned around, my eyes following the carpet that led to the locked door through which I originally tried to enter. I was now on the *other* side of that door.

Was there a message in all of this for me?

If so, perhaps it was this: That whenever the doors of our own internal chapel are locked, the best thing we can do is slow down, listen, and wait. Because maybe, just maybe, the things that are truly meant to be will eventually come to us on the fringe of the spiritual boomerangs we bravely tossed up into the stars.

~ ~ ~ ~

CHAPTER THIRTY-FOUR

"HOW FAR IS THE CEMETERY FROM HERE?" The words tumbled out of my mouth. We were back outside in the church courtyard—Baby Priest and I—and I had to ask the question.

"The cemetery, sir?"

"That's right, please."

He made a face, which suggested one thing: I must have mispronounced a word or two. *Again?* Whatever. Twenty-four hours ago, visiting a cemetery had not even been in the spiritual game plan. But my pal Eric—God bless him—had dropped a few more clues. He emailed me a Google map image of a significant landmark near the church. Under the image, he wrote: "Do you think this is a cemetery?"

Analyzing the image, it occurred to me that my great-grandmother, whose surname was Wilk, could be buried there. Her daughter, my grandmother Jadwiga, had moved east with the family. Because of the mass deportations, mother and daughter never laid eyes upon each other again. They never had an opportunity to say goodbye.

Baby Priest shrugged. "Cemetery is not far; just around the corner."

I grabbed his hand, gripped it tightly, and shook it long and hard as if he'd just shared with me the cure for mood swings. I dashed off, but stopped abruptly in the center of the courtyard. I turned back.

"What is your name?"

"Piotr," he offered, a faint smile appearing on his face.

Peter—just like the saint. I considered him one last time, silently sent him a blessing of deep, deep thanks, and returned to Cab Driver With The Round Happy Polish Face, who greeted me with enthusiasm.

"Oh, my, was it good for you? And where would the fine sir like to go now?"

"Cemetery. Just around the corner. Please!"

He shifted the car into drive and giggled—like a little boy. Jesus. Was I really speaking Polish that poorly?

"Oh, and once again, my name is Gzegorz," I added, seeing I might be on the roll with Baby Priest Peter and all—perhaps my driver would tell me his name this time.

A smirk was all I received, chased back with another, "Yes, oh yes. It is a very good day to go to the cemetery for the fine man."

Apparently, not everyone played the I Tell You My Name, You Tell Me Yours game in these parts. Off we went. Several short, winding village roads later, we pulled into a dirt parking lot near the cemetery. Cab Driver With The Round Happy Polish Face turned around, took one look at the pools of anticipation in my eyes and waved a hand.

"Go, go! Of course I will wait for the fine sir right here!"

I held an appreciative gaze. True, the man was going to nab a good fare and a stellar tip to boot for all he was doing, but on some level, I also hoped that he realized just how much the crazy human he was carting around appreciated his help in getting through one heck of an unconventional To-Do list.

1. Venture alone to a little-known village in eastern Poland without a clue to where you're heading. *Check.*

2. Find the church in which your grandparents were married. *Check.*

3. Pray for a miracle to unlock the church. *Tricky … but doable.*

4. Locate the grave of your great-grandmother?

Too soon to know how that one would play out.

To the right of the cemetery entrance, a gray, metal sign stood askew behind an antiquated brown picket fence. It read: *Zaklad Pogrzebowy—* Funeral Home. The word "Orkus," written in cursive, rested below the words, and underneath that was *Grabarskie Cmentarze Progrzebowe*, the cemetery's moniker.

Unlike my maniacal tête-à-tête before getting into the church, I forced myself to be deliberately unhurried here as I walked into the holy pasture and onto the dirt path in its center that divided the cemetery into two sections. As a clique of billowy clouds floated west to east above my head, the fall breeze seemed unsure whether its bursts wanted to be playful or dramatic, sporadic or intense.

If there is anything that makes a jaunt through a foreign cemetery during a spiritual pilgrimage more mysterious, it is wind. In between the occasional gusts, the Past and Present, once again, seemed destined to merge together.

The deep green rectangular meadow was home to a variety of ornate and plain headstones, raised marble tombs, and wrought-iron crosses, the majority of which stood lopsided like funereal corn stalks begging to be peeled back; noticed. Down the center path, about 300 meters away, rested a small beige hut. I began walking toward it, inspecting the gray tombs on either side of me. On their bellies sat devotional red lanterns, the majority of them lit. The lanterns are a staple in many Polish cemeteries. Visitors paying respects to their loved ones often leave them lit atop of the raised graves and after dusk, from a distance, the ethereal glow emanating out of the cemetery does not go unnoticed.

Great-grandmother's grave has to be in the cemetery. Well, I was ninety-five percent certain of it, for I had never asked any of my relatives prior to stepping foot in the spiritual burial ground if they knew of its existence. But where could that grave be? There were actually two names to search for—my great-grandmother's surname, Wilk, and my family's name from my grandfather's side, Migut. Once again, my gaze lifted as I searched for a divine GPS in the sky.

"Alright, we're looking for a Migut or a Wilk. Lead the way!"

I started doing the math. The Church of St. Onufry was hundreds of years old. The cemetery must be that old, too—at least. My great-grandmother may have passed away some time during the 1940s. So, the question was: Where would somebody who died about seventy years ago be buried? I continued strolling down the center path, looking right and left, studying the names on the graves as the wind continued to rush through the cemetery. But I did not find any Miguts or Wilks. When I stopped directly in front of the beige hut, I shifted my gaze left and was about to start walking that way, but my gut feeling told me: *Go right!*

Fine. I turned to my right and took one step forward.

WILK!

The name was etched on top of a large gray and black raised tomb. Two lanterns sat atop it, one clear, the other red with a white cross emblazoned on its center. A white and pink flowered plant in a planter sat between the two lanterns. Somebody had been there recently, I quickly surmised. And that somebody could very well be a distant relative of mine. Underneath the name Wilk were three names—Jozefa, Antonina and Jan. There was no date on the stone; no way of knowing when these people died.

The name Antonina stood out—the only female name of the family buried there. Antonina.

Antonina?

A feverish attempt to assemble the sacred Rubik's Cube in my mind and then I looked up in desperation.

Good God. I had forgotten my great-grandmother's first name!

~ ~ ~ ~

CHAPTER THIRTY-FIVE

THERE IS A POPULAR POLISH SAYING: "Do not push the river, it will flow by itself."

Once again, I was being asked to "let go—and flow." My hunch told me the tomb was my great-grandmother's, but how could I be certain? Still, what were the odds that I would find the right grave just five minutes into the cemetery? And aside from the ghost of my great-grandmother actually appearing and shouting out her first name, I would have to, again, do the most logical thing: Ask for a sign.

Just then, the wind picked up and practically went right through my soul. Was *that* my sign? Who knew? Deciphering Signs From God, at times, is complicated and one certainly could benefit from a handbook of sorts. (Note to self: Write one!) And, considering it wasn't nighttime and I didn't have the benefit of a streetlamp going off above me as an official guide, perhaps I was left to my own devices.

Head cocked, I eyed the tomb: "Great-grandmother, is that you?"

There were about five Polish people scattered throughout the cemetery, paying their respects to the dead—the names of which *they* knew. I was not privy to the conditions of Polish asylums and and had no intention of finding out. I had to stop talking to myself.

I held my gaze on the grave. "Hang tight," I whispered. "I'm going to check on your neighbors."

The cemetery was much grander in size than I realized and for every lavish resting plot I explored—searching for a Wilk, or Migut—smaller, modest stones and iron crosses made up a vast part of the markers for the soulful collection here. There were graves for babies, for children, for husbands and wives, for beloved brothers and sisters—the outpouring of love engraved across the headstones, heartfelt and revered.

Fifteen minutes later, I returned to the center aisle and the tomb of the questionable three buried near the hut—Jozsefa, Antonina, Jan. And then I kept on, venturing off in the opposite direction, into the western half of the cemetery, just as another gust of wind cascaded over me, blowing into my ears.

And then—nothing.

And then—another gust.

And then—nothing.

The pattern repeated itself. Howling gusts of wind on a slightly cloudy fall day in an ethereal cemetery wedged between two small Polish villages? I could not have asked for better special effects. I continued scanning the monikers on the graves, but the name Antonina kept flashing before my eyes.

My great-grandmother. What sort of woman was she? What thoughts occupied her mind? How did she feel when her daughter, Jadwiga, insisted the family take the farmland they'd been offered in the farthest stretches of what was then eastern Poland in the late 1930s? What happened to this woman upon discovering the fate of her family? What does that do to a mother—to her heart, her spirit, her soul?

If the emotional blood of one's clan—throughout all time—dwells within every cell of our own body, how can any of us *not* be affected by what happens before us?

I shivered. But it had nothing to do with the erratic wind.

My search for names located a few more Wilks—a husband and wife, but the dates of their deaths didn't jibe. Nonetheless, I realized I could very well be related to the people buried there. Antonina beckoned. I returned to her grave and leaned over, my fingertips grazing the smooth marble surface. Slowly, I walked clockwise around the grave until I was back in front of it, viewing it head on again.

Well, the time had come: I had to communicate with the dead.

"Antonina Wilk…" I began all cheery and sweet, because, really, when speaking to those who have passed, would you have it any other way? "I think you are my great-grandmother. And if you are—and I am certain *you* would know—then I would like to honor you."

I held my hand on top of the tomb. I thanked the woman for giving birth to my grandmother. I told her Jadwiga had been a strong, strong woman and that it had been her strength that kept the family together—against all odds. And that I would not be standing there talking to her like a lunatic if I had not learned all about Jadwiga's strength. I told her all about her grandchildren—my aunt, my uncles, my mother—but to me, it seemed the woman had wonderful access to all of that information. For a moment, I contemplated asking if she could point the way for me to move from Befuddled Writer Wanting To Get Out Of Debt to Brilliantly Successful Creative Genius With Six Figures In His Bank Account And A Heart And Mind Of Balanced Spiritual Proportions ... but, really, why be greedy?

I lifted my right palm off of the grave just as another burst of soothing, temperate wind cascaded across my face. Like a silvery celestial flute, its tones filled my ears, enchanting me with a bountiful blessing of unshakeable grace.

~ ~ ~ ~

CHAPTER THIRTY-SIX

SUPER JESUS AND I WERE ENGAGED in a staring match. This was the second time in less than two hours I had come face to face with the Lord in some incarnation, and in this case it only seemed fitting to just stare back at him. Hard not to. When you come across a fifteen-foot tall Jesus statue whose one knee is firmly planted on the ground, it should not matter if his largesse smacks of an animated amusement park-like figurine. The saving grace—there wasn't holy water pouring out of his mouth.

We were stationed on the back lawn of a modern church in the village of Łukawiec, the birthplace of my grandfather, Jacenty. The church was erected in 1984. There was no way my family ever attended mass there. From some point in this small village, however, my grandfather had walked a few kilometers to The Church of Saint Onufry, where he eventually met Jadwiga. And their original farm, the one they had vacated for land further east? Where was that now? Near the spot on which I was standing?

Super Jesus held his gaze.

"Any thoughts?" I asked.

Not a word.

No worries. The silence afforded me time to speculate. What would have happened if the family had remained here in Łukawiec? I certainly would not be standing around asking that question to myself—and Super Jesus for that matter—if they had. An entire series of events—my family's, mine—would have been different.

Perhaps it was my vulnerability that compelled me to mirror Super Jesus. Soon, I, too, was down on one knee, my right hand pressed gently atop of the cool grass and moist soil beneath it. *Tres* "laying of the hands," yes, this I realized, but I just had to feel the land on which my family lived and walked and breathed—safely, for a time.

Eyelids closing, I inhaled deeply and purposefully, conscious of the air I was breathing in—*their* air. The second I opened my eyes again, my attention landed on another figure—just beyond Super Jesus' left shoulder and several hundred meters beyond a wooden fence. Clad in a white workman's cap and bluish-gray overalls, the stranger was a latter day Super Mario Bros. character, someone I had often seen in that popular '80s video game. The man stood there gawking at me—Just like Super Jesus.

No, sir. I really am not that crazy. I'm just feeling the vibrations of my ancestors, thank you very much!

I imagined how that would have gone over if I actually said it and decided to let the old guy stare. What's so wrong with—*forgive me, Super Jesus*— blessing the land? But was I doing more than that? Was I also *thanking* it? Thanking it for giving my family a strong foundation before their move east, where everything changed dramatically—for them, for millions of other Polish people?

Perhaps I was also thanking it for luring me there—via a butter dish, a mustard jar and saltshaker on a dining room table in Warsaw.

Back at the taxi, it occurred to me that either I truly was of questionable mind, what with my penchant for finding signs from the Universe in inanimate objects—water bottles, mustard jars, butter dishes? Or that God really must have, at times, quirky communication skills.

"Oh, the fine sir looks so very happy," sang Cab Driver With The Round, Happy Polish Face. "Did you finish what you came here to do? Are you ready to leave?"

Leave? Had I finished what I came here to do?

The sight of the Polish equivalent to an American mini-mart, directly across the street captured my attention. Was I *still* hungry after devouring that entire box of Polish cookies? Apparently. I excused myself.

"Oh, well, yes! Yes. I will wait! You go, sir, you go! Yes!"

Bless the man.

The mini-mart occupied the front portion of a single-story yellow brick home. Inside, from a plastic bakery case near the register, several *pączki*, the equivalent to a American donut, looked appealing, but I settled on a basic roll, resting it and a bottled water down on the counter. The clerk, a thirtysomething brunette woman of average height, smoothed her black smock and proceeded to ring me up.

And then, out of my mouth sprang this: "Excuse me, miss, please—do you know of any Wilks that live around here?"

I had not planed on asking that question when I came into the store. But now I just had to know: Could distant family members from my grandmother's side of the family still be living in the area?

She giggled.

Really? I could not have annihilated the Polish language that much.

"Wilk?"

I nodded. "Yes, Wilk."

"Wilk?"

"That's right."

Her eyes brightened. "Yes. A man by that name lives right next door."

I stood there in shock. Did she really say that or had I imagined it?

Right ... next ... door?

"Excuse me?"

"Next door," she offered. "Yes, sir."

My head turned so quickly it was as if this Wilk man was hiding behind one of the pastry cases. This amused the clerk. She did not expect such vivid entertainment from a soul-searching Pole with big shoulder pads—and at such a bargain price.

She indicated the exit and spoke slowly as if I had a learning deficiency.

"Yes ... sir. Right ... next ... *door.*"

A nervous laugh escaped the confines of my being. Well, of course—*right next door.* Why wouldn't a man bearing my ancestral name just *happen* to live right next door to a Polish mini-mart that I never knew existed until *after* I worked up an appetite with Super Jesus?

"Is he young? Old?"

The clerk told me his age, but for some reason, I only knew how to count to eight in Polish and I was not about to play How Many? again with my fingers. Wincing with shame, I asked her to write down his age. She did—thirty. The man was thirty years old, which meant he could very well be my second cousin from a distant aunt or uncle or another relative entirely.

Thanking her with the kind of heated frenzy Lucy would when getting a day off from Mr. Mooney at the bank on *The Lucy Show*, the news blasted me into yet another kind of quantum orbit. Somehow, I flew out of the store without bumping into anything, but the clerk decided to follow me outside. Apparently, she wasn't done watching the show. She proceeded to lean up against the building, find a lighter, and quickly light the cigarette in her hand. She took a quick drag, noticed my confusion about which direction to go and indicated a half-dozen tall, untrimmed bushes next to the store and the property just on the other side of them.

"Over *there*, sir."

I held up a finger. "One moment, please."

A chortle. *Again?*

Back at the taxi, I flung the bottled water and the roll onto the backseat, informed Cab Driver With The Round Happy Polish Face I'd be back in a few minutes, and quickly backtracked. Bewildered, he called out after me.

"Oh, well, yes, yes. That is fine. I will of course, wait here for the fine sir. But where are you going?"

"To find a long-lost Polish relative who doesn't know I even exist!"

At least that's what thought I said in Polish.

Briskly walking down the narrow street beside the market, my eyes found the clerk again. She was still resting against the wall, this time, her arms folded over her chest, her lit cigarette dangling between two fingers. I stopped and shrugged. A slight fan of the hand and her cigarette pointed the way to go. I kept on. Just beyond the bushes, a faded amber tractor—very *Green Acres* with its big, badass farm wheels—was slightly submerged in a mud puddle in front of a one-story, barn-like structure. The doors were open, sparks shooting out from within. There must have been a welder inside. Several hundred yards off to the right was a bi-level home with a gravel driveway.

Oh, Mr. Wilk? Can you come out and play?

Was he even in there? And were we even related to each other?

I rushed past the tractor, hopped over a puddle, and approached the driveway of the home. All of sudden, from the barn, emerged a tall, thin, wiry creature with gray hair, the bushiest of mustaches and a face so etched with exhaustion it recalled the bloodhound from *The Beverly Hillbillies*.

The two of us stopped dead in our tracks. It was as if we both had come face to face with Stalin's ghost.

"Why, hello there!" I beamed, more out of nervousness than anything else.

The man stood there, positively befuddled by the sight of me—me of spiked blond hair and shoulder padded European *jacquette*!

"Please, sir. I am looking for a man named Wilk?"

He held a suspicious gaze, his deeply lined face—from age, from fatigue, from hard work, from welding by himself in that damn barn?—suggesting I had interrupted him.

I stepped closer. "Wilk? Does he live here?"

A nod—more of indifference than "here, let me help, sir." He indicated the house and said, "Eh…"

Eh? My father always said "eh" when he cared less about what you were saying to him. *Eh*—the downtrodden's abbreviated version of *Meh*!

"Perhaps you can ask the lady of the house, sir. She will find him for you."

I smiled. "Thank you. Thank you, very very much, sir!"

He disappeared back into the barn without saying another word.

Several yards later, I nearly stepped on a small russet-colored dog that had been tied to a small metal post. If a dachshund and a Chihuahua had frolicked in a doghouse together it would resemble this curiously plump creature with stunted legs and oddly small paws. We looked at each other—he for solace to be removed from his confinement and me out of hope and desperation.

"Sugar pickles, how the hell are you standing up?"

It barked—two yaps, but enough to attract somebody's attention. A middle-aged woman sporting jeans and a thick green sweater, her blond hair pulled back into a ponytail, appeared at the doorway of the house and began walking toward me.

I forced myself not to lunge at her—or step on the dog. "Please, miss. Excuse me. I don't speak Polish that well, but I understand everything…"

She smiled graciously. My clue to go on. I asked about the Wilk man.

A nod. Dear God—it was true. Somebody in that house had incarnated as one of my relatives! She leaned in—just a bit—and studied my eyes. I wanted to tell her that I had no relation to Stalin or the NKVD but I thought it best to avoid *that* subject for the time being. I was told to wait a moment. Left alone with Dog With No Legs, I snapped a photo of it and prayed it would grow longer limbs very soon.

"Have faith, doggie. Seems to be the only way to go around these parts."

Less than a minute later, a man appeared at the doorway and was heading my way. My eyes widened in anticipation of our encounter. Six-feet tall or so, with a stocky frame, he was youthful in appearance—he with his blond hair...

Just like mine!

And round, flushed cheeks ...

Just like Uncle Stanley's...

And thick, prominent nose...

Just like everybody else in our Polish family!

Two blond boys, no more than six or seven years old, appeared at the doorway. Ever so curious, they rested their heads against the doorframes as they watched their father approach the ridiculous looking stranger with the European shoulder pads.

"You are Mr. Wilk?"

His smile made his face appear more plump. "Yes, I am, sir."

I extended a hand. He shook it. Firm grip. I told him I was a writer from America; that my family lived in the area a long time ago.

"I think we could be related!" I quickly added.

He crossed his arms over his chest, frowned, looked down and nodded, as if he were being given instructions on how to operate heavy machinery. I did not know whether he understood me; if I should go on.

"Do you recall anybody in your family ever speaking of ... a Jadwiga Wilk or an Antonina Wilk?"

His eyes searched for clues on the ground.

He is going to say, yes. He is. He must!

"No, sir. I do not believe I have."

"Are you certain?"

"Maybe. I do not know. I am sorry but I cannot recall."

My mind leapt into action. If he was thirty, he was born in 1982, more than forty years after my grandmother Jadwiga and thousands of other Poles were set free from the labor camps. Chances are great-grandmother Wilk died in the mid- to late-1940s. There's no telling how many relatives she or her husband left behind. This man, this Mr. Wilk—he with too many similar familial features to dismiss as chance—could fit onto any number of limbs on my family tree. But which one? And how could I properly convey to him that we were more similar than he could ever realize; that the probability we shared the same genes was so strong, that every beat of his heart beats, as mine does, to the rhythms directly related to our ancestors? We were cut from the same fabric, he and I.

But he couldn't see it. Not now, anyway.

I reached inside my coat pocket and pulled out a business card and handed it to him. He scanned it with just the same amount of enthusiasm Baby Priest had—absolutely none. Immediately, my heart sank a bit from the lack of *pow!* I hoped our encounter would spark. I had to leave this guy alone.

And then ... the wind picked up. And then it simply vanished.

The dog yapped. Mr. Wilk looked down and smiled.

Another gust of wind. And then—nothing.

The wind. The cemetery. Antonina!

Grinning ear to ear now, I inspected the guy's round face again—those hearty cheeks, those bright young eyes. Suddenly, it didn't really matter if *he* believed we were related. I knew we were. Besides, maybe the only thing I needed to realize was that I had to be willing to follow yet another clue—just like that broken family picture frame; just like the butter dish and mustard jar. After all, I had asked for a man named Wilk and a man named Wilk materialized—right next door. Showing up is ninety percent of everything. It gives the Gods a whopping ten percent to work some of their own powerful magic.

I took my cousin's hand, shook it and thanked him. I pointed to the card and pretended as if I were typing.

"Keep in touch? Email?"

He made a face and contemplated the card. "Um ... sure, sir?"

Atta boy!

♦ ♦ ♦

Cab Driver With The Round Happy Polish Face was resting his elbows on the top of the taxi when I returned. He was not alone. The Spy Super of Super Jesus—the guy that spied me blessing the land in front of that statue—was on the other side of the cab.

I nearly laughed out loud. Let's see: Number of Poles in the area that now thought I was crazy? At least five. Number of ways I could explain my way out of what was really happening to me: Zip.

"Oh, yes, yes, *yes!* Come here my friend! Come," my loyal driver beamed. "This man here is the caretaker of the church grounds. He knows *everybody* around here. Ask him about your family!"

The Spy Super of Super Jesus inspected me with fierce inquisitiveness and I shook his hand, and told him who I was and what I was doing. He looked me over—head to toe, shoulder pad to shoulder pad.

"Oh … a *journalist?*"

"Yes, one of *those!*"

The man stepped forward. "I know everybody around here. Who are looking for?"

"A Wilk. I just met one."

"Of course! There are many many Wilks around here!"

Many?

"There are a few more down the road there," he went on, "and some others up the road there and…"

I just stood there, dumbfounded. I didn't now how to take it all in.

"What about Migut?" I interrupted. "Do you know of any Miguts?"

The name seemed to trigger a memory. "Oh my, yes. I do remember that name. They used to live here … a long, long time ago."

He said "long, long time ago" the same way I had when I was explaining my little caper to every Janek, Basia, and Bolek. Extending his arm, he pointed west—and to the east, to the north, to the south, this way, that way. Everywhere. And the names Wilk and Migut freely tumbled off of his tongue.

Good God. There is more of my bloodline here!

I left The Spy Super of Super Jesus, his arms now practically directing airliners, by the cab and walked into the center of the empty roadway. I faced west, the direction from which I came. The Church of Saint Onufry was back there. I looked over my shoulder—east—my gaze following the rolling hills stretching out into the horizon, heading into points unknown. There were more answers for me there, farther down the road. Near Ternopil…

In Siberia…

In Uzbekistan…

In the Middle East…

In Tanzania…

"Dear Lord, how could this be?"

"*What?*" crowed the two men back at the cab.

I turned around and faced east again. And then back to the west. And then, back to the east. Everything—spinning around me. How many emotional miles had I traveled over the last decade in my attempt to unravel my family's story, which, in turn, somehow, became *my* story? Hunted and haunted by it, its firm grip clenched around my heart and my psyche. I felt as if our mutual journeys—mine, my entire family's—chasing after some kind of saving grace would never find a peaceful ending point. And in Warsaw, when I accepted the fact that if I could not physically go to the land from where the Russians removed my family, coming to Łaka and Łukawiec seemed the best alternative. I thought Łaka and Łukawiec would be the ending point of my journey. But now that I found myself on the exact spot on the planet where it all began, the cosmic joke was *still* on me. I had not reached the ending point at all. It was just the beginning. There was so much more to explore. I had come all this way only to learn—*what?*—that I had to go even further? Retrace *every* footstep of the family's journey? All of it—across five continents? As in, *physically?*

Cab Driver With The Round Happy Polish Face tapped the top of the taxi with his fingers.

"Where would the fine sir like to go next?" He sang it, of course.

Ternopil, I wanted to scream. *Novosibirsk. Uzbekistan. Tehran. Karachi. And then ... Tanzania.* What a cab fair that would be.

Jesus—I would have to stock up on Polish cookies.

I glanced at the sky just as another brilliantly swollen and determined cloud slid across the endless blue palette above me. It was heading east. Would I be following it sometime in the near future?

Back at the taxi, I opened the door and slunk back into the back seat, realizing the inevitable—that I had to keep going.

But first, I had to return home—so I could plot my way back.

~ ~ ~ ~

CHAPTER THIRTY-SEVEN

SEVERAL WEEKS AFTER RETURNING from Poland, I was heading back home to Chicagoland from California to visit my family and attend an annual Columbus Day family picnic. I wanted to share photos of Poland and rehash my adventures with the clan. But even at a lofty 30,000 feet, my thoughts were back on the ground—in eastern Poland and Siberia—and focused on the past, on Stalin. The moment the seatbelt sign went off, I fetched my laptop from the overhead bin. Once the computer screen was fully lit, I began poring over the additional research I had collected over the last few months, when I finally took heed to the signs the Gods were offering me.

Few people have read it or actually know of its existence, but back in February of 1989, several years before the fall of the Soviet Union, Georgian historian Roy Aleksandrovich Medvedev, the man who penned the illuminating Stalin exposé "Let History Judge," wrote a research paper published in the tabloid *Argumenti I Fakti*. In the article, on which the *The New York Times* also reported, Medvedev approximated that the deaths directly associated with Stalin's reign of terror hovered somewhere near 20 million people. But that was hardly the place to insert a "period, the end." As *The New York Times* noted, Medvedev's research added onto that figure the 20 million Soviet troops and civilians who died in World War II, which sent the Stalin death toll skyrocketing to about 40 million.

Medvedev's father was among the lost souls of Stalin's broad carnage. It stumped me. What taxing lengths did the historian have to go to in order to break down the figures of Stalin's atrocities?

+ 1 million people exiled or imprisoned between 1927 and 1929.
+ 9 to 11 million farmers and peasants ripped off their own land.
+ 2 to 3 million peasants arrested or exiled in the mass collectivization efforts.
+ 6 to 7 million souls killed by an artificial famine between 1932 and 1933.
+ 1 million people exiled from Moscow and Leningrad in 1935.
+ 1 million executed during the "Great Terror" of 1937-1938.
+ 4 to 6 million sent to forced labor camps, including nearly 2 million Poles.
+ 10 to 12 million individuals forced to relocate during World War II.
+ Approximately 1 million arrested for so-called political crimes (1946-1953).

It is unclear if *all* of the deaths noted were "unnatural" deaths, but other scholars have argued that Stalin's wrath could have reached as many as 60 million people. In I.G. Dyadkin's book, *Unnatural Deaths in the U.S.S.R.: 1928-1954*, the author approximates that the USSR tallied 56 to 62 million "unnatural deaths" between the late 1920s and early 1950s, and that 34 to 49 million of those were directly linked to Stalin.

As I sat there mulling over the figures, it was apparent to me that the level of awareness surrounding Stalin's devastation needs to be greatly raised; that Hitler was not and should not be listed as the 20th century's most inhumane fiend. That label could easily rest directly underneath Stalin's name. And on that plane in late 2012, I could have never have predicted what would come two years later. All the political unrest between Ukraine and Russia in early 2014, under the direction of Vladimir Putin, showcased how Stalin's menacing psychological tentacles were destined to linger on.

But in honor of those who were lost, some progress and justice has been made. In 2005, the Polish Government extended a compensation of twenty percent of the current value of the land and buildings the Poles had lost during the deportations. The compensation was funded by the sale of government property and more than $100 million has already been awarded for lost land and homes in the Kresy (or Eastern Borderlands) to former residents and heirs who have Polish citizen status. It includes the deported families, soldiers who served in the Polish Forces in the West, and their families who spent the war in refugee camps. Some of my family members benefitted from this. The monetary gesture is noteworthy, but I wondered if it was really enough. How could it ever repair the lingering psychological effects and the emotional inheritances that were passed down?

In a Kresy-Siberia Foundation document about the compensation, the organization noted that "the tragic history of the Polish citizens under Soviet Russian occupation during the war were hushed up by the Allies during the war to protect the reputation of the Soviet Union, an important ally in the war against Nazi Germany. Almost seventy years later the survivors have aged and many have died. The [foundation] brings together surviving deportees and their descendants to remember, learn, discover and spread the word of their ordeal to the world and to future generations."

Future generations? In the process of investigating what happened to my family, I had revealed more clearly for myself the under-reported story of the mass deportation of the Poles and affirmed my belief that what happens before us has the ability to live on through us. A remarkable discovery and catharsis, sure, but I continued to remain unsettled.

What, I wondered, could I do about the emotional legacy I inherited? I had traveled so far since the fateful day I discovered that broken picture frame of my family on my desk. All my life I have been living out a fascinating family parable. Like a motion picture projector shooting images onto a screen, my Polish lineage had always been emanating through me in some way. My entire investigation of my family's path proved one thing: I needed to do more work: internally and externally.

I was about to shut my laptop when several saved emails summoned me. They were from my childhood Polish friend, Renee. As I re-read her recent messages, my face flushed with embarrassment over something I could not alter.

Apparently I had called everybody a pig when I was in Poland. Jesus! The word "please" and "piglet" sound similar in Polish, but if you mispronounce the ending, you actually are saying the latter. What on Earth had those lovely Polish people thought of me?

"Piggy, can you help me?"

"Piggy, do you know the way to Łaka?"

"Piggy, do you know if anybody by the name of Wilk lives around here? Do you, piggy, do you piggy?"

I covered my mouth with my hand— the horror of it all.

I shook it off and moved onto other emails—upcoming potential interviews with agents of change and celebs—until one much more easily digestible message found me. Renee had also translated the song in the taxi, the one that Cab Driver With The Round Happy Face turned up on the radio and which I had recorded on my iPhone:

When I was, when I was ... a big boy, a big boy ... my father took me, and this is what he said: Listen always to the voice in your heart...

What was my heart telling me? That I had crossed a kind of spiritual threshold back in Poland; that I had come in direct contact with something extraordinary; something that connected me with the past in an effort to explore and transcend its curious inheritance. Perhaps I was to triumph, to prosper, to create a new legacy?

One last written item on my laptop beckoned me, something so exceptional yet darkly poetic that I often found myself turning back to it over the last year, for it fully captured the ripple effects of Stalin's wrath on the innocent. My grandmother Jadwiga had written to her mother when she was in Africa in the 1940s. (As it turned out, upon my return to Warsaw from the eastern villages, my Uncle Stanley confirmed that my great-grandmother's name *was* indeed, Antonina. I had located her, after all.) Years ago, I discovered my mother retained a copy of the letter, which must have been returned to my grandmother. It was written in Polish and I encouraged my mother to translate it. As the document illuminated my laptop screen, I sat back, I inhaled deeply, and read on:

Tanganyika, Africa— June 18, 1946

My Dearest Mother!

I have written to you a couple times through Red Cross—only 25 words were allowed, but nobody responded. My heart cried on the thought that nobody was alive and I asked God to send some news from whomever was left. Today I received a letter from [my sister] Mary and found sad news that some of our relatives are dead at early age, and that you, my dear mother, lost your eyesight. Is it because you couldn't afford a doctor? Or it because you're crying over me and my children?

I want to thank you from the bottom of my heart for that strong motherly love, but please don't cry or worry about us because it won't help. But take care of your health. I always ask God for his guidance and his help to let me return and find you in good health, and I have strong faith that our Heavenly Father will take care of us and will let me and my children return to you. My heart dies of loneliness for you. Now I can understand what it is to lose your family home and the homeland. Maybe I deserve this suffering for not listening to you when you told me not to leave for colony.

Today I have nothing—no colony, no homeland ... lost everything, including my husband who was dearer to me than my life. The colony was taken by our enemies and we, like orphans, have to wander in different parts of the world. That moment when they threw us out of our home will not be forgotten, even in the darkest grave. I have lived through some difficult moments in my life, but the worst was when I lost my child and my beloved husband whom I loved dearly from my childhood. They did not let me see him or my child in their last moments of their lives or to see where they were buried. We were all very ill with typhoid fever, and not knowing what was going on around us. My husband and Mary were taken to the hospital, 20 miles or so from us. During our illness I didn't know anything about them ... no one took care of us except our Heavenly Father.

When I got a little stronger, I went on foot looking for my Beloved. Could not find my husband [in the hospital], was told that there is no such family by that name and that they didn't know what happened to him. They told me to look for Mary through the window because I was not allowed to go inside. When I saw her through the window, my heart stood still. I did not see Mary—but her skeleton. I called her name and she stretched out her arms to me and called: "Mother, give me some bread because I am dying of hunger ... the only reason that I am alive is because Ted brings me a piece of bread every day." She was talking through fever not knowing what she was saying because Ted was not with us.

When I heard those words, it was like a sword that pierced my heart and I fainted by the window. When I came to, I asked them if I could take her with me, but I was pushed away from the window; laughed at and thrown outside of the gate, which they locked behind me. I do not remember coming back to my children. The only thing I remember is crying and calling, "Heavenly Father, please take me because I don't want to live on this earth!" The children gathered around me, crying and asking, "Mother, who will take care of us is you leave us? We want to die with you!"

Few days later, I took the children and went looking for my husband's grave. I did not see Mary any more. We didn't know where the cemetery was, until one man pointed out in which direction we should go. When we got there, there was no indication where the graves were of our beloved. I started digging with my bare hands looking for the remains but couldn't find them. The sorrow that tore my heart at that time was indescribable. My heart was dying with pain, but I couldn't die. I looked up to God, crying, "God, why are you sending me this pain? Where are you? Can't you see my suffering? Please let me die so I don't have to suffer any more!" I didn't die because it was God's will for me to live. We left the cemetery not knowing where they were buried.

This was in 1942 at the end of January.

After some struggles we arrived in Africa where we have been four years this November. This camp is large, holding 5,000 Poles, mostly women and children. I am working in the orphanage and the children are attending school. Joe and Jenny are in high school, and the rest are in grammar school.

Thank God we're in good health, which we're wishing for you, dear mother. There are no winters here but very hot, which affects some people mentally. I have no friends from back home; everyone is from different parts of Poland. We have a church that has only a roof protecting from the sun and four poles to hold it up. There are three Polish priests that work among us and we always pray for our homeland, our Beloved and have special services asking God to bring us back home.

A lot of families are leaving for the U.S. if they have families there. I have hoped that my sister, Catherine, would help me. I found her through the U.S. Consulate, wrote her often, but she only wrote two letters within the four years and said that her husband died leaving her in debt; that she really has no time to write because she's holding two jobs. My husband's family sent me $40 last year, but they don't write much. I wrote to Catherine in January asking her to take us out of here, but I had no response from her. She's probably afraid that we would be a burden to her, so I live without anyone worrying about me except God's help.

I await the moment that I can come back to you, but please write and let me know what conditions are like there now. Is there a possibility to lead a normal life? Do you know what happened to our land? I bet I'll never see it again. Please let me know what kind of shoes and clothes you have there.

Dear Mother, I would like to ask you if you can send me a copy of my marriage license, birth certificates of my children because I have no documentation at all. Enclosed are the pictures of us all.

Sending you our love and best wishes for your health. Embracing you warmly, we all send you lots of hugs and kisses.

Love,

JADWIGA

~ ~ ~ ~

EPILOGUE

The outskirts of Chicago, October 2012

JUST WEST OF COAL CITY in rural Illinois, approximately three hours south of Chicago proper, several vibrant green acres serve as the occasional weekend retreat of my cousin Margaret, one of my Uncle Ted's four daughters. After coming to America and splitting his time between the states and Poland, Ted, the eldest of the Migut children, passed away in 2002. He survived his own nightmarish experiences during the 1940s. After bicycling to a train station from the family farm near Tarnopol in 1940 for a routine visit to his grandmother, Antonina, he was arrested by the Germans in Lwów, along with many other Poles, and forced into slave labor. Over the last ten years, I have strengthened my bond with Uncle Ted's daughters as well as my many other cousins. I always planned a trip home to Chicago around the time of a festive family picnic Margaret hosted.

The guest list at these gatherings? Vast. It included my Aunt Janina, now in her eighties and still gregarious. I chuckle over how my aunt insists on buying me, my mother, and my stepfather, Chicago beef sandwiches at the joint down the block from her Westchester home so we can all "eat something" on our way to a picnic to "eat something." Uncle Stanley, eighty-one, has attended the soirees during his occasional trips from Poland, although he was not present this year. Uncle John, now in his late seventies, still confiscates an entire tray of fresh pierogi, hides them under his chair, and hoards them all. My mother, Bernice, the youngest of the original Migut children, attends the picnic. Now in her mid-seventies, she is possibly one of the wisest, most generous souls among the bunch.

There is always an abundance of cousins and second cousins, of course, and many other family friends in attendance. Missing from the bunch: Uncle Joe. He passed away in 1988, survived by his two children, Barbara and Donna, and his first wife. His second wife and widow, also named Donna, passed away in early 2012.

Grandmother Jadwiga and Grandfather Jacenty must be at these affairs in spirit. After keeping the family intact through the Siberian nightmare and the odyssey that befell her and her children as refugees in the 1940s, Jadwiga, by some grace, created a manageable life for her children in an African orphanage for eight years. Family relatives in Chicago—my grandmother's sister, Catherine, and Uncle Pete, my long-lost cousin David's great grandfather, and other family members—eventually came through and assisted the family in acquiring the proper documents. This allowed them to finally arrive in Chicago on—of all days—Thanksgiving Day 1950, a journey which, at that point, spanned nearly 19,000 miles from where the Miguts originally began in eastern Poland.

However, Jadwiga's fate was sealed with a diagnosis of liver cancer—her immune system was greatly affected by the family's endless wanderings. She died in 1958, on Palm Sunday, and was laid to rest in Resurrection Cemetery in a town called—I still can't get over it—Justice, near Chicago's South Side. Whenever her spirit glances down from where she currently hovers, one look at the endless smorgasbord of food at the picnic must make her beam with love and devotion.

In between the 2012 Columbus Day feedings, which included an entire roasted pig, nearly a dozen family members, several of their offspring and some of *their* offspring, gathered around a significant fire pit, while others roamed the land. I was seated next to my Uncle John.

"One evening," my uncle began a joke, "there were two nuns in Chicago walking through Grant Park."

This wouldn't be the first time my outspoken uncle engaged the masses with his jokes. He stored a bevy of them in his repertoire and they typically revolved around relationships or the clergy, and oftentimes were told in Polish—oh, how they rhymed in delightful lyrical bravura. And now that nuns were the topic du jour, the man had everyone under his spell.

"All of a sudden, the sisters heard somebody behind them," Uncle John went on. "Well, they turned around and saw there was a man following them. Sister Mary glared at Sister Francis and they started to walk much faster. But behind them, they could hear the footsteps also were going faster. So ... the nuns started walking faster. Again, the footsteps got faster. Sister Francis looked concerned. She turned to Sister Mary. 'It's not working. We have to do something else. Let's split up!' So, Sister Mary went one way and Sister Francis went another."

None of us said a word. Meanwhile, the fire in the pit raged on.

"Sister Mary got back to the convent first and waited and waited and waited for Sister Francis. Finally Sister Francis showed up. She was so out of breath. 'What happened?' Sister Mary asked.

"Sister Francis was breathing heavily, her hand over her chest. 'He caught me,' she huffed.

"Sister Mary's eyes opened up real wide. 'And *then* what, sister?'

"Sister Francis shook her head in shame. 'He told me to raise my dress!'

"Sister Mary's hand leapt to her heart. 'And then *what*, sister?'

"Sister Francis sighed. 'I raised my dress!'

"Sister Mary gasped. 'And then what, sister?'

"Sister Francis paused. 'Well ... I told him to drop his pants!'

"Sister Mary took a step back. 'And *then* what, sister?'

"Sister Francis clasped her hands into prayer. 'Sister Mary,' she said. 'Do you know what happens when a man drops his pants?'

"Sister Mary swallowed hard. 'No sister, *what*?'

"Sister Francis sighed. 'He can't run! I left him there with his pants around his ankles and got out of there as fast as I could!'"

The wave of uproarious family laughter swelled to tsunami-like proportions. Positively drenched in Happy, my heart full, I just sat there contemplating my older relatives, all of whom had, somehow, cultivated levity, happiness, humor and dignity in their lives despite their unsettling beginnings. There they were: Janina, John, my mother Bernice, all of my cousins. I imagined Stanley there—and Ted, sweet Mary and Joe, and Jacenty, and dear Jadwiga, too. What a journey they had all been on—decades in the making to bring them to the very spot on which they were now still breathing in some form. One wrong move—left, right—and I would not be observing them.

God ... let this moment last. Let the joy linger

The breeze picked up—and then disappeared just as quickly as it arrived. Immediately, I recalled the ethereal buzz I felt in the cemetery back in Poland, and as my attention lifted beyond the group, it was as if I was seeing everything on the property with brand new eyes. In the distant fields, rows of fertile cornstalks rose dramatically from the earth. A determined gang of agricultural splendor, they welcomed the occasional tickle of that frisky midwestern breeze. At the other end of the farm: a grove of apple trees. Closer to the fire pit: a pagoda with a bar stocked with enough booze for whiskey and vodka slingers near and far.

And then, my eyes fell upon the house on the farm. I simply could not stop looking at it. *A farmhouse?*

Well, it wasn't a traditional farmhouse per se, but my cousin Margaret's modest, single-story second home did actually sit on ... *farmland!*

Farmland?

The proverbial light bulb popped on above my head and it was determined to stay lit. Decades ago, the Russians had taken my Polish family by force from ... *a farm!*

And now, somehow, they had all come back to one.

Coincidence? Impossible.

An unexplainable and unshakeable grace had been with all of us the entire time.

It made me smile. And as my tear-filled gaze found the horizon, I softly held it there as the last moments of daylight lingered gracefully behind a seemingly endless stretch of wispy midwestern clouds.

A Polish farm...

Well, it finally came to pass.

Everyone found their way back home.

~ ~ ~ ~

ABOUT THE AUTHOR

Greg Archer is a cultural moderator, award-winning journalist, television host, motivational speaker and performance artist. His work covering agents of change, history, travel and the entertainment industry has appeared in *The Huffington Post, Oprah Magazine, San Francisco Examiner, The Advocate, Bust, Palm Springs Life, VIA Magazine* and a variety of cable television outlets. A four-time recipient of the Best Writer Award in a popular San Francisco Bay Area Readers' Poll, he shines the light on change agents near and far, and other under-reported issues in society. In between  receiving "signs" that he's on the right track, he appreciates the time 11:11 (a.m. and p.m.), Bernese Mountain Dogs and platters full of plump pierogi doused with melted butter. He splits his time between his hometown of Chicago and Palm Springs.

~ ~ ~ ~

REFERENCES

Anders, Lt. Gen. W. (1949). *An Army in Exile: The Story of the Second Polish Corps*; Retrieved from http://www.polandinexile.com/ppa.html

Barocas, H. A. & C. B. Barocas (1973). "Manifestations of Concentration Camp Effects on the Second Generation"; (1980). "Separation-Individuation Conflicts in Children of Holocaust Survivors," *Journal of Contemporary Psychotherapy* 11(1): 6-14.

Dekel, S., Rozenstriech, E., Solomon Z. (2012). "Secondary salutogenic effects in veterans whose parents were Holocaust survivors?" *Journal of Psychiatric Research*

Dyadkin, I.G. (1983). *Unnatural Deaths in the U.S.S.R.: 1928-1954.*

Gellately, R. (2008). *Lenin, Stalin, and Hitler: The Age of Social Catastrophe*

Gorodetsky, G. (1999). *Grand Delusion: Stalin and the German Invasion of Russia*

Hoggan, D.L. (1961). *The Forced War: When Peaceful Revision Failed*

Hope, M. (2000). *Polish Deportees in the Soviet Union*

Karski, J. (1985) *The Great Powers and Poland: From Versailles to Yalta* Retrieved from http://books.google.com/books/about/The_Great_Powers_Poland_1919_1945.html?id=kwJpAAAAMAAJ

Kochanski. H. (2012). *The Eagle Unbowed: Poland and the Poles in the Second World War*

Kogan, I. (2002). "'Enactment' in the Lives and Treatment of Holocaust Survivors' Offspring," *Psychoanalytic Quarterly*

Kot, S. (1963). *Conversations with the Kremlin and dispatches from Russia*

Krolikowski, L. (1983). *Stolen Childhood: A Saga of Polish War Children*

Maciejowska, M. (2002). *Deportation of Polish People*

Makow, H. (2007). "Stalin Intended To Strike Hitler First." Retrieved from http://www.savethemales.ca/001895.html and http://www.henrymakow.com

Medeved, R.A. (1989). *Let History Judge, Argumenti I Fakti.* Retrieved from http://www.nytimes.com/1989/02/04/world/major-soviet-paper-says-20-million-died-as-victims-of-stalin.html

Mucci, C. (2013). *Beyond Individual and Collective Trauma: Intergenerational Transmission, Psychoanalytical Treatment, and the Dynamics of Forgiveness.* Retrieved from https://play.google.com/store/books/details/Clara_Mucci_Beyond_Individual_and_Collective_Traum?id=MhN6AgAAQBAJ

Paczkowski, P. (1999). *The Black Book of Communism (ed. Courtois, S.)* Retrieved from http://books.google.com/books/about/The_Black_Book_of_Communism.html?id=H1jsgYCoRioC

Piotrowski, T (ed). (2004) *The Polish Deportees of World War II: Recollections of Removal to the Soviet Union and Dispersal Throughout the World* Retrieved from http://books.google.com/books/about/The_Polish_Deportees_of_World_War_II.html?id=JPdB1yeJeVcC

Shifrin, A. (1982). *The First Guidebook to Prison and Concentration Camps of the Soviet Union*

Siberian Society of U.S.A. (2009). *The Mass Deportation of Poles to Siberia: A Historical Narrative based on the written testimony of the Polish Siberian survivors*

Wright, J. (2000). *A Forgotten Odyssey—The Untold Story of 1,700,000 Poles Deported to Siberia in 1940*

Amnesty of Polish People Retrieved from
http://archive.org/stream/PolandRussiaAndGreatBritain19411945/TXT/00000521.txt
http://archive.org/stream/communisttakeove545503unit/communisttakeove545503unit_djvu.txt
http://kresy-siberia.org/galleries/?lang=en
http://www.polandinexile.com/index.html http://en.wikipedia.org/wiki/Amnesty_for_Polish_citizens_in_the_Soviet_Union
https://groups.yahoo.com/neo/groups/Kresy-Siberia/info

Poland. Ambasada (Soviet Union) Records, 1941-1944, Retrieved from http://www.oac.cdlib.org:80/dynaweb/ead/hoover/reg_205/

Belzec Extermination Camp
Retrieved from http://en.wikipedia.org/wiki/Bełżec_extermination_camp

Deportation of Polish People. Retrieved from
http://kresy-siberia.org/galleries/?lang=en

Commission for Polish Relief Records, 1939-1949, retrieved from
http://www.oac.cdlib.org:80/dynaweb/ead/hoover/reg_203/

Wladyslaw Anders Papers, 1939-1946, Retrieved from
http://www.oac.cdlib.org:80/dynaweb/ead/hoover/reg_344
https://groups.yahoo.com/neo/groups/Kresy-Siberia/info

Polish Refugees in the Middle East. Embassy of the Republic of Poland in Tehran,
Retrieved from
http://teheran.msz.gov.pl/en/bilateral_cooperation/polish_cemeteries/

Kresy Siberia Foundation, Retrieved from
http://kresy-siberia.org/galleries/?lang=en & https://groups.yahoo.com/neo/groups/
Kresy-Siberia/info

Wladyslaw Anders Papers, 1939-1946, Retrieved from
http://www.oac.cdlib.org:80/dynaweb/ead/hoover/reg_344

Property Compensation
Kresy-Siberia Group

Rzeszów and Rseszów Death Camps Retrieved from
http://voices.iit.edu/camps; http://www.deathcamps.org/occupation/rzeszow%20
ghetto.html
http://www.deathcamps.org

St. Onufry Retrieved from
http://en.wikipedia.org/wiki/Onuphrius

~ ~ ~ ~

Made in the USA
Lexington, KY
28 January 2015